Chaucer and the Consolation of Philosophy of Boethius

Chaucer and the Consolation of Philosophy of Boethius

By

BERNARD L JEFFERSON

GORDIAN PRESS
NEW YORK
1968

Originally Published 1917
Reprinted 1968

Library of Congress Catalog Card Number: 67-30878

Published by Gordian Press with the
Permission of Princeton University Press

PREFACE

The problem of this dissertation is to estimate, if possible, the full indebtedness of Chaucer to the *Consolation of Philosophy;* to show that his indebtedness is inadequately represented by lists of specific verbal borrowings such as have been prepared hitherto; and to consider the influence of Boethius on Chaucer as the influence of a philosopher on a highly intellectual poet, capable of thoroughly assimilating the Boethian teaching, of applying it to life, of using it in original ways in his poetry, and of expressing it aptly in language of his own. The culmination of the argument lies in the discussion of the minor poem *Truth* in Chapter III and in the discussion of *Troilus and Criseyde* and the *Knight's Tale* in Chapter IV, the poems which are the highest expression of the Boethian influence. In Chapter I Chaucer's translation is considered. Here I have been hampered somewhat by not having complete access to the French translation which Chaucer used as an aid in his translation of the Latin.

I have not considered it necessary to enter at length into the details of the life of so well known a figure as Boethius. He was born probably about 475 A. D., and spent most of his life in Rome. He is best known as a scholar, and in his works represents the spirit of both classical and mediaeval times. He was the last of the Romans, so called by Gibbon, and at the same time stood at the threshold of the Middle Ages. By his translation into Latin of some of the important works of Aristotle and by his commentaries upon them, he became the transmitter of classical thought to the schoolmen in days when Greek was unknown. One of his best known works was the *De Musica,* a work which Chaucer knew. He is also supposed to have written various theological tracts, but his authorship of these is a debated question. Boethius, besides being a scholar, held various official positions. Under the half barbarous, half civilized Ostrogothic ruler, Theodoric, he served as a minister of state. After attempted reforms he was unjustly thrown into prison, and somewhat later, according to tradition, he was brutally murdered in the year 525. It was while he was in prison that he wrote the *Consolation of*

iii

Philosophy, a work divided alternately into *proses* and *meters*, containing serious thought and flashes of poetry, and based on the philosophical theories of the best of the Greeks and Romans. Throughout the Middle Ages this was his most popular work, and it was translated into almost every European language. Its translators in English, besides Chaucer, include King Alfred, Caxton, and Queen Elisabeth. Although its thought is based on pagan philosophy, Boethius has been canonized as a Christian saint.

For the text of Chaucer's translation I have used Skeat's edition in the *Oxford Chaucer,* Vol. II, and for the Latin original, the edition of Peiper. I wish to acknowledge the kindness of Professor M. H. Liddell in sending to me portions of the French translation used by Chaucer, the kindness of Professor M. W. Croll for the help he gave me in the consideration of Chaucer's prose style, and of Professor C. G. Osgood for suggestions throughout. Especially am I indebted for generous assistance and helpful criticism to Professor R. K. Root, under whose direction the dissertation was written.

Danville, Ohio
August, 1916.

TABLE OF CONTENTS

CHAUCER AND THE CONSOLATION OF PHILOSOPHY OF BOETHIUS

CHAPTER I

THE TRANSLATION

Chaucer's translation of the *Consolation of Philosophy*, although it is diffuse and sometimes inaccurate and blundering, although it contains many awkward and faulty English sentences, yet on the whole is painstaking, faithful, poetic, and spirited. It has been considered by Morris, Stewart, and Skeat sympathetically and well, though briefly.[1] The object of the present chapter is to enlarge upon characteristics of the translation discussed by these writers, and to add other new material wherever it is possible. The chapter falls into three parts: Part I, Sources Supplementary to the Original; Part II, Inaccuracies in Translation; Part III, The Prose Style.

PART I. SOURCES SUPPLEMENTARY TO THE ORIGINAL

To make the work of translating easier and the translation more accurate and understandable, Chaucer resorted to at least two outside sources for assistance. In the first place he was partially dependent upon a French translation of the *Consolation of Philosophy,* and secondly he used the commentary of Nicholas Trivet on this work as a source for part of the numerous glosses which are interspersed throughout the text of his translation. It is possible that in addition to these means of assistance he used others, as I shall indicate later.

1. *Partial Dependence on a French Translation*

The view that Chaucer may have translated the *Consolation of Philosophy* second hand through the French seems to have

[1] Morris in the introduction to his text of Chaucer's translation, E. E. T. S., extra series, 5; Stewart in the *Essay,* pp. 214-28; Skeat in the *Oxford Chaucer,* Vol. II, pp. xxi-xxvii.

had its beginning before 1868, when Morris edited his text of the translation (E. E. T. S., Ex. Ser. 5). Morris, however, in his introduction (pp. xiii-xv) refutes this view by a comparison of several passages from Chaucer's translation and a French translation. The evidence afforded by these passages shows clearly that Chaucer did not resort to the particular French version from which Morris draws his citations; namely, that printed at Paris in 1494; but Morris was evidently not aware that there are other early French translations which Chaucer might have used; one of these I shall consider later. Stewart in the *Essay* (p. 204), apparently not convinced by the citations of Morris, suggests once more Chaucer's use of a French version, although he does not suppose that Chaucer was altogether dependent upon it. Skeat emphatically dismisses this suggestion as "improbable and unnecessary", saying that there is "no trace of anything of the kind" (*Oxford Chaucer*, Vol. II: xiv). Professor Liddell alone supports by specific evidence the view that Chaucer used a French version. His article in the *Academy* (1895, II, 227), however, is merely an announcement of his discovery of Chaucer's use of the French translation found in Ms. fr. 1097 and in Ms. Lat. 18424 of the Bibliothèque Nationale. He cites a few significant resemblances, and states his intention to prepare a parallel text of the two translations. Later in the footnotes to the *Boece* in the Globe Chaucer, he points out further resemblances, showing in particular that Chaucer made certain mistakes which could only result from his having attempted to follow the French translation. His evidence, however, is incidental, occurring as it does at intervals throughout the footnotes, and is not sufficiently organized to attract attention. At any rate recent writers seem not to regard the matter as closed. For example, Professor Root (*The Poetry of Chaucer*, p. 84) says, "there is no adequate support for the assumption frequently made that he availed himself of the French translation." Professor Saintsbury (*Cambridge History of English Literature*, Vol. II: 213) can say no more than that Chaucer has been *thought* to have used it. The parallel text, once contemplated by Professor Liddell, so he writes me, owing to unavoidable circumstances was given up by him several years ago. I, therefore, offer what evidence I have at hand to clear up the uncertainty on this point, and to show that Chaucer *did* use the French translation to be found in the manuscripts alluded to above. For part of my French quotations I am indebted to the kindness of Professor Liddell, who copied extracts from his transcript of it for my use.

That Chaucer should use a French translation does not require any far reach of the imagination. In the first place, it is only natural to suppose that any translator when he sets out to work should consult translations previously made; secondly, in the absence of a Middle English translation, it is plausible to suppose that Chaucer should go to a translation written in French, a language which he could doubtless read almost as well as he could English; and in the third place he would be all the more likely to go to the French if he could find a translation written by Jean de Meun, whose *Roman de la Rose* he had translated, and following whose suggestion in the *Roman* he is sometimes thought to have conceived the very idea of turning the *Consolation* into English (Cf. note p. 113). Now, Professor Langlois in a convincing article (*Romania,* Vol. 42: 331-369) has recently gone a long way toward proving that the French translation in question, namely the one found in Ms. fr. 1097 and in Ms. Lat. 18424, was indeed the work of Jean de Meun. Below follows a comparison of extracts from the Latin text, from Chaucer's translation, and from the French translation. Unfortunately for my purpose, I have not found available the complete French text, but only fragments of it obtained from various places.[2] These, however, seem to me to show conclusively that Chaucer derived much assistance from the French translation, and that at the same time he always closely followed the Latin original, even to the extent of producing a more literal translation than the French version offers.

[2] In all I have the following fragments: 2. m5. from Miss Petersen's article, "Chaucer and Trivet" (*Publications of the Modern Language Association of America,* Vol. XVIII: 190-93); 2. m6., except for the concluding lines, and a long selection at the end of 5. p6. from the article of Professor Langlois above cited; an extract of considerable length from the middle of 3. p12. and 4. m7. entire, copied for me by Professor Liddell. Besides these, I have numerous shorter passages from the article of Professor Langlois, and from the article of Professor Liddell in the *Academy.* There are frequent short quotations also in the footnotes of the *Boece* in the Globe Chaucer.

5 p6. 150-64

Quam comprehendendi omnia visendique praesentiam non ex futurarum proventu rerum, sed ex propria deus simplicitate sortitus est. Ex quo illud quoque resolvitur quod paulo ante posuisti indignum esse, si scientiae dei causam futura nostra praestare dicantur.

Haec enim scientiae vis praesentaria notione cuncta complectens rebus modum omnibus ipsa constituit, nihil vero posterioribus debet.

Quae cum ita sint, manet intemerata mortalibus arbitrii libertas nec iniquae leges solutis omni necessitate voluntatibus praemia poenasque proponunt.

Manet etiam spectator desuper cunctorum praescius deus visionisque eius praesens semper aeternitas cum nostrorum actuum futura qualitate concurrit bonis praemia malis supplicia dispensans.

5. p6. 196-213.[3]

And this presence to comprehenden and to seen alle thinges, god ne hath nat taken it of the bitydinge of thinges to come, but of his propre simplicitee. And her-by is assoiled thilke thing that thou puttest a litel herbiforn, *that is to seyn*, that it is unworthy thing to seyn, that our futures yeven cause of the science of god. For certes, this strengthe of the devyne science, which that embraceth alle thinges by his presentarie knowinge, establissheth maner to alle thinges, and it ne oweth naught to latter thinges; and sin that these thinges ben thus, *that is to seyn, sin that necessitee nis nat in thinges by the devyne prescience*, than is ther freedom of arbitre, that dwellest hool and unwemmed to mortal men. Ne the lawes ne purposen nat wikkedly medes and peynes to the willinges of men that ben unbounden and quite of alle necessitee.

And god, biholder and for-witer of alle thinges, dwelleth above; and the present eternitee of his sighte renneth alwey with the dyverse qualitee of oure dedes, despensinge and ordeyninge medes to goode men, and torments to wikked men.

Et ceste presence de toutez chosez comprendre et de veoir les n'a pas prise Dieus de l'avenement des chosez a avenir, mais de sa propre simplece. Et par ce est solu ce que tu deis un pou ci devant, *c'est assavoir* qu'il n'est pas digne chose de dire que nos futurs doignent cause a la prescience de Dieu, *ne que il soient cause de celle prescience;* car ceste force de science, qui toutez chosez embrace par sa presentaire cognoissance, establist a toutez chosez propre maniere, et ne doit riens aus chosez derrenierez. Et comme ces chosez soient ainsi, *ce est assavoir que necessité n'est pas es chosez de la prescience divine,* franchise de arbitre *est et* demeure enterinement es mortieus *hommes;* ne les lais ne propousent pas ne prometent felonnessement loiers et paines es volentez *des hommes qui sont* absoluz *et delivrez* de toutez neccessitez; et par

dessus maint Dieus regardeur *et* cognoisseur de toutez chosez *avant neïs que elles soient faitez,* et la presente pardurableté de sa vision queurt touz jours avec la *diverse* qualité de nos faiz *qui sont neïs encores* a venir, et dispanse *et ordenne* loiers aus bons et tourmens aus malvais.

---

[3] The abbreviation 5. p6. 196-213, with similar abbreviations, is thus to be interpreted. The "5" refers to the fifth Book of the *Consolation;* the "p6." to the sixth *prose* of that Book; the "196-213" refers to the lines of the *prose,* in Skeat's edition of the translation, Vol. II of the *Oxford Chaucer.* Frequently, in later references the corresponding lines in Peiper's edition of the Latin text will also be cited.

A glance at the two translations reveals a close similarity of word arrangement and of phrasing which can hardly be accidental. A more complete examination of details shows very striking resemblances. In lines 4-5 of the French translation *futurarum* is translated by *des chosez a avenir;* Chaucer accordingly translates it *of thinges to come.* In line 11, however, *futura* is translated by *futurs;* here Chaucer has *futures.* According to the *New English Dictionary* this is the first use of the word in English. In line 28 Chaucer's use of *arbitre,* also a new word, is likewise influenced, apparently, by the French. In line 9 the parenthetical clause *c'est assavoir,* added in the French, is taken over by Chaucer. He also (l. 10) follows the French in changing to indirect discourse the conditional clause which follows *si scientia etc.* In lines 24-27 Chaucer's gloss has very close verbal resemblances to a corresponding gloss in the French.[4] In line 27 he adopts the change of construction of the French which involves the addition of the verb *is;* in lines 38-9 he translates the noun and adjective *spectator—praescius* by two nouns *biholder and forwiter* corresponding to the French *regardeur et cognoisseur;* in line 43 he adds *dyverse* as the French does; in lines 44-5 he translates *dispensans* by *despensinge and ordeyninge* corresponding to the French *dispanse et ordenne.*

The dependence of Chaucer upon this translation becomes all the more evident when it is compared with one of the other French translations. The following passage, corresponding to that above, is taken from the French version which is the best known[5] and which M. Langlois argues in a convincing manner not to be the work of Jean de Meun. It will be noted that this version is widely different from Chaucer's and that only one of the peculiarities of translation pointed out in the preceding paragraph, namely the translation of *dispensans* in the last sentence,[6] exists in it.

[4] For a discussion of Chaucer's dependence upon the French glosses for his own glosses, see pp. 10, 13-14.

[5] This version occurs in numerous manuscripts. M. Langlois quotes from Ms. B. N. fr. 17272. Cf. his article *op. cit.* p. 335.

[6] The similarity at this point between the two French translations may perhaps be explained on the ground that the translation which Chaucer borrowed from was also borrowed from in the other French translation. For more similarities in phrasing between the two, see the footnotes in the aticle of Langlois, pp. 339, and 361 ff.

La quelle (ses) force de tout prendre ensemble et de veoir en present, elle n'a pas des choses advenir, mais de sa propre simplesse. Et pour ce est soult ce que tu disoiez ci devant, que ce seroit chose desordonnee se nos chosez advenir donnoient cause a la prescience de Dieu ; car ceste vertu de science, qui en presencialité enclost tout *et embrace, donne et* establist magniere a tous, ne riens ne doibt aux choses derrenierez *et advenir.* Et comme il soit ainsy, il remaint aux morteulx franchise entiere de volenté ; ne lez raisons ne sont pas malvaises qui proposent guerredons et painez aux volentez franchez de toutez necessitez. Et le souverain regardeur, c'est Dieu qui est par dessus, qui tout *voit et* precongnoist en la presence de sa vision etternelle, quiere (*sic*) aucune condicion de nos fais a advenir et dispense *et ordonne* aus bons loiers et aux malvais tourmens.

From these comparisons it will appear that Chaucer without doubt was dependent upon the French translation from which we first quote. In fact, the similarity is so close that the thought may arise that he depended entirely upon it, and did not consult the Latin at all. Such, however, was not the case, as the following passages will show. Here, it is true, there are unmistakable indications that he made use of the French, but at the same time it appears that he was entirely conscious of the Latin text.

2. m6. 1-13.	2. m6. 1-19.	
Novimus quantas dederit ruinas	We han wel knowen how many grete harmes and destrucciouns weren don *by the emperor Nero.*	Nous avons bien cogneü com grans domagez et com grans agraventeürez fist l'empereur Neron.
5 Urbe flammata patribus-que caesis	He leet brenne the citee of Rome, and made sleen the senatoures. And he, cruel, whylom slew his brother; and he was maked moist with the blood of his moder; *that is to seyn, he leet sleen and slitten the body of his moder, to seen wher he was conceived;*	Il fist ardoir la cité de Romque et fist ocirre les senateurs; et fist ocirre son frere, et *despecier* fist sa mere *par membrez; et la* fist ouvrir pour veoir le lieu ou il avoit esté con-ceüs,
Fratre qui quondam ferus interempto		
Matris effuso maduit		
10 cruore		
15		
Corpus et visu gelidum pererrans	and he loked on every halve up-on her colde dede body, ne no tere ne wette his face, but *he was so hard-herted that* he mighte ben domes-man or Iuge of hir dede beautee.	et regarda de toutez pars dehors et dedens le corps tout froit, ne onques n'i pleura, ainçois fu si dur que il pot jugier de bi-auté morte.
Ora non tinxit lacrimis, sed esse		
20 Censor extincti potuit decoris.		

That Chaucer used the Latin here, even though he very

6

closely followed the French translation,[7] we have conclusive evidence. In lines 7-8 *And he cruel whylom* translates *qui quondam ferus,* not translated at all in the French; in lines 9-11 Chaucer translates *effuso maduit cruore* more literally than the French does; in line 17 he does not translate *dehors et dedens* which has no counterpart in the Latin; in lines 18-19 he translates *ora non tinxit lacrimis* literally, whereas the French merely has the verb *pleura.* The following passages illustrate further that he carefully scanned the Latin text:

4. m7. 1-10.

Bella bis quinis operatus annis Ultor Atrides Phrygiae ruinis 5 Fratris amissos thalamos piavit.	The wreker Attrides, *that is to seyn, Agamenon,* that wroughte and continuede the batailes by ten yeer, recovered and purgede *in wrekinge,* by the destruccioun of Troye, the loste chaumbres of mariage of his brother; *this is to seyn, that he, Agamenon, wan aycin Eleyne, that was Menelaus wyf his brother.*	Agamenon vencheur qui continua les bataillez par le space de x. ans recouura et apaisa par la destruction de Troye les chambres du mariage (de) son frere qui perduez estoient.
Ille dum graiae dare 15 vela classi Optat et ventos redimit cruore, Exuit patrem miserumque tristis 20 Foederat natae iugulum sacerdos.	In the mene whyle that thilke *Agamenon* desirede to yeven sayles to the Grekissh navye, and boughte ayein the windes by blood, he unclothede him of pitee of fader; and the sory preest yiveth in sacrifyinge the wrecched cuttinge of throte of the doughter; *that is to seyn, that Agamenon let cutten the throte of his doughter by the preest, to maken allyaunce with his goddes, and for to han winde with whiche he mighte wenden to Troye.*	Endementiers que cil Agamenon desire donner veilez a la navie Grezesche et rachete les vens par le sanc de sa fille, il se met hors de pitie de pere et li doloreus prestrez fait paix et aliance aus diex par la chetiue gorge de la pucelle.
Flevit amissos Ithacus 30 sodales 35 Quos ferus vasto recubans in antro Mersit inmani Polyphemus alvo.	Itacus, *that is to seyn Ulixes,* biwepte his felawes y-lorn, the whiche felawes the ferse Poliphemus, ligginge in his grete cave, hadde freten and dreynt in his empty wombe.	Ulixes pleura ses compaignons que il avoit perduz les quiex Poliphemus li crueus gisant en sa grant fosse avoit mengiez et plungiez en son ventre vuit.

[7] Instances of Chaucer's indebtedness to the French are the following: Line 1. *wel* translates *bien,* not found in the Latin; ll. 2-3, *ruinas* is translated by two nouns in each; l. 4, *the emperor Nero;* ll. 5-7, use of the French verb *fist* in translating the ablative absolute con-

In these lines several instances of Chaucer's adherence to the Latin are to be noted.[8] In line 8 Chaucer translates *amissos* as an adjective whereas the French expands it into an adjective clause; in line 35 the same difference in the translation of *amissos* occurs. In line 19 Chaucer does not translate *de sa fille* added in the French. In the same line he translates *exuit* more literally, *unclothede;* the French has simply *met hors.* In lines 21-22 he translates *foederat* by *yiveth in sacrifyinge;* in the French this verb is translated *fait paix et aliance aus dieu.* In addition at this place, Chaucer translates *miserum* which the French leaves out. Later in the same *meter* there are several instances where he translates more literally than the French does; among these are the following:

4. m7. 20-1.	4. m7. 26-8.	
Victor immitem posuisse fertur	He, overcomer, as it is seyd, hath put an unmeke	Il vainqui Dyomedez li felon; et le fist mengier
Pabulum saevis dominum quadrigis.	lord foddre to his cruel hors.	a ses propres crueus chevaus.
4. m7. 29-31.	4. m7. 41-3.	
Ultimus caelos labor in-reflexo	And the laste of his la-bours was, that he sus-tened the hevene up-on his	La derrenier de ses tra-vaulz fu que il soustint le ciel seur son col sens
Sustulit collo pretiumque rursus	nekke unbowed; and ·he deservede eft-sones the	flechir et deserui de re-chief estre mis ou ciel.
Ultimi caelum meruit laboris.	hevene, to ben the prys of his laste travaile.	Ce fu li pris et li loiers de son derrenier travail.

The extracts below are somewhat unusual in that there is little or none of the connection between the two translations which is so common elsewhere. The French is a wholesale paraphrase—the only instance which I have found where this translation is so free. Chaucer's translation, on the other hand, is very faithful.

2. m6. 8-13.	2. m6. 9-19.	
Hic tamen sceptro popu-los regebat	And natheles, yit gov-ernede this *Nero* by	Et toutevois gouvernoit il par sceptre emperial touz
Quos videt condens ra-	ceptre alle the poeples	les peuplez *que li souleuz*

structions of the Latin; l. 6, *of Rome;* ll. 16-17, *on every halve;* l. 20, *was so hard-herted that,* which translates *fu si dur que,* not found in the Latin.

[8] There are also numerous instances of indebtedness to the French here: ll. 3-4, *continuede;* l. 5, *recovered;* l. 7, *destruccioun of Troye;* ll. 8-9, *chaumbres of mariage;* l. 15, *thilke Agamenon;* l. 17, *navye;* l. 20, *pitee of fader.*

dios sub undas
5 Phoebus extremo veniens
ab ortu,

10

Quos premunt septem
gelidi triones,
15

20
Quos notus sicco violen-
tus aestu
Torret ardentes reco-
quens harenas.
25

that Phebus the sonne may seen, cominge from his outereste arysinge til he hyde his bemes under the wawes; *that is to seyn, he governed alle the poeples by ceptre imperial*[9] *that the sonne goth aboute, from est to west.* And eek *this Nero governed by ceptre* alle the poeples that ben under the colde sterres that highten "septem triones"; *this is to seyn, he governede alle the poeples that ben under the party of the north.* And eek *Nero governed* alle the poeples that the violent wind Nothus scorkleth, and baketh the brenning sandes by his drye hete; *that is to seyn, alle the peoples in the south.*

venans voit en oriant et en occident et en midi et en septentrion.

From all of the passages quoted above, it will be seen that Chaucer must have had open before him as he worked both the Latin text and the French translation. Without a complete comparison of the two translations, it is impossible to determine the relative degree of his dependence on each of them throughout his whole work. Such a comparison I am unable to make with the limited means at my disposal. But the material which I have, considerably more than is above represented, shows first that the influence of the French translation is very great in Chaucer's translation, not only in the difficult parts but in the easy parts as well; and second that his translation tends to be more literal than the French, although the latter itself (cf. article of M. Langlois *op. cit.* pp. 336-42) is by no means to be regarded as a free translation.

2. *Sources of the Glosses*

Chaucer's translation of the *Consolation of Philosophy*, like the French translation from which he borrows so freely, is interspersed with frequent glosses. It is probable that Chaucer

[9] It will be noted that even here where Chaucer departs so far from the French text, he seems to keep his eyes upon it, as *imperial* corresponds to the French *emperial;* this word does not occur in the Latin.

9

was influenced by the French translator in his plan of incorporating glosses so extensively in the body of his own translation. Moreover, it seems evident that to a certain degree the French glosses were the source of his glosses, first because he frequently adds them at just the places where they are added in the French, and secondly because the two sets of glosses often show striking verbal similarities. It is, of course, possible to explain the similarity of the glosses on the assumption that both translators used the same commentary independently of each other, and it is my object presently to show that Chaucer did find material for his glosses outside of the French translation. At the same time, however, it hardly seems likely that he should remain entirely uninfluenced by the French glosses when he follows the French translation so closely in other regards. Similarities in phrasing like the following make his indebtedness to the French glosses almost certain:

and he was maked moist with the blood of his moder; *that is to seyn, he leet sleen and slitten the body of his moder, to seen wher he was conceived;* 2. m6. 4-6.

et *despecier* fist sa mere *par membrez; et la fist ouvrir pour vecir le lieu ou il avoit esté conceüs.*

'so, at the laste, fooles that sumtyme renden grete thinges oughten ben ashamed of hem-self;' *that is to seyn, that we fooles that reprehenden wikkedly the thinges that touchen goddes governaunce, we oughten ben ashamed of our-self: as I, that seyde that god refuseth only the werkes of men, and ne entremeteth nat of hem.'* 3. p12. 91-6.

Si que a la per fin e· ie et li autre fol mesdisant, qui les grans chosez despicient aucune fois et mesdient, en devons avcir grant honte de nous meismes, *si comme ie avoie dit devant que diex refuse seulement les fais des hommes et que il ne sen entremet.*

ne semeth it nat to entrechaunge stoundes of knowinge;" 'as who seith, ne shal it nat seme to us, that the devyne prescience entrechaungeth hise dyverse stoundes of knowinge, so that it knowe sum-tyme o thing and sum-tyme the contrarie of that thing?* 5. p6. 186-89.

ne nous doit pas estre avis que elle entrechange aussi ses divers fais de cognoistre, *si que elle cognoisse une foiz une chose et autre foiz le contraire de ce?*

and sin that these thinges ben thus, *that is to seyn, sin that necessitee nis nat in thinges by the devyne prescience.* 5. p6. 204-6.

Et comme ces chosez soient ainsi, *ce est assavoir que necessité n'est es chosez de la prescience divine.*

On the other hand, it is to be seen at once that Chaucer has frequently added glosses which do not occur in the text of the French translation. This, for example, is true of the important glosses in 2. m5., and it is also true in a large measure of the glosses in 4. m7. To what source, then, did Chaucer resort for these glosses? This question has been answered in three ways. Skeat (*Oxford Chaucer,* II., xxxvii-xli) thinks that he has found their source in a manuscript of the Cambridge Library (Ms. Camb. Ii. 3. 21). This manuscript he uses as the basis for his text of the translation. It contains not only Chaucer's translation but also the Latin text written in alternate chapters. Skeat does not believe that this manuscript preserves the authentic Latin text used by Chaucer himself, but he believes it to be a copy of that text. The chief evidence by which Skeat would support this contention is that Chaucer seems to have availed himself freely of the glosses with which that manuscript abounds. And Skeat does point out very significant resemblances between Chaucer's glosses and these glosses. Professor Liddell in the *Nation* (1897, Feb. 18, pp. 124 ff.) shows what seems to be conclusive evidence that Chaucer made use of the commentary wrongly ascribed to Thomas Aquinas, and known as the Pseudo-Aquinas. Miss Petersen (*Publications of the Mod. Lang. Ass.,* 1903, Vol. XVIII, pp. 173-93) brings forward very strong evidence to show that Chaucer depended upon the commentary of Nicholas Trivet. The various sources for Chaucer's glosses, thus assigned, would seem to indicate not that he made use of all the commentaries which he could lay hands upon, but rather that the commentaries themselves were in some respects similar to each other and go back to a common ancestor. And indeed the point of Miss Petersen's article is to show that Trivet's commentary in practically every case where Chaucer is concerned includes the glosses of the Pseudo-Aquinas. She finds in consequence that, although the resemblances between Chaucer's glosses and the glosses of both of these sources is often very close, yet in some seventy instances out of a possible three hundred and seventy Chaucer's glosses more closely resemble those of Trivet than those of the Pseudo-Aquinas. She quotes these seventy instances, comparing in full the three sets of glosses.

As a specimen of the relative similarity between the three, I copy the gloss which occurs in the beginning of 3. m11., and its counterpart in each of the two commentaries. This gloss is the longest in Chaucer's translation. It explains in plain language a highly figurative passage which he has just translated. Chaucer probably considered this *meter* of more than usual importance as I shall take up more fully later in discussion of the minor poem *Truth*. I quote first the Latin passage and his translation of it, and then the three sets of glosses. The close similarity of Chaucer's gloss to that of Trivet is to be noted.

Quisquis profunda mente vestigat verum
Cupitque nullis ille deviis falli,
In se revolvat intimi lucem visus
Longosque in orbem cogat inflectens
    motus
Animumque   doceat   quidquid   extra
    molitur
Suis retrusum possidere thesauris.
Dudum quod atra texit erroris nubes,
Lucebit ipso perspicacius Phoebo.

Who-so that seketh sooth by a deep thoght, and coveiteth nat to ben deceived by no mis-weyes, lat him rollen and trenden with-inne him-self the light of his inward sighte; and lat him gadere ayein, enclyninge in-to a compas, the longe moevinges *of his thoughtes;* and lat him techen his corage that he hath enclosed and hid in his tresors, al that he compasseth or seketh fro with-oute. And thanne thilke thinge, that the blake cloude of errour whylom hadde y-covered, shal lighten more cleerly thanne Phebus him-self ne shyneth.

Chaucer.	Trivet.	Pseudo-Aquinas.
Who-so wole seken	Quisquis investigat, *i. investigare vult*	Quisquis vestigat. *i. investigare vult*
the deep grounde of sooth in his thought, and wol nat be deceived by false proposiciouns that goon amis fro the trouthe,	verum mente profunda, *i. subtili mente,* cupitque nullis deviis, *i. falsis propositionibus que a veritate deviant* falli,	verum profunda mente, *i. subtili* et cupit falli nullis deviis, *i. falsis opionibus que faciunt a vero deviare,*
lat him wel examine and rolle	revolvat, *sc. cogitando* lucem visus intimi, *i. aspectum intellectus et rationis,*	ille revolvat in se, *i. exercitet intra se lucem i. speculationem* intimi visus, *i. rationis et intellectus*
with-inne him-self	in se, *sc. recolligendo ab exteriori occupatione* longosque motus, *sc. inquirendo naturam et proprietates rei;*	interioris et ipse cogat, *i. reducat* longos motus, *i. operationes anime procedentes ab anima,*
the nature and the propretees of the thing; and lat him yit eftsones examine and rollen his thoughtes by good deliberacioun. or that he deme;	cogat, *i. recolligat* flectens in orbem, *i. redeundo iterato super cogitationes suas et deliberando de eis antequam faciliter judicet;*	inflectentes *eos motus* in orbem, *i. in circulum redeundo in animam* et quicquid
		animum doceat molitur, *i. laborat speculando* extra, *i. circa res exteriores ille* doceat animum retrursum, *i. ad se conversum*
and lat him techen his sowle	doceatque animum	possidere suis thesauris, *i. potentiis que sunt memoria et intellectus.*
that it hath, by natural principles	possidere suis thesauris, *i. naturalibus principiis[10]*	

[10] Skeat quotes here the corresponding gloss in manuscript, Camb. Ii. 3. 21., mentioned above as one of the possible sources of Chaucer's glosses. "Over the word *retrusum*," he says, "is written *i. absconditum;* and over *thesauris* is *i. naturalibus policiis et principiis naturaliter.*"

kindeliche y-hid	*naturaliter inditis* retru- sum, *i. absconditum sicut* *ea que sunt in suo prin-* *cipio potentiali et virtuali* quicquid molitur, *i. ma-*	
with-in it-self,	*chinatur* extra, *i. omnem* *veritatem quam machina-* *tur esse in rebus ex-* *terioribus, sicut in causa.*	
alle the trouthe the *whiche he imagineth to* *ben in thinges withoute.*		
And thanne *alle the derknesse of his* *misknowinge*	*Et si sic fecerit,* tunc *illud* quod atra nubes er- roris, *i. obscuritas* erroris *quod est ignorantia,* texit dudum	*Et tunc* *illud quod* atra nubes *i. occultavit* ignorantie dudum texit, *i, occultavit*
shal seme *more evidently* *to sighte of his under-* *stondinge thanne the* *sonne ne semeth*	lucebit perspicacius, *i. evidentius* *apparebit visui intellectus* ipso Phebo, *i. quam Sol*	*illud* lucebit, *i. apparebit* perspicacius, *i. evidentius* ipso Phebo, *quasi dicat quod longo* *tempore fuit obscurum* *lucidum apparebit intel-* *lectui.*
to sighte with-oute-forth.	*visui exteriori.*	

Miss Petersen thus seems to have established very definitely the indebtedness of Chaucer to the commentary of Trivet. She has not, however, as she states (footnote, p. 175), been able to compare Chaucer's glosses with those of the French translation except for one *meter* (1. m5., quoted in her article, pp. 190-93). Here she finds that the three most important glosses are derived by Chaucer from the commentary of Trivet and not from the French. This *meter,* however, hardly seems representative of the true condition in this regard. Chaucer was probably more dependent on the French translation for his glosses than the comparison of the two translations of this *meter* would lead one to suppose. I have already cited above certain glosses which he seems to have taken over from the French. In the following instance he has evidently borrowed both from the gloss of Trivet and of the French translation:

The similarity of this gloss with that of Trivet suggests that Ms. Camb. Ii. 3. 21. may be dependent for its glosses upon the commentary of Trivet. Skeat's argument, that because of the similarity in the glosses of Chaucer's translation and of this manuscript the latter is a copy of the one used by Chaucer, therefore is perhaps still entitled to some consideration. There is, however, at Paris a manuscript of the fourteenth century in which are grouped the Latin text, the French translation, and Trivet's commentary (Ms. Lat. 18424). It is possible that Chaucer may have had access to a manuscript of this description. (Cf. article of Miss Petersen, pp. 189-90.)

13

Chaucer. (1. p4. 53ff.)	French.	Trivet.
Whan that Theodoric, the king of Gothes. in a dere yere, hadde hise gerneres ful of corn,	*Comme le roy Theodoric, qui par un chier temps avoit ses greniers plains de blés, commanda que*	
5 *and comaundede that no man ne sholde byen no corn til his corn were sold, and that at a grevous dere prys,*	*cist blé fust chierement vendu et fist crier ban que nus n'achetast blé fors que le sien jusques a tant qu'il eüst tout vendu, je*	
10 *Boece withstood that ordinaunce, and over-com it, knowinge al this the king himself.*[11]	*Boëce alai contre cest establissement et le vainqui, le roy meïsmes sachant, et cognoissant coemption,*	
Coempcioun,[12] *that is to*	*c'est a dire communs*	*Nota quod coemptio vide-*
15 *seyn, comune achat or bying to-gidere, that were establisshed up-on the poeple*	*achez griez et non mie despoilables, commandez et establiz seur le peuple.*	*tur esse*
by swiche a manere im-		*impositio alicujus certe*
20 *posicioun,*		*portionis solvende, ita ut residuum libere ematur, ut si staturetur quod qui-*
as who-so boughte a busshel corn, he moste yeve the king the fifte		*cumque modium frumenti emeret, daret regi quin-*
25 *part.*		*tam partem.*
Whan it was in the soure hungry tyme, ther was establisshed or cryed grevous and inplitable	Ou temps de la fain eigre, fust veuz a degaster et a tourmenter par souffrete et par mesaise Cham-	Cum acerbae famis tempore gravis atque inexplicabilis indicta coemptio profligatura inopia Cam-
30 *coempcioun, that men sayen wel it sholde greetly turmenten and endamagen al the province of Campaigne,*	paigne et Prouvince,	paniam provinciam videretur,
35 *I took stryf ayeins the provost of the pretorie for comune profit. And, the king knowinge of it, I overcom it, so that the*	je recui l'etrif encontre le prevost de pretoire par la raison du commun profit. Je, le roy cognoissant, estrivé et vainqui	certamen adversum praefectum praetorii communis commodi ratione suscepi, rege cognoscente contendi et ne coemptio
40 *coempcioun ne was not axed ne took effect.*	que le coemption ne fust requise ne passast.	exigeretur, evici.

[11] Skeat in the text of Chaucer's translation in the *Oxford Chaucer* divides the gloss at this point, and places the remainder of it at the close of the passage of text, quoted below. He believes that it has been "misplaced" in the manuscripts, and thinks that it naturally should follow the passage which it concerns. Chaucer, however, seems only to be following the French in placing both parts together.

[12] I have not been able to learn whether there occurs in Trivet's commentary a gloss corresponding to the first part of Chaucer's gloss down to line 14. However, the verbal similarities between Chaucer's gloss and the French gloss in this part are interesting; especially, *gerneres* (1. 4) corresponding to the French *greniers*. Chaucer's phrase *comune achat* (1. 15), which is not present in Trivet's gloss, and which corresponds to the French *communs achez,* reveals the influence of the French translation. Even the phrasing of Chaucer's text, it will be noted, seems to have been influenced somewhat by the French gloss in that *was . . . cried* (ll. 27-8) apparently comes from *fist crier* (1. 6).

Chaucer's gloss is thus made up from two sources. A complete comparison of his translation with the French would probably show that the influence of the latter on his glosses was greater than Miss Petersen supposes in her article. The pains which Chaucer took to investigate different sources for his translation indicates no small desire to be clear and faithful.[13]

Above, we have been concerned with the longer glosses of Chaucer's translation, but certain of the more trivial additions are of interest as they help to give an idea of his desire to be clear, just alluded to. He invariably labels proper nouns whose meaning might be obscure, telling whether they refer to animals, countries, stars, winds, or what not. The same tendency may be observed in the French translation, although there are indications that Chaucer is more conscientious in this regard. In the following instances parallels with the French translation are cited as often as I have been able to supply them: Choro, *winde that highte* Chorus, 1. m3. 3, 5; threicio boreas emissus ab antro, *winde that highte* Borias, y-sent out of the caves *of the contree* of Trace, 1. m3. 8, 7; Vesevus, *mountaigne that highte* Vesevus, 1. m4. 6, 8; Fratris totis obvia flammis . . . luna, the mone . . . meting with alle the bemes *of the sonne* hir broder, 1. m5. 5, 6; Hesperos, *the eve-sterre* Hesperus, 1. m5. 8, 11; Arcturus, *sterre that highte* Arcturus, 1. m5. 19, 21; Bacchus, Bachus, *the god of wyne*, 1. m6. 10, 15; Aquilo, *the horrible wind* Aquillon, 2. m3. 12, 11; Serum, *of the contree of* Seriens, (Fr.) des Seriens, 2. m5. 7, 8; Aetnae, *of the montaigne* Ethna, (Fr.) *de la montaigne* de Ethna, 2. m5. 23, 25; urbe, the citee *of Rome*, (Fr.) la cite *de Romque*, 2. m6. 2, 2; septem gelidi triones, colde *sterres that highten* "septem triones", (Fr. septentrion), 2. m6. 15, 11; Lucifer, Lucifer *the day sterre*, 3. m1. 6, 9; Poeni . . . leones. lyouns *of the contree* of Pene, 3. m2. 6, 7; ultima Tyle, the last *ile in the see, that hight* Tyle, 3. m5. 5. 7; Lyncei, *of a beest that highte* lynx, (Fr. de lins), 3, p8. 29, 22; Ursa, the *sterre y-cleped* "the Bere," 4. m6. 6, 9.

[13] In addition to the sources of help above considered, Chaucer seems to have had accessible various texts of the *Consolation*. The evidence for this view rests on 2. p1. 48-53. Here Chaucer translates a passage as it occurs in each of two varying texts, and states before the second version of the passage, "But natheles, some bokes han the text thus." It is possible, however, that Chaucer derived this information from the commentary of Trivet or elsewhere.

Of the numerous inaccuracies in Chaucer's translation, many have been pointed out before; notably, by Stewart (*Essay,* pp. 222-5), by Skeat (*Oxford Chaucer,* Vol. II, pp. xxiv-xxvii, and throughout his notes to the text of the translation), and by Mr. Liddell in the footnotes to the *Boece* in the Globe Chaucer. Those pointed out by the latter are important, as he has compared Chaucer's translation with the French translation, and has shown how certain mistakes resulted from his having misunderstood the French, or from his having followed mistakes already existing in it. The list which follows is more inclusive than any one of the others, because in it is collected the material scattered in the various places just mentioned, and some new instances are added. I have also called attention to certain cases where mistakes seem to have been wrongly attributed to Chaucer in the earlier lists. A star in the following list means that the mistake indicated has not been noted before.

Book I

Meter 1. 3, 3.[14] *lacerae* . . . Camenae: *rendinge* Muses. Rather *rent* or *tattered*. Skeat cites this mistake; the transferred meaning *rending,* however, is recognized by Harper.

*8, 8. solantur *maesti* nunc mea fata senis: comforten now the *sorowful* werdes of me, olde man. *Maesti* misread as *maesta.*

*12, 13. Mors hominum felix quae se nec dulcibus annis inserit et *maestis* saepe vocata venit: Thilke deeth of men is weleful that ne cometh not in yeres that ben swete, but cometh to *wrecches,* often y-cleped. *Maestis* modifies *annis* understood.

Prose 1. 17, 15. quas, uti post eadem prodente cognovi, suis manibus, ipsa texuerat. Quarum *speciem* . . . caligo quaedam neglectae vetustatis obduxerat: the whiche clothes she had woven with hir owene hondes, as I knew wel after by hirself, declaringe and shewinge to me *the beautee;* the whiche clothes a derknesse . . . hadde dusked. Chaucer takes *speciem* as the object of *prodente.*

41, 32. hominumque mentes assuefaciunt morbo, non libe-

---

[14] The first "3" refers to the line of the translation in the *Oxford Chaucer;* the second "3" to the corresponding line in Peiper's edition of the Latin text.

rant: they holden the hertes of men in usage, but they ne delivere nat folk fro maladye. *Morbo* is taken with the wrong
verb. Chaucer follows the French, Tiennent les pensees des
hommes en costume et ne les delivrent pas de maladie.

48, 38. Sed abite potius . . . Sirenes usque in *exitum* dulces:
But goth now rather awey, ye mermaidenes, whiche that ben
swete til it be at the *laste*. Rather *unto destruction*.

*52, 40. His ille chorus increpitus deiecit humis *maestior*
vultum: And thus this companye of Muses y-blamed casten
wrothly the chere dounward to the erthe. Rather *sadly*.
Chaucer thus makes the Muses attendant upon Boethius somewhat more violent than in the original. Cf. passage just above
rendinge Muses for *tattered Muses*.

*61, 48, *maerore* omitted in translation.

Prose 3. 2, 1. *hausi* caelum: *I took* hevene. Skeat includes
this among the mistakes. It seems, however, to be only a literal translation; cf. the French, ie *pris* le ciel.

*2, 2. ad cognoscendam medicantis faciem mentem recepi.
Itaque *ubi* in eam deduxi oculos intuitumque defixi, respicio
nutricem: and received minde to knowen the face of my
fysicien; so that I sette my eyen on hir, and fastnede my look-
inge. I beholde my norice etc. The *ubi* is disregarded.

*37, 28. *quod si*, adversative, translated *so if;* Cf. also for
the same inaccuracy, 2. p3. 52, 39 and 2. p4. 127, 91.

Meter 4. 5, 6. minaeque ponti versum funditus excitantis
aestum: the manaces of the see, commoevinge or chasinge upward *hete* fro the botme. *Aestum* rather means *surge*. Later
in 1. m7. 3, Chaucer explains in a gloss, *hete*, that is to seyn,
the boyling up from the botme.

Prose 4. 3, 3. Ἐξαύδα, μὴ κεῦθε νόῳ omitted. *In this *prose*
several other words are omitted. ll. 9 *residens;* 153. 103
meministi, inquam; 157, 106 *innocentiam;* 161, 110 *quodam
modo se probantis*.

*48, 33 *calumniis: miseyses and grevaunces.* Rather *slander*
or *false reports*.

63, 42. *ne* coemptio exigeretur, evici: I overcom it, *so that*
the coempcioun ne was nat axed ne took effect. The purpose
clause is translated as result.

78, 49. mihi . . . *apud* aulicos: to myself *to* hemward of the
kinges halle. The loose use of the preposition seems due to
the French, *vers* ceus du paliz roial.

83, 53. *alienae* aeris necessitate: for need of *foreine* money.

17

93, 60. *astrui: lykned.* Rather *added.* Chaucer has confused the two possible meanings of the French perf. part. *pareille.*

109, 71. *Fatebimur?: and that I confesse and am aknowe.* Chaucer disregards the interrogation.

128, 84. omnibus *negotiis:* in alle *nedes.* The French has, en tout *besoingnes.* Chaucer has read *besoingnes (besognes)* as *besoings (besoins).*

159, 109. Minuit enim quodam modo se probantis conscientiae *secretum,* quotiens ostentando quis factum recepit famae pretium: For alwey, whan any wight receiveth precious renoun in avauntinge him-self of his werkes, he amenuseth the *secree* of his conscience. *Secretum* is an adjective modifying *pretium* understood. The same mistranslation occurs in the French.

201, 142. cumulus . . . *accedit:* ther bitydeth yit this encrees. *Accedit* read as *accidit.*

*213, 146. Qui nunc populi rumores, *quam* dissonae multiplicesque sententiae, piget reminisci: certes, it greveth me to thinke right now the dyverse sentences *that* the poeple seith of me. Chaucer mistakes the indirect question for a relative.

Meter 5. 9, 12. Solitas iterum *mutet* habenas: *cometh eft* ayein hir used course. The mistake, if it may be called one at all, does not seem a bad one. *Cometh* should perhaps be read *torneth* (Skeat).

Prose 6. 10, 8. fortuita *temeritate:* fortunous *fortune.* This translation would apply better to *fortuitis casibus,* two lines above; indeed, Skeat in his notes makes the mistake of quoting these two words as the Latin from which *fortunous fortune* is derived. Chaucer's translation may have resulted from a similar confusion. Liddell, however, suggests that *fortune* may be a corruption of *folie,* adopted from the French.

*24, 18. Vix, inquam, rogationis tuae sententiam nosco, *nedum* ad inquisita respondere queam: 'unnethe', quod I, 'knowe I the sentence of thy question; *so that* I ne may nat yit answeren to thy demaundes'. *Nedum* means *much less.* (I don't know what you mean; *much less* can I answer you.)

*65, 48. *fomitem: norisshinges,* misread as *fomentum.* The same misreading occurs again, 3. m11. 27, 14.

*72, 53. *mentium: of thoughtes deceived,* evidently confused with the verb *mentior.*

Prose 1. 22, 14. *adyto: entree,* misread as if *aditu.* *Shrine* is the more correct translation.

*37, 28. *ista natura* omitted in translation.

44, 33. *utere moribus: use hir maneres* (Skeat). Perhaps too literal, but does not seem a serious mistake.

Prose 2. 41, 31. *An tu mores ignorabas meos?* omitted in translation.

47, 35. *Persi* regis: king of *Perciens.* Rather king *Perseus.* The French has the same translation, le roy *de Perse.*

*Meter 2. 5, 3. *edita . . .* sidera: *brighte* sterres. Rather *lofty.*

Prose 3. 29, 21. *praetereo: over al this.* Chaucer has misread this verb for *praeterea,* the adverb.

*41, 30. cum in *Circo:* in the place that highte *Circo.* The case ending is disregarded.

*41, 31. multitudinis expectationem triumphali *largitione* satiasti: fulfuldest the abydinge of the multitude of people . . . with so large *preysinge and laude,* as men singen in victories. Chaucer misses the point that Boethius spread *largesse* among the crowd.

Prose 4. 126, 90. omne *mortalium genus:* alle *the kinde of mortal thinges* (Liddell). Not an apt translation, but still not a serious mistake.

Meter 4. 9, 13. Fugiens periculosam sortem sedis amoenae humili *domum* memento certus figere saxo: have minde certeinly to ficchen *thyn hous of a merye site* in a lowe stoon. Chaucer does not translate *sortem,* and has *sedis amoenae* modify *domum.*

12, 21. duces *serenus* aevum: shalt leden a *cleer* age. *Serenus* misread as accusative.

Prose 5. 3, 3. *Age: Now understond heer.* Mistranslation of the French, Or *entens* ici.

10, 8. *effundendo: to hem that despenden.* Rather *by spending.* Stewart and Skeat both cite this as a mistake. Although it is not a literal translation, yet it seems permissible as it does not disturb the meaning.

10, 8. *coacervando: to thilke folk that mokeren.* As noted just above, this does not seem a serious mistake.

33, 25. *naturae pulchrum* esse . . . videatur: semen *a fair creature.* Rather, seem *fair to a creature.*

*54, 39. *animatium: of bestes,* as if *animalium.*

90, 68. *sepositis: subgit,* as if *suppositis.*

*Prose 6. 3, 3. Quae si in improbissimum quemque ceciderunt, *quae* flammis Aetnae eructuantibus, *quod* diluvium tantas strages dederint? The whiche dignitees and powers, yif they comen to any wikked man, they don as grete damages and destrucciouns as doth the flaumbe of the mountaigne Ethna, whan the flaumbe walweth up; ne no deluge ne doth so cruel harmes. Chaucer has not recognized that *quae* and *quod* are in this case interrogative pronouns.

*Prose 7. 80, 60. *populares auras: audience of poeple,* as if *auras* were *aures.*

Meter 7. 20, 25. *sera* . . . dies: *cruel* day, as if *saeva.*

*Prose 8. 3, 3. fallax illa *nihil:* she [Fortune], deceyvable. Chaucer misses the negative.

Book III

*Meter 1. 1, 1. Qui serere *ingenuum* volet agrum, liberat arva prius fructibus: Who-so wole sowe a feeld *plentivous,* lat him first delivre it fro thornes. *Ingenuum (new* or *virgin)* is apparently read as the adverb *ingenue (liberally).*

4, 6. Si malus *ora* prius sapor edat: yif *mouthes* han first tasted savoures that ben wikkid. *Ora* is misconstrued as nominative (Liddell). This is holding Chaucer a little too close. Cf. similar change in 2. m5. 11, 10.

Prose 2. 33, 28. In his . . . humanorum actuum votorumque *versatur* intentio: In thise thinges . . . *is torned* alle the entencioun etc. *Is torned* is a mistranslation of *versatur* (Liddell). The French also has *est tornee.* It does not seem a mistranslation.

57, 49. *afferre: bi-refte awey.* The meaning is precisely the opposite. Chaucer translates as if *auferre.*

Prose 3. 48, 34. *forenses* querimoniae: *foreyne* compleyntes. Rather *public* complaints.

Prose 4. 2, 2. Num vis ea est *magistratibus,* ut utentium mentibus virtutes . . . depellant? Han they nat so gret strengthe, that they may putte vertues in the hertes of folk that usen the lordshipes of hem? *Magistratibus,* really a dative of possession in the first clause, is made the direct object of the deponent *utentium.*

42, 29. *multiplici consulatu: many maner dignitees of consules.* The phrase means rather that Boethius had held the consulship many times.

64, 44. opinione *utentium:* by the opinioun of *usaunces.*

Rather *in the opinion of those using (it)*. However, see above in the same prose 3, 3, *utentium mentibus,* translated by Chaucer, *in the hertes of folk that usen.* He evidently knew how to translate the construction. The French is *des usans;* possibly Chaucer has misread it for *des usances.*

Prose 5. 46, 36. An *praesidio* sunt amici, quos non virtus sed fortuna conciliat? But whether swiche men ben frendes *at nede,* as ben conseyled by fortune and nat by vertu? *Praesidio* is dative of service instead of ablative.

*Prose 7. 13, 12. sed nimis e natura dictum est nescio quem filios invenisse tortores: quorum quam sit mordax quaecumque condicio, *neque* alias expertum te *neque* nunc anxium necesse est ammonere: but it hath ben seyd that it is over muchel *ayeins* kinde, that children han ben founden tormentours to hir fadres, I not how manye: of whiche children how bytinge is every condicioun, it nedeth *nat* to tellen it thee, that hast or this tyme assayed it, and art yit now anguissous. *E,* translated *ayeins,* means rather *from* or *in accordance with.* The last part of the passage is directly opposite to what the Latin means, as Chaucer misses the application of the *neque . . . neque.* Boethius had never experienced sorrow in his children; therefore he needed to be told of it. In regard to the nobility of the sons of Boethius, cf. 2. p3. 25 ff.

18, 16. *Euripidis: Euripidis.* Chaucer preserves the genitive form.

Prose 8. 11, 9. *obnoxius . . .* subiacebis: thou shalt . . . *anoyously* ben cast under.

29, 22. *Lyncei: of a beest that highte lynx.* The allusion is to the man, *Lynceus.* The French also has, *de lins.*

Prose 9. 16, 12. an tu arbitraris quod nihilo indigeat egere potentia? Wenest thou that he, that hath nede of power, that him ne lakketh no-thing? The relative and the main clauses are confused.

50, 32. *fateamur: adden.* A free translation which occurs also in the French.

106, 72. *in adversum,* omitted.

142, 92. *(in) Timaeo:* in his book of *"in Timeo".* Peiper's text omits *in;* however, some Latin manuscripts have it.

Meter 9, 28, 22. *augustam: streite.* Misread as *angustam.*

Prose 10. 53, 42. *vel ita naturaliter habere praesumas,* omitted.

164, 121. Quo fit, uti *summa,* cardo atque causa expetendorum omnium bonitas esse iure credatur: And therefor is it that men oughten to wene by right, that bountee be the *soverein fyn,* and the cause, etc. Chaucer has taken the noun *summa* to be the superlative adjective; *fyn* translates *cardo.*

*Prose 11. 66, 48. Sed quid de herbis arboribusque, quid de *inanimatis* omnino consentiam rebus prorsus dubito: But certes, I doute me of herbes and of trees . . . that ne han no felinge sowles. *Inanimatis* does not modify *herbis arboribus;* but, on the other hand, is in contrast to it, and refers to life-less things like rocks, fire, air, etc., as Boethius proceeds to describe.

*Meter 11. 27, 14. *fomes: norisshinge,* translated as *fomentum.* Cf. 1. p6. 65, 48.

Prose 12. 22, 14. *exponam: answeren.* The French verb here is *espondrai;* Chaucer seems to have read it as *respondrai.*

55, 38. *clavus: keye,* as if *clavis. Clava,* a few lines later, is translated in the same way.

74, 51. *detrectantium* iugum: a yok *of misdrawinges.*

75, 51. *obtemperantium* salus: the savinge of *obedient* thinges.

Meter 12. 4, 7. Postquam flebilibus modis silvas currere *mobiles* amnes stare coegerat: after that he hadde maked, by his weeply songes, the wodes, *moevable,* to rennen; and hadde maked the riveres to stonden stille. *Mobiles* modifies *amnes.*

24, 31. Quae *sontes* agitant metu: that tormenten and agas-ten the sowles *by anoy.* Rather *anoyous soules* (Liddell). But *by annoy* seems to translate *metu.* The real force of *sontes* seems lost in translation.

Book IV

Prose 1. 21, 15. in locum *facinorum* supplicia luit: and it abyeth the torments in stede of *wikkede felounes.*

Prose 2. 97, 68. *indicium: Iugement,* as if *iudicium.*

Prose 3. 52, 40. non *affecit* modo verum etiam . . . *infecit?* ne *defouleth ne enteccheth* nat hem only, but *infecteth and envenimeth* hem. Chaucer does not distinguish between the two verbs.

Prose 4. 67, 47. *nullus respectus . . . exempli: ne non ensaumple of lokinge.* It should be *non lokinge of ensaumple; i. e. no regard for the example.*

152, 106. num videntes eadem caecos putaremus? now we

that mighten seen the same thinges, wolde we nat wene that *he* were blinde? The pronoun should be *we* instead of *he*. The French has the same mistake.

Prose 6. 105, 80. *fetuum* seminumque . . . progressus: progressiouns of sedes and of *sexes*. The French also has *sexes*.

122, 96. Quae vero, *inquies,* potest ulla *iniquior* esse confusio: *But thou mayst seyn,* what *unreste* may ben a worse confusioun. Chaucer began with the French *Mais tu diros,* and then turned to the Latin, construing *inquies* as a noun. (Liddell). Skeat suggests that Chaucer tried to translate the extraordinary reading *inquiescor,* found in the Latin manuscript which he thinks is a copy of the one that Chaucer used.

163, 126. opinioni vero tuae *perverso* confusio: but, as to thy *wikkede* opinioun, it is a confusioun. The adjective modifies the wrong noun.

168, 130. *colere* . . . innocentiam: *continue* innocence. The French verb here is *coutiuer* which Chaucer seems to have read as *continuer.*

220, 170. *exercitii* . . . causa: cause *of continuacioun and exercysinge.* The French is *coutumance* which Chaucer seems to have read as *continuance.*

Meter 6. 27, 34. *interea: amonges thise thinges. Interea* read as *inter ea.*

33, 42. Quae nunc stabilis *continet* ordo: the thinges that ben now *continued* by stable ordinaunce. *Continet* read as *continuit.*

Prose 7. 55, 38. *debet: semeth,* as if *decet.*

Book V

Prose 1. 1, 1. *orationis: resoun,* as if *rationis.*

2, 2. Recta quidem, inquam, exhortatio *tuaque* prorsus auctoritate dignissima: Thanne seyde I, 'Certes, rightful is *thyn* amonestinge and ful digne by auctoritee'. *Tua* modifies *auctoritate.*

17, 14. *agnoscere, simul cum.* In the translation *simul* is taken with *agnoscere* rather than with *cum.*

34, 25. *principio: prince and beginnere.* Rather *beginning.*

58, 46. fortuiti causa *compendii: abregginge* of fortuit hap. Rather *gain, profit.* The same occurs in the French, *l'abregement* du cas fortunel.

Prose 3. 19, 16. *probo: proeve* instead of *approve* (Skeat). Chaucer, however, gives the correct reading himself in a gloss:

proeve . . . as who seith, *I ne alowe nat, or I ne preyse nat.* Cf.
a similar instance below where Chaucer corrects himself.

30, 24. quasi . . . *laboretur:* as it were *y-travailed,* or more
precisely, as Chaucer adds, *weren bisy to enquiren.* It is
hardly fair to infer, as Skeat does, that Chaucer has mis-
translated here, when he later corrects himself. The French
also has *nous travaillons.*

Prose 3. 35, 26. Ac *non* illud demonstrare *nitamur:* But I
ne enforce me nat now to shewen it. "The translation is here
quite wrong;—Chaucer seems to have read *nitamur* as *vita-
mus"* (Skeat). *Nos* instead of *non* occurs in some of the
Latin manuscripts. Skeat apparently considered only *nos.*

Meter 3. 12, 11. Sed cur tanto flagrat amore *veri tectas*
reperire notas? But wherfore enchaufeth it so, by so greet
love, to finden thilke notes of *sooth y-covered. Tectas* modifies
notas rather than *veri* (Skeat). However, it is possible to
consider that *y-covered* modifies *notes,* and is separated from
it only by another modifier, *of sooth.*

Prose 4. 30, 20. *positionis* gratia: by grace *of positioun* (or
of possessioun, as it is found in some manuscripts). Rather
by way of supposition.

*Meter 5. 3, 3. *vi pectoris incitata,* omitted in translation.
6, 5. *liquido* . . . volatu: *moist* fleeinge. Rather *easy* fleeing.

Prose 6. 93, 74. Atque si est divini humanique *praesentis*
digna collatio: Certes, thanne, if men mighte maken any
digne comparisoun or collacioun of the *presence* devyne and
of the *presence* of mankinde. *Presence* both times seems a
mistake for *present.*

Thus, in Chaucer's translation curious mistakes of many
descriptions abound. He sometimes does not understand his-
torical allusions. He very often misses finer shades of meaning by losing the force of conjunctions, prepositions, and
pronouns. In numerous instances he translates interrogative
sentences as declarative sentences so that a doubtful point in
the original becomes a statement of fact in the translation,
or a rhetorical question loses its intended force. Less often,
but several times, he ignores or misapplies negatives so that
the meaning of the Latin is entirely reversed. He sometimes
translates Latin phrases and single words in so literal a fashion
that the English has little or no significance. He very frequently misrenders words, and disregards case relations.

The causes for Chaucer's mistakes are various. In the first place, many of them seem due to inaccurate scholarship and to careless or hasty methods. The translation is not as accurate as it was possible for a fourteenth century translation to be. Purvey's Biblical translations, made at about the same time, are more scholarly and finished. Moreover, Chaucer's work is very uneven; some passages are done much more poorly than others. *Prose* 4 of Book II is an example of one of the poorer parts; besides containing numerous mistakes, the translation shows several apparently careless omissions of words and phrases. Secondly, Chaucer made many mistakes, because he followed misrenderings already existing in the French translation.[15] Yet, here again Chaucer may not unfairly be held at fault, because, as he used the Latin text as well as the French, he had an opportunity to correct the mistakes of the latter. On the other hand, in justice it must be said that Chaucer's mistakes may often be excused; for he evidently, as an examination of the list will show, encountered many corruptions in the manuscripts with which he worked. It also must be remembered that he would not have at his disposal the lexicons and grammars which a translator would have today. His was of necessity a rough and ready method of translation. On account of lack of other aids, he was forced to take advantage of all the hints afforded in the Latin and French manuscripts through the relationship in the vocabularies of the three languages. Aided by keen penetration and poetic insight, notwithstanding imperfections and drawbacks, he often translated brilliantly and well.

Part III. The Prose Style

This section dealing with the prose style of the translation does not pretend to be exhaustive. Such a study would have to include a more extensive examination of Chaucer's other prose works and the prose works of his contemporaries than is made in what follows. I am pointing out only some of the more salient features. The problem is further complicated by the fact that Chaucer's translation is in part a translation of a French text as well as of a Latin text. Without complete

[15] Most of the instances in which Chaucer follows mistakes in the French translation must be included in the above list, since it includes the instances noted by Professor Liddell in his footnotes to the text of Chaucer's translation in the Globe Chaucer after his comparison of the two translations.

access to the French text, I have been obliged to make my comparisons primarily with the Latin, but the influence of the French must never be forgotten.

In the consideration of the prose style of Chaucer's translation I shall take up the following subjects: 1. Latin Influence in Vocabulary. 2. Peculiarities in Sentence Structure. 3. Alliteration. 4. Diffuseness. 5. Metrical Qualities.

1. *Latin Influence in Vocabulary*

One aspect of Chaucer's literalness appears in his bringing over from the original into his translation many Latin words, with the effect that his vocabulary becomes highly Latinized. This appropriation is in particular true of the more difficult passages. The philosophical content of the *Consolation of Philosophy* grows deeper as the work advances, and as Dame Philosophy proceeds from her so-called simple remedies to the stronger; consequently, we find a greater proportion of Latin words present in the later books of the translation than in the earlier. The first *prose* of Book I and the sixth *prose* of Book V may be compared to advantage in this regard. The first passage, eighty lines long, contains some fifteen words brought over from the Latin; an equal number of lines in the second passage contains more than five times as many instances. In Book IV, prose 6, one of the longer *proses,* there are about fifty-two opportunities for the incorporation of Latin words. Chaucer has availed himself of forty of them.

The result of this rather wholesale draught upon the Latin was to introduce into English some entirely new words. In the discussion of the Latin element of Chaucer's vocabulary it may be of some interest to consider the probable causes of their introduction. Stewart (*Essay,* p. 221) is of the opinion that we here find Chaucer in the very act of trying out new words. But it hardly seems that Chaucer was seriously experimenting with the new words for their own sake. In the first place he makes very little use of these new words in his subsequent writings, as we might expect if he were interested in the words for themselves. In the second place his use of them sometimes indicates a carelessness which is hardly consistent with experimentation. For example, he translates *temperiem* (4. p6. 134, 105) and *temperamentum* six lines later both by *atempraunce,* a word which his readers had never seen before, and which in the two instances was to express different ideas. His trans-

lation of the adjective *fortuitus* is very shifting. The word
occurs at least three times up to 5. p1. 58, 48, and each of these
times he translates it *fortunous;* in 5. p1. 58 he translates it
fortuit, and in the *meter* following *fortunel,* here perhaps influenced by the French.

The real reason for Chaucer's use of so many Latin words
was more likely merely that of convenience. As has been said
before, he appropriates them most plentifully in the difficult
passages; here he would find many philosophical terms which
would have no suitable equivalents in English. These he
would be forced to bring over just as he found them; and,
indeed, we find that many of the words introduced are such
as to facilitate the expression of philosophical ideas, as *abso-*
lute from *absolutum, eternity* from *aeternitas, mutable* from
mutabilis.

A list of new words which appear for the first time in the
translation is given below. The forms of some of them, even
though they contain a Latin root, suggest a French origin
rather than a direct taking over from the Latin. Doubtless,
if a comparison were to be made with the French translation
which Chaucer uses, we should find that the Latin words, in
many instances, are taken over in it also, just as we indeed
found to be the case with *futurs* and *arbitre,* mentioned above
(p. 5). Chaucer perhaps would feel doubly at liberty to
use a new word if he found it both in the original and in the
French. My evidence that these words appear for the first
time in English in the *Boece* depends on the *New English*
Dictionary. Some of them, perhaps, may be found to have
occurred earlier elsewhere. The list follows: *absolut* from
absolvere, 3. m9. 12, 9; *amonicioun, ammonitione,* 1. p4. 7, 5;
arbitre, arbitrii, oFr. *arbitre,* 5. p3. 12, 10; *atempraunce* translates *temperiem,* 4. p6. 134, 105, and *temperamentum,* 4. p6.
144, 111, but suggests oFr. *atemprance; attencioun, attentio-*
nem, 2. p1. 2, 1; *autompne, autumnus,* oFr. *autompne,* perhaps
found by Chaucer in the French translation, 1. m2. 17, 21;
coempcioun, coemptio, coemption, found in the French translation, 1. p4. 59, 39; *coeterne, coaeternum,* 5. p6. 39, 33; *com-*
mittest, committeres, 2. p1. 74, 52; *compotent, sui compos,* 5.
p6. 33, 28; *compressed, compressa,* 2. p7. 46, 33; *conioineth,*
coniunctus, 5. p4. 105, 77; *contagious, contagione,* 3. p12. 4, 3;
convenient, conveniebat, 1. p4. 187, 131; *corigeth, corrigit,* 4.
p7. 26, 19; *corollarie, corollarium,* 3. p10. 101, 78; *demonstra-*

cioun, demonstrationibus, 2. p7. 17, 10; *diffinisshed, definisti,* perhaps suggested by oFr. *definiss,* 3. p10. 6, 5; *disencreseth, decrescit,* 5. p6. 53, 43; *echines, echinis,* 3. m8. 14, 14; *efficient, efficiens,* 5. m4. 29, 26; *eternitee, aeternitas,* translated in the French *pardurableté,* 5. p6. 8, 7; *exceden, excedere,* 5. p5. 46, 33; *fatal, fatum,* 4. m4. 2, 2; *fortuit, fortuiti,* 5. p1. 58, 45; *fortunel, fortuitous,* cf. oFr. *fortunal, -el,* 5. m1. 10, 8; *fortunous, fortuitis,* cf. oFr. *fortuneus,* 1. p6, 7, 6; *futures, futura, futurs* in French translation, 5. p6. 200, 154; *imaginabile, imaginabilem,* 5. p4. 126, 104; *immoevabletee, immobilitate,* 5. p6. 51, 42; *impetren, impetrent,* but suggests oFr. *impetrer,* 5. p3. 142, 103; *impreinted, imprimi,* but suggests oFr. *empreinter,* 5. m4. 6, 5; *impressed, impressas,* 5. m4. 31, 29; *inestimable, inaestimabilem,* 5. p3. 137, 100; *infirm, infirma,* 5. m2. 3, 5; *intelligence, intellegentia,* 5. p3. 109, 80; *interminable, interminabilis,* 5. p6. 11, 9; *manifest, manifestum,* 2. p2. 175. 123; *mortal, mortales,* 5. p6. 128, 101; *muses, musis,* 1. p1. 51, 38; *nat mutable, immutabiles,* 4. p6. 110, 84; *mutabilitee, mutabilitas,* 2. p2. 59, 42; *mutaciouns, mutatio,* 2. p1. 23, 15; *obiecte, obiectae,* 5. p3. 3, 2; *orator, orator,* 4. p4. 183, 124; *Porche* (special use, as applied to the Stoic school of philosophy), *porticus,* 5. m4. 1, 1; *porismes, porismata,* but suggests oFr. *porisme,* 3. p10. 100, 77; *positioun, positionis,* 5. p4. 30, 21; *presentarie, praesentaria, presentaire* in the French translation, 5. p6. 202, 155; *previdence, praevidentia,* 5. p6. 83, 67; *propinquitee, propinquitatis,* 2. p3. 25, 17; *proscripcioun, proscriptioni,* 1. p4. 174, 122; *quereles, querimonias,* cf. oFr. *querele,* 3. p3. 48, 34; *refect, refectus,* 4. p6. 257, 199; *sensibilitees, sensus,* 5. m4. 5, 3; *sensible, sensible,* 5. p4. 131, 116.

The following new words may be added to this list, if we can accept as the actual date of the translation, 1374, assigned by the *New English Dictionary*. In each instance below is appended the name of the author who introduced the word, if Chaucer did not translate the *Consolation* until 1383, the latest assigned date:[16] *argument, argumentum,* 4. p6. 204, 157 (Wyclif); *compelleth, compellit,* 5. p4. 66, 49 (Wyclif); *conditionel, condicionis,* 5. p6. 128, 101 (Wyclif); *coniecte, coniecto,* 5. p3. 3, 3 (Wyclif); *considered, considerandum,* 5. p4. 118, 88 (Barbour); *coniunccicioun, coniunctione,* 3. p11. 47, 34 (Barbour); *dispensacioun, dispensatio,* 4. p6. 169, 131 (Wyclif); *disposicioun, dispositionis,* 5. p6. 184, 143 (Bar-

---

[16] The later date seems nearer the truth. See pp. 151-3.

bour); *disputacioun, disputationis,* 5. p1. 19, 15 (Barbour); *divynaciouns, divinationem,* 5. p4. 3, 2 (Wyclif); *facultee, facultas,* 5. p4. 99, 73 (Wyclif); *familiaritees, familiaritas,* 3. p5. 1, 1 (Wyclif); *implyeth, implicet,* but suggests oFr. *emplier,* 5. m1. 10, 8 (Wyclif); *infirmity, infirmitas,* 4. p2. 102, 71 (Barbour); *litargie, lethargum,* but cf. oFr. *litargie,* 1. p2. 14, 11 (Wyclif); *oportunitee, oportunitate,* 2. p3. 27, 20 (Barbour); *perturbaciouns, perturbationibus,* 1. p5. 51, 40 (Wyclif); *predestinat, praedestinata,* 5. p2. 33, 27 (Wyclif); *prescience, praescientia,* 5. p3. 17, 14 (Wyclif); *repugnem, repugnare,* 5. p3. 3, 3 (Wyclif).

Some new words, not derived from Latin, appear in the translation. Most of these, it will be noted, are French in origin; and perhaps they come from the French translation: *agreabletee* translates *aequanimitate,* cf. oFr. *agreablete,* 2. p4. 83, 59; *agreablely, aequanimos,* 2. p4. 92, 66; *amonestinge, exhortatio,* cf. oFr. *amonestement,* 5. p1. 3, 3; *aspreness, acerbitate,* 4. p4. 106, 93; *to ben calm, blandire,* 2. p2. 32, 24; *compounen, fingere,* cf. oFr. *componre,* 3. m9. 6, 4; *defeted, tabescis,* cf. oFr. *defeit, -fait,* 2. p1. 7, 4; *destinal, fatalis,* 4. p5. 56, 41; *entalenten, afficiant,* cf. oFr. *entalenter,* 5. p5. 4, 2; *hostelements, supellectilis,* cf. oFr. *(h)ostillement,* 2. p5. 85, 63; *indifferently,* in gloss 5. p3. 91; *perdurabletee, immortalitatem,* cf. oFr. *perdurablete,* 2. p7. 63, 47; *pronouncere, orator,* 2. p3. 39, 30; *hust, tacebat,* 2. m5. 16, 16.

The examples above indicate how dependent Chaucer was upon the Latin text and the French translation for his vocabulary. There are, however, certain words which he did not bring over, and the translation of which involves him in circumlocutions because of the lack of English equivalents: *elegi, drery vers of wrecchednesse,* 1. m1. 4, 4; *has scenicas meretriculas, thise comune strompetes of swich a place that men clepen the theatre,* (the French translation has here, *ces communes putereles abandonnees au peuple*), 1. p1. 34, 27; *inextricabilem labyrinthum, the hous of Dedalus, so entrelaced that it is unable to be unlaced,* 3. p12. 117, 77; *series indeflexa, ordenaunce of destinee, which that ne may nat ben inclyned,* 5. p3. 131, 97; *natura contenta est, nature halt hir apayed,* 2. p5. 57, 42; *vernis floribus, floures of the first somer sesoun,* 2. p5. 48, 34; *deus multi prodigus auri, god giveth them (as fool-large) moche gold,* 2. m2. 8, 10; *inexorabilesque discordiae, discordes that ne mighten ben relesed by preyeres,*

1. p4. 36, 27; *frondifluae . . . brumae, winter that maketh the leves to falle,* 1. m5. 12, 14; *inresoluto . . . nexu, by a bonde that may nat ben unbonde,* 3. m2. 5, 4; *inexhausti vigoris, with swich vigour and strengthe that it ne mighte nat ben empted,* 1. p1. 6, 8.

2. Peculiarities in Sentence Structure

Chaucer in the translation of the *Consolation of Philosophy* shows a conspicuous lack of sentence unity and coherence. Stewart describes very vividly his desperate encounters with difficult sentences and the labored efforts of parts of his prose in contrast with the great ease exhibited everywhere in his poetry. The *Melibeus* shows considerably more finish in this respect.[17] Chaucer's difficulty may have been occasioned by the facts that he translated more easily from the French in *Melibeus* than from the Latin in the *Consolation,* even though aided constantly by a French version, and that the thought of the latter is more profound and difficult to follow, or that the Boethian translation is a less mature work. A description of some of the chief faults and peculiarities[18] follows:

(a). Excessive Use of *and*—The stringing out of sentences by the use of *and* is very characteristic of all of Chaucer's prose works; instances may be found on almost every page. In this respect he is not, of course, an exception among the writers of his time. There are instances, however, where Chaucer's fondness for this conjunction plays havoc with the coherence of his sentences, as in the one to be cited: Quos notus sicco violentus aestu torret ardentes recoquens harenas: and eek Nero governed alle the poeples that the violent wind Nothus scorkleth, *and* baketh the brenning sandes by his drye hete. 2. m6. 17-19, 12-13 (cf. also 1. p6. 71-77, 52-57).

(b). Excessive Use of *that*—The frequency with which Chaucer uses *that,* both as a conjunction and as a pronoun,

[17] Although the *Parsons Tale* is on the whole more carefully written than the translation of the *Consolation,* yet there are more poor sentences to be found in it than in the *Melibeus.* Cf. *Parsons Tale* I, 416ff.; 444ff.; 670; 889; 967. In *Melibeus* loose sentences of this kind are rare. See, however, B 2248-50.

[18] In this connection Chaucer's translation of ablative absolute constructions may be of some interest. He sometimes translates them literally, and sometimes turns them to subordinate clauses. For literal translations, cf. 1. p3. 2, 1; 20, 18; p4. 62, 42; 80, 51. For translations as subordinate clauses, cf. 1. m3. 1, 1; p4. 5, 4; 2. p2. 23, 18; p3. 37, 28; m3. 13, 12; p4. 43, 32; p5. 73, 54; p6. 6, 4.

is conspicuous especially when the pronominal and the conjunctive use occur, perhaps several times, in the same sentence. The prose of the *Melibeus* shows the same tendency (cf. *Melibeus* B2406; 2504; 2583), but not to so great an extent. Examples from the translation follow: Postremo quod a qualibet re diversum est, id non est illud a quo intellegitur esse diversum. quare quod a summo bono diversum est sui natura, id summum bonum non est, quod nefas est de eo cogitare quo nihil constat esse praestantius: And eek, at the laste, see wel *that* a thing *that* is dyvers from any thing, *that* thilke thing nis nat *that* same thing fro which it is understonden to ben dyvers. Thanne folweth it, *that* thilke thing *that* by his nature is dyvers fro soverein good, *that that* thing nis nat soverein good; but certes, *that* were a felonous corsednesse to thinken *that* of him *that* nothing nis more worth. 3. p10. 64-70, 50-55; quare nihil est quod ullo modo queas dubitare cuncta quae sunt appetere naturaliter constantiam permanendi, devitare perniciem: For which thou mayst nat drede, by no manere, *that* all the thinges *that* ben anywhere, *that* they ne requiren naturelly the ferme stablenesse, etc. 3. p11. 133, 95; Unde non recte quidam qui, cum audiunt visum Platoni mundum hunc nec habuisse initium temporis nec habiturum esse defectum, hoc modo conditori conditum mundum fieri coaeternum putant: Wher-for som men trowen wrongfully *that,* whan they heren *that* it semede to Plato *that* this world ne hadde never beginninge of tyme, ne *that* it never shal han failinge, they wenen in this maner *that* this world be maked coeterne with his maker. 5. p6. 36, 30. For cther examples of the excessive use of *that* compare 1. p1. 6, 6; 3. p5. 23, 19; 79, 57; 4. p1. 29, 20; p2. 31, 21; p4. 114, 79; 5. p5. 32, 23; p6. 136, 107. Wyclif's writings sometimes show the same characteristic. Cf. for example. *Wyclif's English Works.* Ed. F. D. Matthew. E. E. T. S. 74, p. 228.

(c). Translation of indirect discourse constructions—Indirect discourse constructions were a frequent source of trouble to Chaucer. Nesciebat Croesum regem Lydorum Cyro paulo ante formidabilem mox deinde miserandum rogi flammis traditum misso caelitus imbre defensum? Wistest thou nat *how Cresus,* the king of Lydiens of whiche king Cyrus was ful sore agast a litel biforn, *that this rewliche Cresus* was caughte of Cyrus and lad to the fyr to ben brent, but that a rain, etc.? 2. p2. 42, 32 (For an instance of a similar kind, see the

Parson's Tale I, 324) ; Aetate denique Marci Tullii, sicut ipse
in quodam loco significat, nondum Caucasum montem romanae
reipublicae fama transcenderat: At the laste, certes, in the
tyme of Marcus Tullius, as him-self writ in his book, *that* the
renoun of the comune of Rome ne hadde nat yit passed ne
cloumben over the mountaigne that highte Caucasus. 2. p7.
40, 29 ; Quid vero, inquit, obscurumne hoc atque ignobile censes
esse an omni celebritate clarissimum: 'What demest thou
thanne?' quod she, 'is that a derk thing and nat noble...*or elles
that it is* right noble and right cleer by celebritee of renoun?'
3. p9. 36, 23.

(d). Detached Nouns—A common occurrence throughout
the translation is that of a noun introducing a clause and
standing without close grammatical connections with the clause.
This characteristic may sometimes be explained as a device
for gaining emphasis and sometimes as a result of Chaucer's
having followed the Latin word-order very closely.[19] The
noun, for example, may stand in the Latin in the accusative
case at the beginning of the sentence. Chaucer translates as
if it were nominative, and then passing on discovers his mistake, but turns the sentence to suit his convenience without
regard to sentence structure. Instances of this peculiarity
occur, but occur less frequently in the *Parson's Tale.* (Cf.
Parson's Tale I, 343; 695; 931.) The instances in the translation of the *Consolation* are very numerous : Paulinum con-
sularem virum cuius opes palatinae canes iam spe atque ambi-
tione devorassent, ab ipsis hiantium faucibus traxi : *Paulin, a
counseiller of Rome,* the richesses of the whiche Paulin the
houndes of the palays...wolden han devoured by hope and cov-
etise, yit drow I him out, etc. 1. p4. 68, 43 ; Itaque remedia quae
paulo acriora esse dicebas, non modo non perhorresco, sed au-
diendi avidus vehementer efflagito : *And tho remedies* whiche
that thou seydest her-biforn weren right sharpe, nat only that I
am nat a-grisen of hem now, but I, desirous of heringe, axe
gretely to herein the remedies. 3. p1. 10, 7 ; quos no nab iratis
sed a propitiis potius miserantibusque accusatoribus ad iudicium
veluti aegros ad medicum duci oportebat : *the whiche shrewes,*
it were a more convenable thing, that the accusours or advo-
cats, nat wroth but pitous and debonair, ledden tho shrewes
that han don wrong to the Iugement, right as men leden syke

---

[19] Sometimes Chaucer follows the French translation in this peculiarity; at other times he does not.

folk to the leche. 4. p4. 187, 127; hanc enim necessitatem non propria facit natura sed condicionis adiectio: For certes, *this necessitee conditionel,* the propre nature of it ne maketh it nat, but the adieccioun of the condicioun maketh it. 5. p6. 133, 105. Many other instances occur. Cf. 1. p4. 179, 124; m5. 32, 39; p5. 19, 15; 2. m2. 16, 19; 3. p8. 54, 33; m12. 3, 5; 4. m4. 5, 5; p6. 149, 115; 213, 165; 5. p3. 116, 87.[20]

(e). Repetition of Nouns with Pronouns—Chaucer seems to have thought that the principle of clearness demanded that the reader be constantly reminded of the name of the thing written about. Accordingly in any given passage we are likely to find a somewhat monotonous repetition of the principal noun, avoided in the Latin by the frequent use of pronouns. Chaucer very often translates these pronouns by repeating with them the antecedent for which they stand. In this way Chaucer emphasizes the value of the noun at the expense of the pronoun; substantive pronouns in the Latin tend to become adjective pronouns in his translation. The first nine lines of 3. p7. illustrate the tendency running through the whole. The theme of these lines is the futility of the pleasures of the body (voluptates). Boethius in the Latin uses the noun twice, twice represents it by a relative pronoun, and twice leaves it to be supplied as the subject of verbs. In all six instances, Chaucer repeats the noun *delices:* But what shal I say of *delices (voluptatibus)* of body, of whiche *delices (quarum)* the desiringes ben ful of anguissh, and the fulfill-inges of hem ben ful of penaunce? How greet syknesse and how grete sorwes unsufferable, right as a maner fruit of wikkednesse, ben thilke *delices* wont *(solent)* to bringen to the bodies of folk that usen hem! Of whiche *delices (quarum)* I not what Ioye may ben had of hir moevinge. But this wot I wel, that who-so-ever wole remembren him of hise luxures, he shal wel understonde that the issues of *delices (voluptatum)* ben sorwful and sorye. And yif thilke *delices* mowen maken *(explicare possunt)* etc. There are many other instances of the same thing; cf. repetition of *lettres,* 1. p4. 123, 81, of *dignitees and powers,* 2. p6., and of *dignitees,* 3. p4. The repitition of nouns with pronouns is much less frequent in *Melibeus* and the *Parson's Tale.* See, however, *Melibeus,* B, 2378;

[20] In one instance the main verb is altogether forgotten, and the subject, a pronoun, stands completely detached from the rest of the sentence. (3. p9. 38, 25). The same thing occurs in *Melibeus* B, 2447-8.

2437; 2524; 2544, 2685; *Parson's Tale* I, 80; 170; 290; 429; 682; 1039.

(f). Irregularities in Phrasing—Chaucer sometimes loses in coherence because he shifts from one form to another in giving expression to ideas of the same rank: bybliothecae potius ...parietes quam tuae mentis sedem requiro: ne I axe nat rather the walles of thy librarie...than *after* the sete of thy thought. I. p5. 26, 20; quoniam proecellit id quod nequeat auferri: for more worthy thing and more digne *is* thilke thing that may nat ben taken awey. 2. p4. 106, 76; Quam, inquam, me non modo ea quae conclusa est summa rationum, verum multo magis haec ipsa quibus uteris verba delectant: 'I delyte me', quod I, *'nat only* in the endes or in the somme of the resouns that thou hast concluded and proeved, but thilke wordes that thou usest delyten me moche more.' 3. p12. 88, 60; cum omnis fortuna vel iucunda vel aspera tum remunerandi exercendive bonos tum puniendi corrigendive improbos causa deferatur: so as alle fortune, whether so it be Ioyeful fortune or aspre fortune, is yeven either by cause *of guerdoning* or elles *of exercysinge* of good folk, or elles by cause *to punisshen* or elles *chastysen* shrewes. 4. p7. 5, 4.

3. *Alliteration*

That we should expect to find alliteration in Chaucer's translation is made probable *a priori* by two considerations. In the first place Chaucer was well acquainted with this form of literary embellishment as is abundantly shown in his poetry.[21] (See the article of Felix Lindner, "The Alliteration in Chaucer's Canterbury Tales", *Essays on Chaucer,* Chaucer Society Publications, 2nd Series 2.) In the second place the Latin original is highly colored by alliteration in both *proses* and *meters.* It is hardly to be supposed that this fact would escape the sensitive ear of a poet like Chaucer. That he should try to reproduce it would not be at all surprising. Moreover, the fragments of the French translation which I have show alliteration. Although it sometimes becomes difficult to choose between artificial and accidental sound repetitions, the following

[21] There are also instances of it in *Melibeus* and the *Parson's Tale.* See *Melibeus* B, 2183, 2208, 2216, 2226, 2228, 2239, 2259, 2276, 2281, 2328, 2393, 2414, 2713, 2895; *Parson's Tale* I, 158, 176, 197, 249, 269, 274, 281-3, 294, 355, 543, 656, 706, 731, 736, 769, 809, 816, 840, 854, 1010-12, 1087.

examples seem sufficient to show that Chaucer did as a matter of fact frequently follow the Latin alliteration.

Heu quam *praecipiti mersa profundo* Mens hebet et propria *luce relicta* *Tendit* in *externas* ire *tenebras,* *Terrenis* quotiens flatibus aucta *Crescit* in inmensum noxia *cura.*	'Allas! how the *thought* of man, *dreint* in over-*throwinge deepnesse, dulleth,* and forleteth his propre cleernesse, mintinge to goon in-to foreine *derk-* *nesses,* as ofte as his anoyous bisinesse *wexeth* withoute mesure, that is *driven* to and fro with *worldly windes.* 1. m2. 1, 1.

In the first two lines above the order of alliteration in the Latin will be observed to be *pmpm;* Chaucer preserves the same order in the *thdthd* arrangement. I shall point out below other instances where he seems to follow the Latin order. In the third and fourth lines it will be observed that the letters *te* are repeated four times in the Latin at the beginning of syllables. The accumulative effect of this and the other alliterations is very noticeable as will be found, especially if the lines are read aloud. A similar effect is produced in Chaucer's lines. The -*esse* (-*esses* in one instance) in which four words terminate may have been intended to match repetitions in the Latin.

Stringatque ligans inresoluto *Singula* nexu, *placet* arguto Fidibus lentis *promere* cantu.	It lyketh me to *shewe,* by *subtil song,* with *slakke* and delitable *soun* of *strenges,* . . . and how she (Nature), *bindinge,* restreyneth alle thinges by a *bonde* that may nat ben *unbounde.* 3. m2. 1, 4.

Here the repetitions of the Latin are especially conspicuous. The first two lines begin with *s* and end in -*uto;* the presence of *p* in corresponding positions in the two lines will also be noted. Chaucer matches this recurrence in sound by the frequent repetition of *s,*[22] and by the translation of *inresoluto* through the phrase *by a bonde that may nat ben unbounde,* an instance of *figura etymologica,* the discussion of which will be taken up later.

[22] Professor Liddell suggests (Globe Chaucer, p. 382) that *slakke* in translation of *lentis* is the scribe's mistake for *wakke* or *waike.* The former word beginning in *s,* however, may be due to Chaucer's desire for alliteration. Likewise Skeat (*Oxford Chaucer* II, 425) thinks *cometh eft* in translation of *mutet* a text corruption for *torneth* (1. m5. 9, 12). The alliteration in the Latin text at this place is very obvious, and the *c* of *cometh* helps to preserve the alliteration in the translation. Again in his notes on the same *meter* Skeat comments on *derke derknesses* as "not a happy expression" (1. m5. 34, 29). At this place also in the Latin the alliteration is pronounced.

Quam variis terras animalia permeant figuris:
Namque alia extento sunt corpore *pulveremque verrunt*
Continuumque trahunt *vi pectoris* incitata sulcum:
Sunt quibus alarum levitas *vaga verberetque ventos*
5 Et *liquido longi* spatia aetheris enatet volatu:
Haec pressisse solo *vestigia gressibus gaudent*
Vel *virides* campos transmittere vel *subire silvas*
Quae *variis videas* licet omni discrepare formis,
Prona tamen facies hebetes valet ingravare sensus.
10 Unica gens hominum *celsum levat* altius *cacumen*
Atque *levis* recto stat *corpore* despicitque terras.

The beestes passen by the erthes by ful diverse figures. For som of hem han hir bodies straught and crepen in the dust, and drawen after hem a tras or a foruh y-continued; . . . (Gloss)

And other *beestes,* by the *wandringe* lightnesse of hir *winges, beten* the *windes,* and over-*swimmen* the *spaces* of the longe eyr by moist fleeinge. And other beestes *gladen* hem-self to diggen hir tras or hir steppes in the erthe with hir *goings* or with hir *feet,* and to *goon* either by the *grene feldes,* or elles to *walken* under the *wodes.* And al-be-it so that thou seest that they alle *discorden* by *diverse formes,* algates hir *faces,* enclined, *hevieth* hir dulle wittes. Only the linage of men *heveth heyeste his heye heved,* and stondeth light with his up-right body, and biholdeth the erthes under him. 5. m5. 1, 1.

The most conspicuous point to be observed here is that Chaucer has to some extent preserved the arrangement of the alliterated words, although the places where the alliteration occurs in the original and in the translation do not coincide. In lines 2 and 3 of the Latin occurs a *pvvp* sequence, in lines 6 and 7 a *vggv* sequence, and in lines 7 and 8 a *vssv* sequence. There are two such sequences in the translation. The long alliteration *heveth heyeste his heye heved*—for length compare this with the Latin *vaga verberetque ventos*—presents the arrangement *hev- hey- hey- hev.* We find this same sequence again in the lines: And other *beestes,* by the *wandringe* lightnesse of hir *winges, beten* the windes. Other instances of this sequence occur in Chaucer's translation of passages included in which the Latin contains a similar arrangement: Nothus *scorkleth,* and *baketh* the *brenning sandes.* 2. m6. 18; *wene* to *liven* the *longer* for *winde.* 2. m7. 19.

rerum exitus prudentia *metitur* eademque in alterutro *mutabilitas* nec *formidandas fortunae minas* nec exoptandas *facit* esse blanditias.

But wisdom loketh and amesureth the ende of thinges; and the same chaunginge from oon in-to another . . . *maketh* that the *manaces* of *Fortune* ne ben nat for to *dreden,* ne the *flateringes* of hir to ben *desired.* 2. p1. 62, 44.

Such reproductions of the alliteration as occur in this passage occur frequently elsewhere. Cf. 1. m5. 9, 13; 2. m3. 7-10, 7-10; 2. p8. 7, 8; 3. p10. 28-29, 22-23; 3. m12. 1-2, 1-4; 4. p1. 10, 8; 19-21, 13-16; 30-3, 21-2; 4. p6. 254-8, 196-200; 4. p7. 13-15, 8-9. The following *meters,* entire, may be profitably studied in this regard: 1. m1; 2. m3; 3. m12; 4. m6.

Chaucer's reproduction of the alliteration of the original is well shown in those instances where the alliteration occurs in two successive Latin words. In Chaucer's translation of the sentence in which these words appear is likely to occur a similar alliteration of successive words, although the latter may not be a translation of the particular words alliterated in the Latin: Carmina *qui quondam* studio florente peregi, flebilis heu maestos inire modos: Allas! I, weping am constreined to beginnen vers of sorowful matere, that whylom in florisching studie made *delitable ditees*. 1. m1. 1, 1; pro *verae virtutis* praemiis falsi sceleris poenas: peyne of *false felonye* for guerdon of *verray vertu*. 1. p4. 163, 112; rara si constat sua forma mundo, si tantas *variat vices:* yif the forme of this worlde is so *selde stable*, etc. 2. m3. 14, 13; Tamen atras pellere curas miserasque fugare querelas non *posse potentia* non est: yif thou mayst nat putten awey thy foule *derke desyrs*, and dryven out, etc. 3. m5. 6, 8; non quidquid Tagus aureis harenis donat aut Hermus *rutilante ripa:* alle the thinges that the river Tagus yeveth yow with his *goldene gravailes*, or elles alle the thinges that the river Hermus yeveth with his red brinke. 3. m10. 8, 7; Quisquis profunda mente *vestigat verum:* who-so *seketh sooth* by a deep thought. 3. m11. 1, 1; primum quod memoriam *corporea contagione*, dehinc cum *maeroris mole* pressus amisi: first whan I loste my memorie by the *contagious coniunccioun* of the body with the sowle; and eftsones afterward, whan I loste it, confounded by the charge and by the burdene of my sorwe. 3. p12. 4, 3; Haec concordia temperat aequis elementa modis, ut pugnantia vicibus cedant umida siccis iungantque *fidem frigora flammis:* By thise same causes the floury *yeer yildeth swote smelles* in the firste *somer-sesoun*, etc. 4. m6. 19, 19; Quosque pressurus foret altus orbia *saltiger spumis* umeros notavit: And the *bristlede boor* markede with scomes, etc. 4. m7. 39, 27.

One method used by Chaucer for securing alliteration is to translate one Latin word by two alliterated words: *properata* malis: *hasted* by the *harmes* that I *have*. 1. m1. 10, 9; *obduxerat: dusked* and *derked*. 1. p1. 19, 17; *infructuosis affectum spinis:* with *thornes* and *prikkinges* of *talents* or *affecciouns*, whiche that ne ben no-thing *fructefyinge* nor *profitable*. 1. p1. 38, 31; *obstipui:* I wex al *abaisshed* and *astoned*. 1. p1. 57, 34; tunc me *discussa* linquerunt nocte tenebrae: thus, whan that night was *discussed* and *chased* a-wey, *derknesses* forleften

me. 1. m3. 1, 1 ; *dissolutis: dissolved* and *don* a-wey. 1. p3. 1, 1 ;
excitantis: commoevinge or *chasinge*. 1. m4. 4, 6 ; rapidos rector
comprime fluctus et quo caelum regis inmensum *firma* stabiles
foedere terras : thou governour, withdraw and *restreyne* the
ravisshinge flodes, and *fastne* and *ferme* thise erthes stable
with thilke bonde, with whiche thou governest the hevene that
is so large. 1. m5. 39, 46 ; *signat* tempora propriis aptans
officiis deus : God *tokneth* and *assigneth* the tymes, ablinge
hem. 1. m6. 12, 16 ; *deplorasti: biweyledest* and *biweptest*.
1. p6. 15, 12 ; *impetum:* the *swiftnesse* and the *sweigh*. 2. p1.
81, 57 ; *constet: stedefast* ne *stable*. 2. p3. 17, 17 ; *tepentis:* that
wexeth warm. 2. m3. 8, 5 ; *hians: gapinge* and *gredy*. 3. p3.
69, 49 ; *recessus:* the *crykes* and the *cavernes*. 3. m8. 8, 10.
There are many other examples. See 2. p4. 45, 33 ; 2. p4. 123,
88 ; 2. m7. 12, 13 ; 2. m8. 8, 13 ; 3. p7. 8, 6 ; 3. p9. 137, 92 ;
3. p10. 101, 78 ; 4. p1. 4, 3 ; 4. p2. 32, 27 ; 4. p6. 257, 199.
There are also many instances in *Melibeus* and in the *Parson's
Tale* where Chaucer uses two alliterated words together meaning about the same thing. See *Melibeus* B, 2208, 2259, 2260,
2261, 2279, 2306, 2355, 2429, 2431, 2509, 2523, 2564, 2569,
2641, 2642, 2805, 2833, 2867, 2885, 2941 ; *Parson's Tale* I, 133,
177, 276, 340, 432, 475, 609, 625, 626, 685, 724, 730, 735, 758,
805, 863, 980, 990, 1045, 1054.

Closely related to alliteration is that figure of speech known
as *figura etymologica*. When Chaucer finds an instance of
the latter in the original, as is frequently the case, he usually
reproduces it. Occasionally he adds it of his own accord
when it has no counterpart in the Latin as in the following
striking instance : Omnia certo fine gubernans hominum solos
respuis actus merito rector cohibere modo. Nam cur tantas
lubrica versat fortuna vices ? premit insontes dempta sceleri
noxia poena, . . . Latet obscuris condita virtus clara tenebris :
O thou *governour, governinge alle thinges* by certein ende,
why refusestow only to *governe* the werkes of men by dewe
manere ? Why suffrest thou that slydinge fortune torneth so
grete entrechaunginges of thinges, so that anoyous peyne, that
sholde dewely *punisshe* felouns, *punissheth* innocents ? . . . And
vertu cler-shyinge naturelly is hid in *derke derkenesses*. 1. m5.
22, 25. In the succeeding instances Chaucer reproduces the
figure from the Latin, although it will be observed that his
tendency is to out-do the original in this regard : hunc con-
tinuum *ludum ludimus* rotam volubili orbe versamus : this *pley*

I *pleye* continuely, I *torne* the whirlinge wheel with the *torning* cercle. 2. p2. 36, 27; aut quot *stelliferis* edita noctibus caelo *sidera* fulgent: as ther shynen brighte *sterres* on hevene on the sterry nightes. 2. m2. 4, 3; Quam vero late patet vester hic error *ornari* posse aliquid *ornamentis* existimatis alienis: but how brode sheweth the errour and folye of yow men, that wenen that any thing may ben *aparailed* with straunge *aparaile-ments*. 2. p5. 112, 86; si vestros animos amor quo caelum *re-gitur regat:* O! weleful were mankinde yif thilke Love that *governeth* hevene *governed* youre corages! 2. m8. 17, 29; *pulchrum pulcherrimus* ipse mundum mente gerens similique in imagine formans: thou that art alder-*fayrest*, beringe the *faire* world in thy thought, formedest this world to the lyknesse semblable of that *faire* world in thy thought. 3. m9. 8, 7; tum, illa, quanti, inquit, aestimabis, si bonum ipsum quid sit *ag-noveris?* . . . Infinito, inquam: si quidem mihi pariter deum quoque qui bonum est continget *agnoscere:* 'How mochel wilt thou *preysen* it', quod she, 'yif that thou knowe what thilke good is?' 'I wol *preyse* it', quod I, 'by *prys* withouten ende, etc. 3. p11. 3, 2; patrisfamilias dispositissima domo vilia vasa cole-rentur pretiosa: in the right *ordenee hous* of so mochel a fader and an *ordenour* of meynee, etc. 4. p1. 30, 21. Although here the figure does not occur in the Latin, yet its use in Chaucer's translation may be intended by him to correspond to the very obvious alliteration of the original; *conditore conditum* coaeter-num: world be *maked* coeterne with his *maker*. 5. p6. 39, 32. Both in *Melibeus* and in the *Parson's Tale* Chaucer shows a fondness for this figure. See *Melibeus* B, 2228, 2521, 2567, 2727, 2762; *Parson's Tale* I, 125, 189, 193, 200, 209, 328, 336, 406, 458, 656, 806.[23]

4. *Diffuseness*

The text of Chaucer's translation is about half as long again as the original. That it should be so is not altogether to be explained by the fact that translation from Latin into English would necessitate frequent expansions. Chaucer might have left out many of his additions and still have produced a faith-ful version without feeling hampered for lack of adequate

[23] In addition to the sound repetitions already referred to there are a few instances of rhyme. For example, 'It is certein and establisshed by lawe perdurable, that no-thing that is engendred nis stedefast ne stable. 2. m4. 17; and that the last ile in the see, that hight Tyle be thral to thee. 3. m5. 5.

means of expression. The chief sources of this expansion are the four hundred odd glosses, already discussed, varying in length from one to ten lines, the frequent translation of one Latin word by two English words (Cf. Lounsbury *Studies in Chaucer,* II, 154), and the translation of single words, participles, adjectives, nouns, pronouns, adverbs, and even conjunctions as clauses:

(a). Expansion of Participles—Papinianum diu inter aulicos *potentem* militum gladiis Antoninus obiecit: Antonius comaundede that knightes slowen with hir swerdes Papinian...*Whiche Papinian hadde ben longe tyme ful mighty* amonges hem of the court. 3. p5. 37, 29. The following instances, chosen from *proses* 2-5 of Book II, give an idea of the frequency with which Chaucer resorts to this method of translation: p2. 34, 26; 47, 35; 50, 38; 61, 44; p3. 12, 8; 21, 15; 30, 22; 34, 26; 42, 31; 61, 47; p4. 18, 12; 62, 44; 131, 94; p5. 5, 5; 15, 12; 32, 24; 37, 26; 76, 57.

(b). Expansion of Adjectives—*dulcibus* annis: in yeres *that ben swete.* 1. m1. 13, 13; suarum *securus* tuis ingemescit iniuriis: he biwayleth the wronges *that men don to thee,* and nat for him-self; *for he liveth in sikernesse.* 2. p4. 22, 16; *minimam* . . . aliquam portionem: som porcioun of it, *although it litel be.* 2. p7. 10, 52; *sereni* maris: the see, *whan it is cleer.* 2. p5. 43, 31. Cf. also 2. p4. 25, 17; 72, 51; 28, 20; 75, 53; 85, 59. It will be noted that the latter examples are all taken from one *prose;* this *prose* is not unusual in this regard.

(c). Expansion of Nouns—ne nostrum *comites* prosequerentur iter: Muses, *that ne weren felawes,* and folweden my wey. 1. m1. 6, 6; *ammirationem* . . . merebantur: deserved by no wey *that ye sholden mervailen on hem.* 2. p5. 38, 29; inbecillius *homine:* more freele *than is mankinde.* 2. p6. 27, 18. See also 2. p2. 40, 31; 3. p1. 15, 10; 3. p8. 43, 32.

(d). Expansion of Pronouns—*nostris* malis: to the harmes *that I have;* 1. p4. 201, 142; ne aggreditur quidem *quisque: ther is no might* that undertaketh. 4. p2. 19, 14; *Quis* enim quidquam nescius optet: *what is he* that desireth any thing of which he wot right naught. 5. m3. 20, 16. See also 1. m1. 10, 9; 2. p2. 5, 4; 3. p11. 128, 91; 5. m4. 21, 18.

(e). Expansion of Adverbs—*desuper: we that ben heye above.* 1. p3. 54, 43; Terrarum *quidem* fructus animantium procul dubio debentur alimentis: *sooth is that,* withouten doute, the frutes of the erthe owen to ben, etc. 2. p5. 52, 39.

(f). Expansion of Conjunctions—Chaucer's favorite method of translating a concessive conjunction is to turn it into a short clause introducing the real concessive clause: *tametsi* nemo audeat confiteri: *al-be-it so that* no man dar confesse it. 4. p7. 53, 36. See the following examples selected from *proses* 4 and 5 of Book II: p4. 11, 7; 98, 71; p5. 3, 3; 34, 26; 88, 67.

The reason for the various expansions to be found in the translation is not always apparent. Sometimes, however, they seem designed for rhetorical effect, as I shall attempt to show in the following section.

5. *Metrical Qualities*

Stewart (*Essay*, pp. 228-9) and Saintsbury (*History of English Prose Rhythm*, pp. 72-5) maintain that Chaucer at times reproduces the original Latin meter. Skeat (*Oxford Chaucer*, II, p. xxiii) holds that this reproduction is imperfect and unintended. The question whether Chaucer deliberately attempted to reproduce the Latin cadences is a subtle and difficult one, and it is not my object to consider it here. The question, moreover, could not be decided without a complete comparison of Chaucer's translation with the French translation, for, as I shall attempt to show presently, the addition of phrases and peculiar twists of construction which might be supposed to be due to Chaucer's desire for rhythm are influenced in part by the latter. But, whatever the source, there is in the translation a certain balance of part against part, an equality of phrase and clause length, a fullness of period, which often contribute a rhetorical dignity and a solemn melody worthy of the impressive thought to which the *Consolation of Philosophy* gives expression.[24] Although the translation may be a less smooth and less finished piece of prose than the *Melibeus,* or the *Parson's Tale,* and although it shows in the main the same characteristics of style as these works, yet parts of it at least are much more inspired and poetic. Let us now consider some of the means by which Chaucer attempts to secure dignity of style.

(a). Translation of Single Latin Words by Two English

[24] Among the best passages might be mentioned 1. m1 and p1, the spirited description telling how Dame Philosophy puts to flight the weeping Muses; 1. m5, the lament of Boethius; 2. m5, the former age; 2. m8, the bond of love; 3. m2, the bond of Nature; 3. m9, the prayer of Dame Philosophy; 4. m4, the second bond of love passage.

Words—It will be found that Chaucer frequently translates each of several Latin words of a sentence by two English words not differing greatly in meaning; he occasionally thus doubles as many as four words. The result is to make the sentence fuller and more impressive. Examples follow: Et esset, inquit, infiniti stuporis omnibusque horribilius monstris, si, uti tu aestimas, in tanti velut patrisfamilias dispositissima domo vilia vasa colerentur pretiosa sordescerent: 'certes', quod she, 'that were a greet *merveyle,* and *an enbasshinge (stuporis)* with-outen ende, and wel more horrible than alle monstres, yif it were as thou wenest: that is to seyn, that in the right ordenee hous of so mochel a *fader* and *an ordenour of meynee (patrisfamilias)* that the vessles that ben *foule* and *vyle (vilia)* sholden ben *honoured and heried (colerentur),* and the precious vesseles sholden ben *defouled* and *vyle (sordescerent).* 4. p1. 27, 19; At nos desuper inridemus vilissima rerum quaeque rapientes securi totius furiosi tumultus eoque vallo muniti quo grassanti stultitiae adspirare fas non sit: But we that ben heye aboven, siker fro alle *tumulte* and *wode noise (tumultus),* *warnestored* and *enclosed (muniti)* in swich a palis, whider as that *chateringe* or *anoyinge folye (stultitiae)* ne may nat atayne, we scorne swiche *ravineres* and *henteres (rapientes)* of fouleste thinges. 1. p3. 54, 43. There are numerous examples of words thus doubled in groups. Cf. 1. p1. 15, 14; 1. m7. 8, 18; 2. p1. 19, 11; 40, 31; 81, 57; 2. m1. 9, 6; 2. p3. 19-28, 15-21; 2. p4. 45, 33; 55, 39; 3. p9. 137-40, 92-3; 4. p1. 4, 3; 5. m3. 1-7, 1-5. See also *Melibeus* B, 2169, 2201, 2216, 2226, 2352, 2401, 2598; *Parson's Tale* I, 81, 116, 130, 554, 774.

(b). Balance in Phrasing—Chaucer is fond of repeating a series of words in successive phrases so as to give them equality in length and similarity in sound. Thus a preposition, possessive pronoun, or adjective of one phrase is likely to be repeated in the succeeding phrase: Tune ille es, ait, qui nostro quondam lacte nutritus nostris educatus alimentis in virilis animi robur evaseras: 'art nat thou he', quod she, 'that whylom *y-norisshed with my milk,* and *fostred with myne metes,* etc. 1. p2. 3, 2; operis tanti pars non vilis homines: we men that ben nat *a foule party,* but *a fayr party* of so grete a werk. 1. m5. 37, 44; Paucis enim minimisque natura contenta est: for *with ful fewe thinges,* and *with ful litel thinges* nature halt hir apayed. 2. p5. 56, 44; tanto strepitu: *with so grete a noise,* and *with so grete a fare,* 2. p5. 82, 60. *Melibeus* and the *Parson's Tale* show the same tendency. See *Melibeus* B, 2427, 2473, 2526, 2530, 2532, 2845; *Parson's Tale* I, 299, 392, 400, 550, 603, 621, 737-8, 853, 864, 899, 911, 1049, 1055-6.

(c). Balance in Clauses—There is a tendency to be observed throughout the translation for the clauses of a given passage to approach equality in length. Chaucer avoids abrupt and unexpected terminations. This fulness of style is effected by devices such as doubling words in translation as described above, turning phrases of the original into clauses, repeating prominent words such as the subject and predicate in successive clauses. In the following passages the average clause length is about constant, although a precise equality in length is not to be expected: O thou maker of the whele *that bereth the sterres (stelliferi), which that art y-fastned (nixus)* to thy perdurable chayer, and tornest the hevene with a ravisshing sweigh, and constreinest the sterres to suffren thy lawe; so that the mone som-tyme shyning with hir ful hornes, meting with alle the bemes *of the sonne* (supplied by Chaucer) hir brother, hydeth the sterres *that ben lesse (minores).* 1. m5. 1, 1; But certes, al be thou fer fro thy contree, thou nart nat put out of it; *but thou hast failed of thy weye and gon amis* (all from *aberrasti*). And yif thou hast lever for to wene that thou be put out of thy contree, than hast thou put out thy-self *rather than any other wight hath* (The *potius* appears alone in the Latin without the concluding clause). . . . For yif thou remembre of what contree thou art born, it nis nat governed *by emperours, ne by governement of multitude (multitudinis imperio).* 1. p5. 6, 5; she, that yit *covereth hir and wimpleth hir (velat)* to other folk, hath shewed hir every-del to thee. *Yif thou aprovest hir and thenkest that she is good* (all from *probas*), use hir maneres and pleyne thee nat. 2. p1. 42, 31.

It will also be noted in this connection that Chaucer frequently splits up sentences of the Latin into clauses, and arranges these in a parallel series, each member of which has a common subject. If a parallel arrangement of this kind appears in the Latin itself, Chaucer is very likely to elaborate upon it in his translation. The repetition of the same initial word or words in each clause serves to give a definite rhetorical effect.

Et ego quidem bonis omnibus pulsus dignitatibus exutus existimatione foedatus ob beneficium supplicium tuli. *Videre autem videor* nefarias scelerotum officinas gaudio laetitiaque fluitantes perditissimum quemque novis delationum fraudibus imminentem, iacere bonos nostri discriminis terrore prostratos.

And I, that am put awey fro gode men, and despoiled of dignitees, and defouled of my name by gessinge, have suffred torment for my gode dedes. Certes, *me semeth that I see* the felonous covines of wikked men habounden in Ioye and gladnesse. *And I see* that every lorel shapeth him to finde out newe fraudes for to accuse gode folk. *And I see* that gode men, etc. 1. p4. 217, 151.

Ille dedit Phoebo radios dedit et cornua
  lunae,
Ille homines etiam terris dedit ut sidera
  caelo:
Hic clausit, etc.

He *yaf* to the sonne his bemes; *he yaf* to the mone hir hornes. *He yaf* the men to the erthe; *he yaf* the sterres to the hevene. *He* enclosed, etc. 3. m6. 2, 2.

Unde haec sic animis viget
Cernens omnia notio?
Quae vis singula perspicit
Aut *quae* cognita dividit?
Quae divisa recolligit
Alternumque legens iter.

Whennes thryveth thanne or *whennes* comth thilke knowinge in our sowle, that discerneth and biholdeth alle thinges? And *whennes is thilke strengthe* that biholdeth the singuler thinges; *or whennes is the strengthe* that devydeth thinges y-knowe; *and thilke strengthe* that gadereth to-gidere the thinges devyded; *and the strength* that cheseth his enterchaunged wey. 5. m4. 19, 16.

Numerous other instances may be pointed out to illustrate this same characteristic. Cf. repetition of *ne shal nat moeve that man.* I m4. 4-9, 5-10; *why refusestow . . . why suffrest thou.* I. m5. 22-6, 25-9; *com forth . . . the suasion . . . com forth musice.* 2. p1. 28-32, 20-24; *and eek Nero,* throughout 2. m6; *Seestow nat . . . seestow nat.* 2. p7. 45-9, 32-35; *amiable Fortune and the contraire Fortune,* throughout 2. p8; *and hadde maked,* 2. m12. 3-9, 5-13; *the beestes.* 5. m5. 1-6, 1-6. See also I. p4. 13-14, 10-11; I. m6. 5-10, 7-15; 2. p4. 58-67, 42-7; 2. p5. 106-9, 81-4; 2. p6. 80-4, 61-3. Among many examples in *Melibeus* and the *Parson's Tale* see the following: *Melibeus* B, 2434-43, 2552, 2648-55; *Parson's Tale* I, 256, 278-80, 331, 372, 509, 777.

(d). Influence of the French Translation on Chaucer's Prose Style—A comparison of Chaucer's translation with the French translation and the original in the extracts quoted below shows that Chaucer must have been dependent in part upon the French translation for the parallel sentence structure and balance of clauses which we have just been considering. An examination of the extract quoted on page 6 also supports this view.

Felix nimium prior aetas	Blisful was the first age of men! They helden hem apayed with the metes that the trewe feldes broughten forth.	Trop furent beneure li homme du premier aige! Il se cuidrent apaiez des viandes que li loial champ leur apportoient. Il ne se destruient pas par outrage qui fait les hommes manues et pereceus. Quant il avoient longue piece jeune il mengoient les glans des bois. Il ne savoient fere beurage de miel et de vin; ne taindre les blanches toisons des Siriens par diverses couleurs entrans comme venim.
Contenta fidelibus arvis		
5 Nec inerti perdita luxu,	They ne distroyede nor deceivede nat hem-self with outrage.	
Facili quae sera solebat 10 Ieiunia solvere glande,	They weren wont lightly to slaken hir hunger at even with acornes of okes.	
Non bacchica munera norant 15 Liquido confundere melle. Nec lucida vellera Serum Tyrio miscere veneno.	They ne coude nat medly the yifte of Bachus to the cleer hony—(Gloss); ne they coude nat medle the brighte fleeses of the contree of Seriens with the venim of Tyrie;—(Gloss).	
20 Somnos dabant herba salubres Potum quoque lubricus amnis Umbras altissima pinus.	They slepen hoolsom slepes up-on the gras, and dronken of the renninge wateres; and layen under the shadwes of the heye pyn-trees.[25]	Il se dormoient sus les herbes, et bevoient les courans ruisseaus; et gesoient es umbres des haus pins. 2. m5. 1-13, 1-12.

Chaucer's translation, outside of the introductory clauses, consists of a series of eight clauses nearly parallel in arrangement, averaging about twenty syllables in length, and corresponding to many different constructions in the Latin. In the main, it will be observed, he follows the French translation very closely, although the latter diversifies the parallel ar-

[25] Chaucer's translation, thus characterized by an arrangement in parallel clauses and by the recurrence of similar words, may be compared with the looser and less rhetorical arrangement of Colville's translation (p. 44, Bax edition of Colville's translation of 1556) and with the more literal and condensed translation of Queen Elizabeth (E. E. T. S., original series, 113). I have omitted the glosses from Colville's translation.

Colville.	Queen Elizabeth.
The first age of man was much happye that was contented with such as ye fields brought forth without labor of man, and was not hurte wyth great excesse of metes and drynkes. They weren wont to satysfye theyr long hunger wyth lytell acornes of the oke, and knewe (not) howe to myng the wyne with honye, nor how to dye the white fleses of woll of Seria with the venim of tyre. They could then be contentyd to take holesom slepes upon the grasse and knew no beddes of downe, and drynke fayre rennynig water for lacke of wyne and ale, and also dwell under the shadowe of the hygh pyne tree for lacke of curyous howses.	Happy to much the formar Age With faithful fild content, Not lost by sluggy lust, That wontz the long fastz To Louse by son-got Acorne, That knew not Baccus giftz With molten hony mixed Nor Serike shining flise With tirius venom die. Sound slipes Gave the grasse, Ther drink the running streme, Shades gave the hiest pine.

It will be noted that Colville's translation shows indebtedness to the translation of Chaucer.

rangement of clauses by introducing a temporal clause at the end of the eighth line, and by leaving the *il ne savoient* to be understood in the thirteenth line. The following analysis will show the relation between the two translations and the original:

They helden hem apayed, Il se cuidrent apaiez, from the adjective *contenta*.

They ne distroyede nor deceivede, Il ne se destruient, from the adj. *perdita*.

They weren wont, from *solebat*. Here the French has *quant il avoient,* etc.

They ne coude nat medly, Il ne savoient fere, from *norant confundere*.

They ne coude nat medle, taindre (Il ne savoient is understood), from *norant* (understood) *miscere*. Chaucer translates *confundere* and *miscere* by the same verb *medle*.

They slepen hoolsom slepes up-on the gras, Il se dormient sus les herbes, from *somnos dabat herba salubres. Herba* is thus the literal subject of *dabat,* although it is changed completely around in the two translations.

And dronken of the renninge wateres, et bevoient les courans ruisseaus, from *potum quoque lubricus amnis. Amnis* is literally the subject.

And layen under . . . pyn-trees, et gesaient . . . pins. Pinus is literally the subject.

The comparison of these passages indicates that a complete study of Chaucer's prose style involves a careful consideration of the French translation, although the differences between the latter and Chaucer's translation, pointed out above, show the stamp of Chaucer's hand. Basing my opinion on the portions of the French translation which I have available, I believe that the English translation is more rhetorical, and the style somewhat more pretentious.

Chaucer's prose, then, is marked by a fullness, a sense of measure and proportion. A consideration of the sections of this chapter which deal with his inconsistency of phrasing, his cumbersome handling of indirect discourse, and his misconstructed sentences precludes any idea of a precise application of mechanical principles such as came later to characterize the prose of John Lyly; yet, Chauer, gifted with a sensitive ear, feeling the spirit of his original, has reproduced its enthusiasm, its dignity of expression, and, as best he could, its symmetry of style. His translation is the translation of a poet.

CHAPTER II

INFLUENCE OF THE CONSOLATION ON CHAUCER'S THOUGHT: PROVIDENCE

The *Consolation of Philosophy* has been called the "golden book" of the Middle Ages. It is expressed, as may be judged from the foregoing chapter, in highly poetic language, and is attractive and understandable. The poetry has an essentially human appeal. Written by Boethius at the time of his unjust imprisonment, it reflects the turmoil of his own soul and is a product of sincere emotion. Men are always comforted in times of trouble by comparing their own affairs with the milder and fiercer aspects of nature, and by considering the majesty and serenity of the heavenly motions when storm and turmoil rage below, alike in external nature and in their own lives. And it was here that Boethius derived comfort.

Boethius, however, goes deeper than the emotional, poetic parts might lead one to suppose. Choosing now here, now there from Plato, Aristotle, Cicero, the Stoics, and the Neo-Platonists, he explains how, if men have a true conception of God, a conception unobscured by worldly desires, riches, fame, and power, a conception commensurable with God's greatness, they may see that even adversity is a blessing; that evil is consistent with God; that man, although he is a free moral agent, is none the less watched over by the all-seeing eye and guided by the omnipotent hand. Boethius thus finds consolation for his affliction in the greatness and goodness of God. His veneration of the deity is one of the most pronounced characteristics of his philosophy. It was this veneration no doubt which led people in the Middle Ages to the belief that Boethius was a Christian saint. Not recognizing the pagan elements in his philosophy, they considered him an expounder of Christian doctrine.[1] The tragic death of Boethius was wrongly thought to have been occasioned by his adherence to the Christian faith. Dante places him in the

[1] The belief that Boethius was a Christian also rested on five theological tracts ascribed to him in the Middle Ages: *De Trinitate, Utrum Pater et Filius et Spiritus Sanctus de Divinitate Substantialiter Prae-*

eighth circle of Paradise (*Par.* 10. 121-9). Chaucer regarded the *Consolation* as a holy Christian work, and in his retractation at the close of the *Parson's Tale*, his translation of the *Consolation* is classed with "bokes of Legendes of seintes, and omelies, and moralitee, and devocioun."

It is easy to understand how a book so serious and holy as the *Consolation*, and yet poetic, might be translated with enthusiasm by Chaucer. It dealt with subjects which appealed to him deeply. No ideas in Chaucer's poetry are more characteristic of him than those concerned with Fortune, with "destinee," with "cas and aventure," with "gentilesse," with "felicitee," with "divine purveyaunce," the "bond of love," "trouthe," and similar things. These are also themes of the *Consolation of Philosophy*. It now becomes my purpose to try to determine how far Chaucer was influenced by Boethius in these ideas. I hope to emphasize more than has been previously emphasized the debt which Chaucer owed to Boethius for much that we admire in the serious side of his poetry.

The present chapter, and the chapter following it, deal with the influence of the *Consolation* on Chaucer's thought; the present one, with the influence of Boethius on Chaucer's conception of Providence; the next one, with the influence of Boethius in determining Chaucer's ideas of "felicitee". The object of Boethius in the *Consolation* is to teach what true happiness, or "felicitee" as Chaucer terms it, is. Boethius accomplished his object by explaining the nature and operation of Providence in man's affairs. The two ideas of course overlap, but I have found it convenient to consider them separately. This chapter deals largely with the divine plan apart from man; the next, with man in relation to the divine plan.

I shall divide the present chapter on Providence into two parts: (1) The hierarchy of heavenly powers. (2) The justice of heaven questioned.

PART I. THE HIERARCHY OF HEAVENLY POWERS

The system by which Providence controls the universe, according to Boethius, is complicated. Providence rules absolutely. Her chief minister is destiny. Under destiny are Fortune, chance, and possibly other agencies, to be discussed

dicentur, Quomodo Substantiae Bonae Sint, De Fide Catholica, Liber contra Eutychen et Nestorium. Whether Boethius actually wrote these tracts has long been a disputed question.

presently. Although the rule of Providence is absolute, yet it is benevolent. This benevolence is poetically described through the figure of the "bond of love" which links all of the universe together in harmony. Of these agencies, I shall first discuss Fortune, the one most frequently spoken of by Chaucer.

1. *Fortune*

Fortune, as represented in mediaeval art[2] and literature, was a living, potent, and terrible force. Wars, violence of all kinds, and plagues made life very uncertain. The position of kings was especially hazardous. As Chaucer translates a passage of the *Consolation,* "the olde age of tyme passed, and eek of present tyme now, is ful of ensaumples how that kinges ben chaunged in-to wrecchednesse out of hir welefulnesse" (3. p5. 3-5). The *Monk's Tale* of Chaucer and the *De Casibus Virorum et Feminarum Illustrium* of Boccaccio are merely amplifications of this theme. The lines of Gower in the prologue of the *Confessio Amantis* express the general attitude:

> The world stant evere upon debat,
> So may be seker non astat,
> Now hier, now ther, now to, now fro,
> Now up, now down, this world goth so,
> And evere hath don and evere schal.   567-71

Fortune, allegorically, was made to explain all the ups and downs of the violent times in which the people of the Middle Ages lived. In fact, so vividly did she come to be conceived that in their literature she is represented as a real and actual force, a goddess as powerful as was Minerva or Juno to the Romans.

In the *Consolation* (chiefly in Book II), Boethius was the first[3] to visualize Fortune in this most personal way. He imagines Fortune concretely, as coming to him and herself arguing her case with him. His discussion of Fortune may be divided into three phases: (1) Her mutability (Book II). She plays with men, first flattering them with her gifts, then deceiving them, by taking those gifts away. Her gifts are riches, power, fame, and bodily pleasure. One day her face is bright; the

[2] See *Les Arts au Moyen Age.* Album. Vol. VI, series 4, plates 37-40.

[3] For the classical conception of *Fortuna,* see *Dictionnaire des antiquités grecques et romaines.* Mr. Galpin has briefly discussed the realism in the mediaeval conception of Fortune in an article entitled "Fortune's Wheel in the Roman de la Rose," *Publications of the Modern Language Association,* Vol. 24, pp. 332 ff.

next it is covered with a cloud. Her wheel always turns, bringing the proud to low estate, and the low to high estate, but the former process is the more frequent one. Men can be sure of nothing, for she plays just as she likes with free and bond. Absolutely without sympathy, she cares no more for one man than another. (2) Defense of Fortune by herself (2. p. 2). The gifts which I give are mine. If I favor men with prosperity for a while, I can take away again what I have already given. The world is my realm. I can do as I like therein. In taking my gifts a man thereby swears allegiance to me as his queen. Therefore he must abide by my laws. At death, it is true, he goes out of my reach, but until then, I can dispose of him as I like. Moreover I do one lasting favor for men even in deserting them. I show them who their true friends are, for the false friends always follow me. The true friends remain behind. (3) The deeper significance of Fortune, as dependent upon the deity (4. p7). Of a connection with Providence, Fortune herself does not seem to be aware, for she works blindly and wantonly. But behind her and governing her, is the all-wise Providence. Through the adversities of Fortune, Providence creates in men what we now call character. Through adversity they are made strong.

The purposes of Boethius, therefore, were highly serious, as in Fortune he saw the instrument of God. By her he attempted to make a logical explanation for the apparently illogical and unjust uncertainties of life. Boethius himself, however, did not dwell at greatest length upon the most important aspect of Fortune. He devoted far more time to describing her fickleness, and her picturesqueness. The description of Fortune comes in the earlier part of the *Consolation*, when Philosophy is consoling Boethius with what she calls her "lighter remedies". In the latter part of the *Consolation*, Boethius, though he continues to speak of adversities, in the main no longer does it through the allegory of Fortune.

But the picturesque allegorical side of Fortune is just the side which took the fancy of many of the mediaeval poets. As she passed through their hands, she took on more and more characteristics. Elaborate similes were invented to describe her. Alanus de Insulis, in the *Anticlaudian*[4] describes the luxurious mansion where she lives. Jean de Meun describes her wheel[5] as a wheel which could be moved about from place to place, always spinning up and down, always bearing men to their destruction in its downward course. In art she is sometimes[6] pictured as a blind negress sitting in the midst of the busy turmoil of men, presiding over battles, or over workmen digging for gold, or over human figures representing prosperity and sensuality. These are caught up by her wheel one by one and turned out as grinning skeletons, pierced with daggers, emblematic of violent death. Thus the allegory of Fortune came to be a very lively conception; and she is made to explain all the changes in the lives of men.

Light and fanciful poets, who glibly described Fortune, did not take the pains to analyze that of which they wrote. To them Fortune was no more than an attractive literary convention. They devoted themselves only to describing her fickleness and her picturesqueness without thinking of her significance. But there is every evidence that the more thoughtful poets attempted to establish for themselves the place in the world of that which was allegorically called Fortune. Dante devotes his attention to showing that she is an instrument of God. Just as God has given guides to control the heavens, so He has ordained Fortune as a "general minister" to change vain possessions from people to people beyond the hindrance of human wisdom. Dante employs only one simile, and that a commonplace one, to describe her deceitfulness, saying that her sentences are like snakes hidden in the grass (*Inf.* 7. 84). This discussion of Fortune at the beginning of the *Inferno* suffices for the whole *Divine Comedy* (7. 67-96). Thereafter she is mentioned briefly, but only as the instrument which directs earthly affairs to their outcome.[7] Jean de Meun in the *Roman de la Rose* takes pains to explain that she is not to be considered as an actual goddess:

> D'autre part, si est chose expresse,
> Vous faites Fortune déesse,
> Et jusques ou ciel la levés,
> Ce que pas faire ne devés,
> Qu'il n'est mie drois ne raison
> Qu'ele ait en paradis maison;
> El n'est pas si bien eúreuse,
> Ains a maison trop périlleuse.   6179-86

[4] Wright, the *Anglo-Latin Satirical Poets*, vol. II, pp. 268 ff.
[5] *Roman de la Rose*, 6411-14. (Elzévirienne edition, Paris, 1878.)
[6] *Les Arts au Moyen Age, op. cit.* plate 40.
[7] Cf. *Inferno*, 13. 98; 15. 46, 70; 30. 14, 146; *Purg.* 19. 4; 26. 36; 32. 116; *Par.* 12. 92; 17. 26; 27. 145.

The moral Gower in the Prologue to the *Confessio Amantis* has a characteristic idea of Fortune:

> And natheles yet som men wryte
> And sein that Fortune is to wyte,
> And som men holde oppinion
> That it is constellacion,
> Which causeth al that a man doth:
> God wot of bothe which is soth . . .
> The world arist and falth withal,
> So that the man is overal
> His oghne cause of wel and wo.
> That we Fortune clepe so
> Out of the man himself it groweth;
> And who that other wise troweth,
> Behold the poeple of Irael
> IFor evere whil they deden wel,
> Fortune was hem debonaire,
> And whan thei deden the contraire,
> Fortune was contrariende.   529-555

The idea here presented that Fortune comes to man according to his merits is not altogether Boethian or Dantesque. According to Boethius good men often suffer the most. (Cf. *Consolation* 4. p6. 177-206.)

In England the idea of Fortune, so wide-spread in Italy and in France,[8] early received attention. The *Cursor Mundi*, in the advice to the reader with which the author concludes, has a rather unusual allusion to Fortune's casting men down into a well. The *New English Dictionary* records this instance as the earliest use of the word and dates it 1300. *William of Palerne*, translated from a French original about 1340-50, contains brief allusions to Fortune. A passage in Barbour's *Bruce*[9] (1375) contains the usual conventional charges against Fortune and a long account of her wheel. There are indications, however, that the ideas of Fortune in England were crude and less wide-spread than on the continent. The *Gest Hystoriale of Troye* (1370),[10] singularly enough, speaks of

[8] Cf. *Studies in Chaucer's Hous of Fame*, W. O. Shyperd. *Chaucer Society*, 2nd Ser. 39, pp. 120-8.

[9] E. E. T. S. Vol. II, Extra Series 21, 29. Book XIII, 631-660.

[10] E. E. T. S. 39, 56. ll. 2706ff:

> But fortune, that is felle, forthers his tyme;
> Hastis to unhappe, having no rewarde,
> Ordans an yssew, evyn as hym list;
> Turnys all entent, that hym tary wold;
> Caches furthe his cold wirdis with cumpas to ende.—
> But no man tentes to tene er the tyme come,
> No ferd is for fortune till it falle to.

Fortune in the masculine gender. The Fairfax Ms. of the *Cursor Mundi* leaves out allusions to Fortune contained in the other manuscripts.[11] *Piers Plowman* and the alliterative romance, *Morte Arthure,*[12] have little to say of the fickle goddess. Therefore it seems that Fortune found a place more definitely in those poets who follow the French school, Gower, Chaucer, and Chaucer's follower, Lydgate. Of these three, Chaucer's discussion of Fortune shows the most sympathetic understanding of the discussion of the *Consolation of Philosophy* as the following paragraphs are designed to prove.

Lydgate says of the *Consolation of Philosophy:*

> I trowe ther is no man a-lyve
> Whiche koude aright halvendel discryve
> Her pitous wo nor lamentacioun
> Certys not Boys, that hadde swiche renoun
> With drery wordis to be-wepe and crye
> In compleynynge to philosophie
> Thoruh his boke accusynge aye Fortune.
>
> > *Troy Book* IV. 3006 ff.

Lydgate probably thought that the *Consolation of Philosophy* was one huge outcry against Fortune; at least, there is little in his discussion of Fortune in the *Troy Book* to show that he understood the deeper side of the *Consolation.* He is, however, very enthusiastic and diffuse in his outcries against Fortune and in his descriptions of her fickleness. It was that

---

[11] *Cursor Mundi* E. E. T. S. 66, 68, ll. 2317-20. The Göttingen, Trinity, and Cotton Mss. all have allusions to Fortune. The Fairfax Ms. omits this entirely:

> Than blindes us a littel wele,
> That we can noght us selven fele,
> Dame Fortunue turnes than hir quele,
> And castes us dun until a wele. (From the Cotton Ms.)
> Then blindis us a litel wele
> That we can noght our-selvin fele
> For certis I, likkin hit to a quele
> Of our life the werldis wele.
> Now up now down as fallis with chaunce. (Fairfax.)

A similar omission is to be found in 1. 27628:

> If thou be riche, thou thanc fortune. (Cotton)
> If thou be riche, yet may hit go. (Fairfax)

[12] Lines 3260-3394 of this poem contain an elaborate description of a duchess, not spoken of as Fortune, but having the characteristics of Fortune. The very gorgeousness and lack of restraint in this description mark it as different from the conventional account.

side only which appealed to him, although he introduces her on all possible occasions. Nor were these allusions to Fortune in his source, the *Historia Troiana* of Guido, which in most other matters he follows with the strictest fidelity. A characteristic difference in the attitudes of Lydgate and Guido is well illustrated in their explanation for the unhappiness of Troilus. Lydgate (III. 4077 ff.) attributes it to the instability of Fortune; Guido to the inconstancy of women. Lydgate substitutes for Guido's diatribe against women, one against Fortune. The extent of Lydgate's allusions to Fortune is well shown in Book II of the *Troy Book*. It begins with a description of Fortune seventy-six lines long. Thereafter he alludes to her in lines 409-16, 2235, 2597ff., 3241-2, 3307-14, 3915, 3996ff., 4255-69, 5256ff. Some of the similes which Lydgate contrived are interesting; for example, Fortune fills the bottles of some people with sugar and honey, the bottles of others with bitter gall, myrrh, and aloes.

It was explained a few paragraphs above that Gower's idea of Fortune was not Boethian. It is questionable whether he knew the *Consolation of Philosophy;* at least he did not know it thoroughly.[13] In the *Confessio Amantis* the allusions to Fortune are not so elaborate as in the *Troy Book;* they are, in fact, of a most perfunctory nature, but are exceedingly frequent.[14]

The allusions to Fortune in Chaucer's poetry consist of three rather long connected passages and, in addition, many allusions, scattered pretty generally throughout the remainder of his poems. The long passages consist of ll. 618-718 *Book of*

[13] Gower attributes the following gloss to Boethius (*Confessio Amantis* II, 260): "Boicius: Consolacio miserorum est habere consortem in pena". These words are not to be found in the *Consolation of Philosophy*. The gloss quoted from the *Consolation* in the Prologue l. 567, however, is correct.

[14] The following references to Fortune are taken from Book III of the *Confessio Amantis:* 786, 998, 1006, 1136, 1395, 1733, 1840, 2365, 2442. These references contain certain perfunctory allusions to Fortune's wheel and phrases such as "that if fortune so befalle" and "as no fortune may be weyved". Strangely enough on one occasion Gower assigns the famous wheel to Venus instead of to Fortune:

> But sche which kepth the blinde whel,
> Venus, whan thei be moste above,
> In al the hoteste of here love,
> Hire whiel sche torneth, and thei felle
> In the manere as I schal telle.   I. 2490-4.

the Duchess, the conversation of Troilus and Pandarus in *Troilus,* Bk. I, stanzas 121, 122 and 123, and his poem *Fortune.* We find a pronounced difference between the spirit of the first passage and that of the other two.

The passage in the *Book of the Duchess* has been shown, conclusively, to be derived in small part from the *Remède de Fortune* of Machault,[15] and in the main from the *Roman de la Rose.*[16] There is nothing essentially Boethian. Chaucer, like Lydgate, has concerned himself primarily with the fickleness of Fortune, rather than with her other attributes. The passage consists of a long simile in which Fortune is represented by the knight, who laments the loss of his lady, as playing a game of chess with human beings for chessmen. Skeat is rather misleading when he says that this is imitated from the *Roman (Oxford Chaucer,* Vol. 1, p. 478). The device of having Fortune play the game of chess is peculiarly Chaucer's own. In the parallel passage in the *Roman* (ll. 6921 onwards) it is Charles of Anjou, opposed to first Manfred and then Conradin, who with armies of men plays the chess game. Chaucer thus shifts the emphasis from the living kings to the allegorical Fortune. Besides the chess game from the *Roman,* he gets the ideas also that Fortune is like filth covered over with flowers (ll. 628-9; cf. *RR.* 9237 ff.) and that like a scorpion she makes merry with her head and stings with her tail (ll. 636-40; cf. *RR.* 7027-7030). From Machault's *Remède*

[15] Furnivall. *Trial Forewords,* pp. 47-8. It is interesting to note that the *Remède* is very closely modelled upon the *Consolation of Philosophy.* For a discussion of the resemblances see, *Oeuvres, Société des Anciens Textes Français,* Vol. II, XX-XXIX. In both the *Consolation* and the *Remède,* the author laments against Fortune, and in each case is comforted by a wonderful woman, Philosophy, in the first case, Esperaunce in the second. "Les idées principales emises par Guillaume se trouvent dans l'oeuvre latine; l'ordre et la succession des idées sont à peu près conservés—certaines comparisons sont soigneusement reproduites, certains passages presque littéralement traduits."

[16] *Oxford Chaucer.* Vol. I, pp. 478-481. Chaucer was very strongly under the influence of the *Roman de la Rose* when he wrote the *Book of the Duchess.* It is interesting that the longest single passage borrowed from the *Roman* relates to Fortune. The other borrowings for the most part center around the names of people or places: ll. 284, 331, 402, 405, 435, 570, 571, 589, 725, etc. There are 17 such. Two similies are borrowed: ll. 780, 963. The other borrowings pertain mostly to nature or love: ll. 291, 405-9, 578, 791-2, 1024, 1152-3.

de Fortune he gets the ideas that she is a "false portraiture"
(l. 626), that she laughs with one eye and weeps with the
other (ll. 633-4), that "she is th' envyous charite" (l. 642; cf.
Remède de Fortune, "c'est l'envieuse charite"). Chaucer, apparently, has added the ideas that she walks upright and yet
limps, that she looks foul and fair at the same time (ll. 622-3),
that she has a monster's head (l. 628), that her wheel is now
at the fire, now at the table (ll. 644-6). From the above, it
will appear that Chaucer in the main was interested in the
picturesque side of Fortune and in similes descriptive of her
mutability. The element of the excuse for Fortune, mentioned
above as being found in Boethius' *Consolation,* is present in
a shadowy form.[17] Fortune is not represented as making excuses for herself, nor are the excuses Boethian in their origin;
yet their mere presence indicates that Chaucer was aware of
the defence sometimes made for the fickle goddess. Perhaps
it was suggested to him by analogy from the *Roman.* The
content of the excuse is Chaucer's invention. Further, there
is an allusion to Socrates (ll. 718-20). This is a very faint
suggestion of what we termed above the deeper significance
of Fortune. Socrates was the conventional example of the
strong man who rose above the wiles of Fortune on account
of his steadfastness of character.[18] But Chaucer here does
not explain wherein the strength of Socrates lay further than
by implication in the following light allusion:

> Remember yow of Socrates
> For he ne counted not three strees
> Of noght that Fortune coude do.   ll. 675-684.[19]

After this one extended attempt to describe through elaborate similes the fickleness of Fortune, Chaucer throughout the

[17] Ll. 675-684. The knight, at the close of his long lament against
Fortune, says that after all she is not to blame. He too, had he been
Fortune, would have taken the "fers" or queen, for she was the best
that could be taken. Dante, *Inferno,* 7. 91-3, says that Fortune is often
wrongly reviled.

[18] *Roman de la Rose,* ll. 6119-22. This was also true in art. Cf.
Annales Archéologiques Vol. XVI, p. 346. A figure of Socrates appears by a figure of Fortune.

[19] Cf. the nobler lines of the poem *Fortune* wherein Chaucer seems
to have a truer appreciation of Socrates:

> "O Socrates, thou stedfast champioun,
> She never mighte be thy tormentour,
> Thou never dreddest hir oppressioun,
> Ne in hir chere founde thou no savour."   ll. 17-20.

remainder of his poetry is content with very general charges of her falseness.[20]   His treatment, as I shall attempt to show presently, becomes more philosophical.

The other two extended passages in Chaucer's poetry relative to Fortune, unlike the passage in the *Book of the Duchess,* are Boethian in origin.   Let us consider first the stanzas 120, 121, 122, Bk. I of *Troilus.*   They sum up briefly the argument which takes place between Boethius and Fortune in the *Consolation,* Bk. 2, pr. 2.   Troilus takes the part of Boethius; Pandarus uses the arguments of Fortune in defence of herself.   Troilus cries out with the conventional lament that Fortune is his bitter foé; that he is borne down on her wheel; that he has become her plaything.   Pandarus replies:

> 'Than blamestow Fortune[21]
> For thou art wrooth, ye, now at erst I see;
> Wostow nat wel that Fortune is commune[22]
> To every maner wight in som degree?
> And yet thou hast this comfort, lo, pardee!
> That, as hir joyes moten over-goon,[23]
> So mote hir sorwes passen everichoon.
>
>   For if hir wheel stinte any-thing to torne,
> Than cessed she Fortune anoon to be;[24]
> Now, sith hir wheel by no wey may sojorne,
> What wostow if hir mutabilitee
> Right as thy-selven list, wol doon by thee,
> Or that she be not fer fro thyn helpinge?[25]   841-53

The passage in *Troilus,* thus, is concerned with the defence of Fortune.   The poem *Fortune,* however, contains all three of the elements: (1) the complaint, (2) the defence of Fortune by herself, (3) the deeper significance of Fortune.   The

[20] Cf. *Troilus* I, 837-40; IV, 1-7; *Truth* 9; *Knight's Tale* A 925 ff.; *Monk's Tale* B 3587; 3636-7; 3913-6; 3956-7; *Merchant's Tale* E 1311-4; 2062-5; *Franklin's Tale* F 879. This list is not inclusive; yet other allusions to Fortune's fickleness will be found to be of a meager nature.

[21] Why pleynest thou thanne? *Consolation,* 2. p2. 20.

[22] thou that art put in the comune realme of alle, ne desyre nat to liven by thyn only propre right. *Consolation,* 2. p2. 60-2.

[23] For if thou therfor wenest thy-self nat weleful, for thinges that tho semeden ioyful ben passed, ther nis nat why thou sholdest wene thy-self a wrecche; for thinges that semen now sorye passen also. *Consolation,* 2. p3. 52-4.

[24] O thou fool, of alle mortal fooles, if Fortune bigan to dwellen stable, she cesede than to ben Fortune. 2. p1. 82-4.

[25] What eek yif my mutabilitee yiveth thee rightful cause of hope to han yit beter thinges. 2. p2. 59-60.

complaint against Fortune and the defence of Fortune by herself are seen in the general plan of the poem. It consists, in fact, of a conversation between a complainant who prefers charges and Fortune who answers them. Both complaint and defence are, in part, the usual ones. Fortune is charged with changing worldly affairs without order or discretion (ll. 1-3), with being a false dissimulator (l. 23). Fortune replies, in part, by her usual answers: I only lend my gifts; I do not give them permanently. I may again advance you in my favor. Anyhow I teach you your true friends,[26] and you should give me great credit for that service. Furthermore you were born in my kingdom, and you should not give orders to me, your lawful queen; you must go about my wheel just as other people do. The sea ebbs and flows, the heavens shine or rain or hail just as they please; therefore why cannot I act in accordance with my nature and be fickle too. All of these excuses have counterparts in the *Consolation*.[27] Both complaint and defence, however, in addition to what has been discussed, contain deeper ideas which in the *Consolation* would proceed from the mouth of Dame Philosophy herself.

The poem, in its deeper significance, would seem to indicate a thorough assimilation of the Boethian Philosophy. The resemblances to the *Consolation* are not verbal. They, rather, are conclusions which would result from a thoughtful reading of that work. Selfsufficiency, a life independent of worldly cares and pleasures, as I shall have occasion to discuss more fully later, is one of the principal teachings of Boethius. In the poem *Fortune*, accordingly, we find such lines as these:

> So muche hath yit thy whirling up and doun
> Y-taught me for to knowen in an hour.
> But trewely, no force of thy reddour
> To him *that over him-self hath the maystrye!*[28]
> *My suffisaunce shal be my socour!*   11-15.
>
> *And he that hath him-self hath suffisaunce.*   26.

[26] Cf. *Monk's Tale* B 3431-5 and *Wife of Bath's Tale* D 1203-4.

[27] Cf. line 29 of *Fortune* and 2. p2. 17 of the *Consolation;* lines 30-31 and 2 p2. 58; 33-4 and 2. p8. 25-28; 41-5 and 2. p1. 69-72, 78-80 and 2. p2. 21-3; 46 and 2. p2. 37; 57-64 and 2. p2. 26-33. In the main the whole idea comes from 2. p2, the part of the *Consolation* which deals with the defense of Fortune by herself.

[28] Cf. *Consolation* 2. p4. 98-101: Thanne, yif it so be that thou art mighty over thy-self, that is to seyn, by tranquillitee of thy sowle, than hast thou thing in thy power, that thou noldest never lesen, ne Fortune ne may not beneme it thee.

Between these two passages come the excellent lines concerning Socrates. Chaucer thus explains wherein the Greek philosopher was enabled to stand so serenely in the midst of joy and woe alike. He had happiness within himself. In the *Roman,* Socrates is more stoically indifferent:[29]

> O Socrates, thou stedfast champioun,
> She never mighte be thy tormentour;
> Thou never dreddest hir oppressioun,
> Ne in hir chere founde thou no savour. 17-20.

Finally, we learn that Fortune is not all powerful, but, as is explained by Boethius,[30] gives place to a higher power:

> Lo, th' execucion of the *magestee*
> *That al purveyeth* of his rightwisnesse,
> That same thing 'Fortune' clepen ye,
> Ye blinde bestes, ful of lewednesse!
> The hevene hath propretee of sikernesse,
> The world hath ever resteles travayle;
> Thy laste day is ende of myn intresse:[31] 65-71.

Sentiments akin to those found in the passages above are found in the *Consolation* and the *Roman.* But the point to be noted is that Chaucer's expression of them is largely his own. They had become a part of him, as the familiarity and dex-

---

[29] See *Roman de la Rose* 6119-22:

> A Socrates seras semblables,
> Qui tant fu fers et tant estables
> Qu'il n'ert lies en prosperites,
> Ne tristes en aversites.

[30] In the passage here quoted, Chaucer evidently means that it is not fortune but destiny who executes the decrees of Providence. See *Consolation* 4. p6. 42-6: For purviaunce is thilke divyne reson that is establissed in the soverein prince of thinges; the whiche purviaunce disponeth alle thinges. But destinee is the disposicioun and ordinaunce clyvinge to moevable thinges, by the whiche disposicioun the purviaunce knitteth alle thinges in his ordres;

Boethius says of Fortune in 5. m1. 13-16: Right so Fortune, that semeth as that it fleteth with slaked or ungovernede brydles, it suffreth brydles, that is to seyn, to be governed, and passeth by thilke lawe, that is to seyn, by thilke divyne ordenaunce.

Chaucer shows a recognition of the complete scheme in *Troilus,* 3. 617-20:

> But O Fortune, *executrice of wierdes,*
> O influences of thise hevenes hye!
> Soth is, that *under god,* ye ben our hierdes,
> Though to us bestes been the causes wrye.

[31] Cf. *Consolation* 2. p3. 60-61: yit natheles the laste day of a mannes lyf is a manere deeth to Fortune, and also to thilke that hath dwelt.

terity with which he uses them serve to show. In the *Consolation* and the *Roman,* the ideas are scattered over many pages. It requires the close attention of a reader to fit the parts together in deriving the whole, for there is a little here and a little there, and much in between; but Chaucer has grasped the essentials, digested the whole, reduced it into compact form, and expressed in admirable poetry the entire teaching of Boethius on Fortune. Notice the conciseness of statement, and yet the accuracy of analysis in the last three lines of the passage just quoted. In a nutshell, it contains much of the teaching of the *Consolation,* the turmoil of the world, the serenity of heaven, and the opportunity of men to escape from one to the other. This stanza (65-72) resembles in completeness and conciseness the explanation which Dante gives of Fortune:

> E quegli a me: "O creature sciocche.
> Quanta ignoranza è quella che vi offende!
> Or vò che tu mia sentenza ne imbocche
> Colui, lo cui saver tutto trascende,
> Fece li cieli, e diè lor chi conduce,
> Sì ch'ogni parte ad ogni parte splende,
> Distribuendo ugualmente la luce;
> Similemente agli splendor mondani
> Ordinò general ministra[32] e duce." *Inf.* 7. 70-78.

2. *Providence and Destiny*

After the second book of the *Consolation,* Boethius, as has been said, ceases to speak much of Fortune, and thence in certain portions of the later books considers the more profound of the divine agencies which operate in men's affairs; namely, Providence and destiny. I shall now show that Chaucer recognized the distinction which Boethius made between these two members of the divine hierarchy.

In prose 6 of book 4 is explained the mechanical process whereby Providence intervenes in human affairs. This intervention is through the agency of destiny, which Boethius supposes to be altogether distinct from Providence, yet dependent upon it. Providence itself remains forever aloof from the world, situated in the tower of the "simplicitee" of God. From

[32] Fortune. As stated above (p. 51), Dante's explanation of Fortune in the *Inferno* 7. 67-96 suffices for the whole *Divine Comedy;* thereafter she is mentioned only briefly. Dante appears to give to Fortune the functions which Boethius gives to destiny. Cf. p. 62.

it proceed only the plans for earthly guidance. It is the business of destiny to execute the plans and the decrees of the divine mind. Boethius thus describes their relations:

The whiche thinges (Providence and destiny), yif that any wight loketh wel in his thought the strengthe of that oon and of that other, he shal lightly mowen seen, that thise two thinges ben dyverse. For purviaunce is thilke divyne reson that is establisshed in the soverein prince of thinges; the whiche purviaunce disponeth alle thinges. But destinee is the disposicioun and ordinaunce clyvinge to moevable thinges, by the whiche disposicioun the purviaunce knitteth alle thinges in hir ordres; for purviaunce embraceth alle thinges to-hepe, al-thogh that they ben dyverse, and al-thogh they ben infinite; but destinee departeth and ordeineth alle thinges singulerly, and divyded in moevinges, in places, in formes, in tymes, as thus: lat the unfoldinge of temporal ordinaunce, assembled and ooned in the lokinge of the divyne thought, be cleped purviaunce; and thilke same assemblinge and ooninge, divyded and unfolden by tymes, lat that ben called destinee. And al-be-it so that thise thinges ben dyverse, yit natheles hangeth that oon on that other; for-why the order destinal procedeth of the simplicitee of purviaunce. (4. p6. 39-56.)

Boethius illustrates this relation by an example. It is just as a workman who perceives the form of a thing in his thought, and then later executes with his hands the thing which he has previously conceived.[33]

That Chaucer recognized this distinction between Providence and destiny is shown in different passages.

> The destinee, ministre general,
> That executeth in the world over-al
> The purveyaunce, that God hath seyn biforn,
> So strong it is, etc. (A 1663-6)

Professor Tatlock (*Modern Philology* III, pp. 371-2) points out that this passage from the *Knight's Tale* shows the influence of Dante. This influence is very probable, but is most obvious in a striking verbal similarity to which Professor Tatlock does not call definite attention. The "ministre general" corresponds to Dante's "general ministra" (*Inf.* 7. 78).

---

[33] Chaucer uses this illustration in *Troilus* I. 1065-71 where Pandarus is attempting to think out a plan which will help the hero:

> For every wight that hath an hous to founde
> Ne renneth nought the werk for to biginne
> With rakel hond, but he wol byde a stounde,
> And sende his hertes lyne out fro with-inne
> Alderfirst his purpos for to winne.
> Al this Pandare in his herte thoughte,
> And caste his werk ful wysly, or he wroughte.

This phrase does not occur in the *Consolation*. Dante's "general minister", however, is Fortune (cf. p. 60 above), not destiny as here in Chaucer's lines. Dante seems to be inclined to disregard destiny as an agent of Providence and to make Fortune combine the functions alloted to both Fortune and destiny in the *Consolation*. He uses the word "destino" only twice. Each time it is intimately connected with Fortune and does not appear alone.[34] Chaucer, on the other hand, although he may be indebted to Dante for the phrase, preserves the spirit of Boethius in making destiny the minister of God. In the following passage Chaucer indicates that Fortune is subordinate in rank to the *wierds* or destiny:

> But O, Fortune, executrice of wierdes,
> O influences of thise hevenes hye!
> Soth is, that, under god, ye ben our hierdes,
> Though to us bestes been the causes wrye.
>
> (*Troilus* 3. 617-20)

Other passages in *Troilus* show the relation between Providence and destiny:

> Sin god seeth every thing, out of doutaunce,
> And hem desponeth, thourgh his ordenaunce,
> In hir merytes sothly for to be,
> As they shul comen by predestinee.   (4. 963-6)
> Aprochen gan the fatal destinee
> That Joves hath in disposicioun,
> And to yow, angry Parcas, sustren three,
> Committeth, to don execucioun;   (5. 1-4)

The idea here is different from that contained in the *Teseide* (9. 1-4) on which the passage is based.[35] There is in the corresponding lines of the *Teseide* no mention of the dependence of destiny upon Providence.

3. *Cas or Aventure or Destinee, Etc.*

Before we leave this section of the subject, it may be well to consider what seems to be another influence of the Boethian

[34]   Qual fortuna, o destino
       Anzi l'ultimo di quaggiù ti mena? (*Inf.* 15. 46-7)
       Se voler fu, o destino, o fortuna,
       Non so; ma passeggiando tra le teste,
       Forte percossi il piè ne viso ad una. (*Inf.* 32. 76-8)

[35]   Già appressa va il doloroso fato
          Tanto più grave a lui a sostenere
          Quanto in più gloria già l'avena levato
          Il fe'vittorioso ivi vedere.

The classical terminology is probably derived from the *Thebais* of Statius. See *The Influence of Statius upon Chaucer*, B. A. Wise, p. 20.

account of the divine scheme of things, an influence which pervades Chaucer's poems from *Troilus* on down through the *Canterbury Tales*. It involves such passages as the following:[36]

> And so bifel, by aventure or cas, (A 1074)
>
> Were it by aventure or destinee,
> (As, whan a thing is shapen, it shal be) (A 1465-6)
>
> As was his aventure, or his fortune,
> That us governeth alle as in commune. (B 4189-90)

Professor Tatlock (*op. cit.* p. 372) ascribes the presence of the alternatives presented in such lines to the influence of Dante. His basis for doing so is the two passages in the *Divine Comedy:*

> Qual fortuna, o destino
> Anzi l'ultimo dì quaggiù ti mena? (*Inf.* 15. 46-7)
>
> Se voler fu, o destino, o fortuna,
> Non so; ma passeggiando tra le teste,
> Forte percossi il piè ne viso ad una. (*Inf.* 32. 76-8)

There is, however, a better explanation to be derived from the *Consolation* than from these two isolated passages of Dante for the peculiarity of Chaucer's lines.

In the first *prose* of Book V of the *Consolation* Boethius takes up an explanation of chance. He asks of Dame Philosophy a definition in this manner:

'Nis ther thanne no-thing that by right may be cleped either "hap" or elles "aventure of fortune"; (nihilne est quod vel casus vel fortuitum iure appellare queat?) (5. pi. 40-43).[37]

In the "hap or elles aventure of fortune" we have a closer parallel to the "aventure or cas" of the first passage quoted above than that which Professor Tatlock points out in the lines of Dante. The alternatives of Boethius and of Chaucer seem synonymous with chance, whereas the "destino" and

---

[36] See also *Anelida and Arcite* 348; *Troilus* 1. 568, 2. 285, 4. 297, 388; *House of Fame* 1052; A844; B1428; E1967.

[37] Dame Philosophy gives the following answer to this question: Hap is an unwar bitydinge of causes assembled in thinges that ben don for som other thing. But thilke ordre, procedinge by an uneschuable bindinge to-gidere, which that descendeth fro the welle of purviaunce that ordeineth alle thinges in hir places and in hir tymes, maketh that the causes rennen and assemblen to-gidere. The word "hap" occurs frequently in Chaucer's poetry:

O sodeyn hap, o thou fortune instable, E 2057

Cf. also *Legend of Good Women* 1773, *Parliament of Fowls* 402-4, *Troilus* 2. 1454, B 3927-8.

"fortuna" of Dante, as has been shown above, would be regarded by Chaucer as distinct from each other.

The full explanation, however, for the alternatives presented in the above passages and in frequent other passages in Chaucer's poetry depends on more than mere verbal resemblances. The reading of the *Consolation* decidedly leaves the impression that heaven interferes in human affairs in many different ways. Although the guiding hand of Providence is behind all intervention, yet, as the functions of destiny, fortune, and chance, variously called "casus" or "fortuitum", overlap, there must remain considerable uncertainty as to which of these agencies of Providence to ascribe any particular event. The complicated relation of these agencies is made all the more uncertain by an explanation of Dame Philosophy in which she admits the possibility of still other forces, presided over by destiny:

> Thanne, whether that destinee be exercysed outher by some divyne spirits, servaunts to the divyne purviaunce, or elles by som sowle, or elles by alle nature servinge to god, or elles by the celestial moevinges of sterres, or elles by the vertu of angeles, or elles by the dyverse subtilitee of develes, or elles by any of hem, or elles by hem alle, the destinal ordinaunce is y-woven and acomplished (4. p6. 65-71).[38]

The various means of intervention presented in all these possibilities seem sufficient to account for Chaucer's use of the alternatives. In the following lines from the *Merchant's Tale,* which show the influence of the passage last quoted, Chaucer has presented a larger number of possible alternatives than he has elsewhere:

> Were it by destinee or aventure,
> Were it by influence or by nature,
> Or constellacion,[39] (E 1967-69)

[38] 4. p6, from which this quotation and the long quotation at the beginning of the chapter on the distinction between Providence and destiny are taken, is the part of the *Consolation* from which Chaucer derives his fatalistic conception. He has taken more from this *prose* than from all the rest of Book IV. See pp. 161-2.

[39] Lydgate with his characteristic exaggeration has the following unusual passage:
> But seye, Priam, what infelicite,
> What newe trouble, what hap, what destyne,
> Or from above what hateful influence
> Descended is, by unwar violence,
> To meue the, thou canst not lyue in pes!
> What sodeyn sort, what fortune graceles,
> What chaunce unhappy, withoute avisenes,
> What wilful lust, etc. *Troy Book* 2. 1797ff.

Thus it seems evident that Chaucer was dependent upon Boethius for this peculiarity in phrasing. It is true that the Stoics and Neoplatonists,[40] as well as Boethius, had disputed over the question of the relationship of Providence, destiny, and chance; but of these discussions it is not likely that Chaucer had first hand knowledge. It is also true that he may have run across the words, "o destino, o fortuna" in Dante's poem and was attracted by them; but if such were the case, it is most probable to suppose that they only accentuated ideas which he had derived from studying and translating the *Consolation* where all of the terms are discussed in full.

4. *The Bond of Love*

The method of providential intervention set forth in the *Consolation* and explained hitherto is prosaic and altogether mechanical. Boethius, as a matter of fact, unfolds it in the *proses* of the *Consolation*. He reserves, however, a more mystical explanation for the *meters,* where his unfettered spirit soars above the necessity of subtle distinctions. This explanation is in the "chain of love".

The present orderly arrangement of the universe, according to Boethius, is the resultant, if it may so be termed, of two forces, Nature and Love. Nature is the god-given principle which enters into every object, celestial or terrestrial, and which causes it to possess a certain definite motive power, propelling it in a certain definite direction. But if left to itself, each object would pursue its course independently of all other objects. The universe would be a flux. The light things would rise forever up; the heavy things would sink forever down. The moist things would become irrevocably separated from the dry things. All the diverse elements of the universe would rush together or fly apart in continual warfare. Heavenly bodies would collide in riotous chaos; and all things would follow wihtout control or direction the

[40] The Stoics held that Providence and destiny were identical; the Neoplatonists that destiny was inferior to and dependent upon Providence. (*History of Philosophy,* Ueberweg, Vol. I, pp. 194-245). Seneca in a letter to Lucilius (*Teubner,* Vol. III, epis. 16, p. 35) shows the unsettled condition of his mind on this subject. The purpose of his letter is to advise Lucilius to live the philosophical life, no matter whether it is God that rules, or merely fate or chance: Quid mihi prodest philosophia, si fatum est? Quid prodest, si deus rector est? Quid prodest, si casus imperat?

principle of self implanted within them. But to rescue the universe from this confusion, exists the bond of Love, emanating from Providence. It restrains unalterably and binds together the diverse elements so that serenity is brought out of chaos. This idea of the unifying power of Love is advanced in three splendid *meters* of the *Consolation:* 2. m8; 3. m9; 4. m6.

Chaucer gives prominence to the "bond of love" in the *Knight's Tale* and especially in *Troilus* Bk. III. In the former poem Theseus (A 2987-93) comforts Palamon and Emily after the death of Arcite by explaining to them the all-embracing and all-determining power of the divine Love. In *Troilus* Bk. III, which marks the culminating point in the love delirium of the hero, the "bond of love" is proclaimed in two different passages:[41] ll. 1261 and 1744-64. All of these passages show the direct influence of Boethius. 2. m8 of the *Consolation* seems to have made the deepest impression upon Chaucer, as he translates it entire in the lines of *Troilus* last mentioned (3. 1744-64). I quote below both Chaucer's prose and verse translations. The verse translation is introduced in the third book as a song of Troilus in praise of love. It occurs at the very climax of the action, just before Troilus' downfall through Criseyde's unfaith. It should not be thought that Chaucer, in introducing this passage from Boethius, converts the praise of divine love into a praise of purely physical love with an attendant lowering of its dignity. Indeed Boethius himself introduces the element of human love in the lines:

This Love halt to-gideres peoples ioigned with an holy bond, and knitteth sacrement of mariages of chaste loves (15-16).

The love which holds together the stars is the same as that which exists between human beings. Chaucer introduces, first, the love which binds peoples together and thence passes

---

[41] There are three songs in praise of love in Bk. III. The first, ll. 1-49, is based on stanzas 74-79, Book III of the *Filostrato* and so is not Boethian; it contains no allusion to the "bond" of love. The second, ll. 1254-1266, contains the words, "benigne Love, thou holy bond of thinges" (1261); this line is the only trace of Boethian influence in the passage, but it is interesting as being substituted for the words, "Donna, sei tanto grande e tanto vali" in three lines (1261-31) otherwise taken from Dante (*Par.* 33. 13-15). The third is the passage quoted in full below (1744-64). These lines are absent from Ms. Harl. 3943, and are inserted later in Phillipps.

to the love which binds external nature. Boethius has the opposite order.

(cf. ll. 1744-5 with 19-20 below)

Love, that of erthe and see hath governaunce   1744
Love, that his hestes hath in hevene hye,
Love, that with an holsom alliaunce
Halt peples joyned, as him list hem gye,

(cf. ll. 1746-9 with 27-30 below)

Love, that knetteth lawe of companye,
And couples doth in vertu for to dwelle,
Bind this acord, that I have told and telle;   1750

(cf. l. 1750 with 17-18 below)

That the world with stable feith varieth acordable chaunginges;

That that the world with feyth, which that is stable,
Dyverseth so his stoundes concordinge,
That elements that been so discordable

that the contrarious qualitee of elements holden among hem-self aliaunce
5 perdurable;
that Phebus the sonne with his goldene chariet bringeth forth the rosene day;

Holden a bond perpetuely duringe,
That Phebus mote his rosy day forth bringe,

that the mone hath commaundement
10 over the nightes, which nightes Hesperus the eve-sterre hath brought;

And that the mone hath lordship over the nightes,

Al this doth Love; ay heried be his mightes!   1757

that the see, greedy to flowen, constreyneth with a certein ende hise flodes, so that it is nat leveful to
15 strecche hise brode termes or boundes upon the erthes, *that is to seyn, to cover al the erthe:*—al this acordaunce of thinges is bounden with Love, that governeth erthe and see, and hath
20 also commaundements to the hevenes. And yif this Love slakede the brydeles, alle thinges that now loven hem to-gederes wolden maken a bataile continuelly and stryven to fordoon the fasoun of
25 this worlde, the whiche they now leden in acordable feith by faire moevinges. This Love halt to-gideres poeples ioigned with an holy bond, and knitteth sacrement of mariages of chaste loves; and
30 Love endyteth lawes to trewe felawes. O! weleful were mankinde, yif thilke Love that governeth hevene governed youre corages!

That that the see, that gredy is to flowen,
Constreyneth to a certeyn ende so
His flodes, that so fersly they ne growen
To drenchen erthe and al for ever-mo;

(cf. ll. 17-18 with 1750 above)
(cf. ll. 19-20 with 1744-5 above)

And if that Love ought lete his brydel go,
Al that now loveth a-sonder sholde lepe,
And lost were al, that Love halt now to-hepe.   1764

(cf. ll. 27-30 with 1746-9 above)

So wolde god, that auctor is of kinde,
That, with his bond, Love of his vertu liste
To cerclen hertes alle, and faste binde,
That from his bond no wight the wey out wiste.   1768

Chaucer's verse translation, it will be seen includes practically all that the prose one does, and differs from it only in that some of the parts are changed about and that the application, as shown in the conclusion, is made to fit the particular occasion.

Thus, in conclusion, it is evident that Chaucer recognizes in all its phases the scheme set forth in the *Consolation* to explain the working of God's ordinances—equally binding whether executed through destiny, fortune or chance, or proceeding from the divine love. The idea of an overruling Providence seems to have made a deep impression on Chaucer at one time in his life. In particular, *Troilus* and the *Knight's Tale* have a decidedly fatalistic background and contain long and frequent passages which dwell upon various questions relating to Providence, especially in its relation to men. The fact that four of Chaucer's characters, Troilus, Palamon, Arcite, and Theseus, as I shall discuss in detail in a later chapter, were all interested in this problem is a good indication of the interest of Chaucer himself. Whether he derived his conception entirely from Boethius, it is impossible to tell. It is altogether likely, among other possibilities, that he was influenced by the *Divine Comedy,* to which frequent allusion has been made above and which was probably read by Chaucer sometime near the period when he was interested in the *Consolation.* It is noteworthy that the poems which show the strongest evidence of Boethian influence also show the strongest evidence of Dante's influence.[42] The two together may have had a cumulative effect in forming Chaucer's views. But however this may be, the extended passages which consider the subject of providential control are discussed almost exclusively in the Boethian fashion—a fact evident, in part, from what has been shown and, in part, from what will be shown.

PART II. THE JUSTICE OF HEAVEN QUESTIONED

If the power of Heaven is so absolute, why should so much evil exist in the world? what place is there for the operation of free will in man? These two vexed questions are asked by Boethius, and answered, at length, by Dame Philosophy in the *Consolation,* the first in Book IV, the second in Book V.

[42] This statement is in particular true of *Troilus* and the *House of Fame.* The influence of Dante is not predominant, however, in the *Knight's Tale* which contains a strong Boethian influence, nor is the influence of Boethius strong in the *Parliament of Fowls* which contains a strong influence of Dante. It is possible that Chaucer gradually passed from under the influence of Dante to the influence of Boethius. For further discussion on this point see pp. 151-2. For the influence of Dante on Chaucer see *Dante in English Literature,* pp. 2 ff., by Paget Toynbee.

Chaucer, through his characters, considers both of these questions. He always takes more pleasure in the question than in the answer, and leaves the answer to the clerks.

1. Why Does God Permit Evil?

The question of the justice of God in permitting evil is brought up frequently by Chaucer, in the *Complaint of Mars* (218-26), in *Troilus* (3. 1016-19), in the *Legend of Good Women* (2228-35), and in the *Man of Law's Tale* (813-16). The two longest passages, however, which consider this question are the speeches of Palamon in the *Knight's Tale* (A 1303-33) and of Dorigen in the *Franklin's Tale* (865-93). These two speeches, and in part the shorter ones just mentioned, follow identically the same outline: (1) The almighty power of God is granted. No doubt is ever expressed as to the existence of that. (2) The question is asked: why does this all powerful God permit evils to afflict man and the guiltless to suffer? (3) The speaker, not being able to reconcile to each other the facts of God's existence and the existence of evil, leaves the matter for clerks to decide.

Palamon thus begins to lament the fact that Arcite has escaped from prison, whereas he remains there:

> 'O cruel goddes, that governe
> This world with binding of your word eterne,
> And wryten in the table of athamaunt
> Your parlement, and your eterne graunt,
> What is mankinde more un-to yow holde
> Than is the sheep, that rouketh in the folde?
> For slayn is man right as another beste,
> And dwelleth eek in prison and areste,
> And hath siknesse, and greet adversitee,
> And ofte tymes giltelees, pardee!
> What governaunce is in this prescience,
> That giltelees tormenteth innocence?
> . . . . . .
> Th' answere of this I lete to divynis, (A 1303-23)

And thus Dorigen speaks when she fears that her husband has been dashed to pieces on the rocks:

'Eterne god, that thurgh thy purveyaunce
Ledest the world by certein governaunce,
In ydel, as men seyn, ye no-thing make;
But, lord, thise grisly feendly rokkes blake,

. . . . .

Why han ye wroght this werk unresonable?
For by this werk, south, north, ne west, ne eest,
Ther nis y-fostred man, ne brid, ne beest;
It dooth no good, to my wit, but anoyeth.

. . . . .

I woot wel clerkes wol seyn, as hem leste,
By arguments, that al is for the beste,
Though I ne can the causes nat y-knowe.
But thilke god, that made wind to blowe,
As kepe my lord! this my conclusioun;
To clerkes lete I al disputisoun.   (F 865-890)

This particular form of presentation seems to have been derived from the *Consolation* 1. m5, the very impressive lament of Boethius which in the beginning leads Dame Philosophy to offer her consolations. This *meter* first calls attention to the wonderful serenity of nature, the calm movement of the celestial orbs, and the greatness of the divine being of whom these are the manifestations. Then Boethius breaks forth:

O thou governour, governinge alle thinges by certein ende, why refusestow only to governe the werkes of men by dewe manere? Why suffrest thou that slydinge fortune torneth so grete entrechaunginges of thinges, so that anoyous peyne, that sholde dewely punisshe felouns, punissheth innocents? (1. m5. 22-6.)

In this there is the same recognition of the greatness of God, and also the same questioning found in the speeches of Palamon and of Dorigen. The *meter* is very poetic and full of dignity, and as such may well have made a deep impression on Chaucer's mind. The same idea is brought out again in 4. p1. of the *Consolation*, but less impressively.[43]

The corresponding passages of Chaucer and Boethius are thus very much alike. The difference is that Chaucer leaves to the clerks the answer which Boethius has Dame Philosophy answer in full and to his satisfaction (4. p2-p5. inc.). Of course too much must not be inferred about Chaucer's beliefs

[43] That Chaucer had 1. m5 more closely in mind is shown not only by a greater resemblance in form between this *meter* and the two speeches here quoted but by a verbal resemblance. Cf. which mankinde is so fair part of thy werk (F 879) and we men that ben nat a foule party, but a fayr party of so grete a werk (1. m5. 37-8).

from what his characters say, but it is significant that nowhere in his poetry is he concerned with the parts of the answer most elaborated upon by Dame Philosophy, although he presents so frequently the question which brought forth this answer. Dame Philosophy through subtle sophistries is enabled to show: (1) that evil does not exist at all (4. p2. 137ff.) and (2) that evil-doers never triumph over the innocent for the reason that they are really less happy if they receive no punishment than if they receive punishment (4. p4. 57ff.).[44] The ability to understand and explain such paradoxes Palamon and Dorigen must leave to the more astute old clerks, but to themselves, as ordinary laymen, the evils which beset them must still seem to exist. Chaucer with somewhat more obvious satire and sly humor also leaves it to the clerks to adjust the precise relationship between God's foreknowledge and man's free will, the other problem solved by Dame Philosophy in the two closing books of the *Consolation*.

2. Foreknowledge and Freewill

Chaucer discusses the foreknowledge of God in relation to the free will of man in two extended passages of his poetry: *Troilus and Criseyde* 4. 958-1078 and the *Nun's Priest's Tale* B 4420-40. What he has to say of this matter is derived almost wholly from Book V of the *Consolation of Philosophy*. The long passage in *Troilus* is derived from a question put by Boethius to Dame Philosophy, and the passage in the *Nun's Priest's Tale* from her answer to this question, although this answer is not accepted by the Nun's Priest. I shall consider each in turn.

The speeches of Boethius in the rôle which he assumes in the *Consolation* are usually characterized by their brevity. His speech in *prose* 3 of Book V, however, in this respect is

[44] Boethius in 4. p6 and p7 develops the idea that the evils which afflict men serve to give them greater strength of character. Chaucer considers this point with some detail in the *Clerk's Tale*. Here, however, the idea is suggested by his immediate source, Petrarch's tale of the patient Griselde. (Cf. *Oxford Chaucer,* II. xxxv). The explanation of evil in 4. p6 and p7 is more tangible than that developed from the highly idealistic standpoint of Boethius in the earlier *proses* of Bk. IV of the *Consolation,* and Chaucer may have considered it as within the range of every day intelligence. Chaucer is indebted very little to the first part of Book IV. See pp. 161-2.

an exception. It is by far the longest single speech which he makes and extends several pages in length. In it he analyzes minutely various theories which have been advanced for reconciling the foreknowledge of God to the free will of man. He is utterly unable, however, to find a satisfactory conclusion. This speech merits a brief review as Chaucer adopted it for use as a soliloquy by his hero, Troilus.

It is noteworthy that Boethius never supposes as an explanation of free will the possibility that the foreknowledge of God does not exist. This is accepted as axiomatic. What he questions is whether, granting this foreknowledge, man can have free will. He imagines various relations which may exist between the two, but which are all equally unsatisfactory to him. First, one explanation consists in the possibility that God may be mistaken in his foreknowledge of the deeds that men will do in the future. God forms judgments, but they are in no way binding on men; for the latter act entirely under the guidance of their own wills. They may mold their futures one way, or they may mold them another, as dependent upon their own acts; God judges how they will proceed, but oftentimes, not correctly. Boethius dismisses this view at once, for to argue that the omnipotent God may be mistaken is a treason against Him; it is equivalent to placing His foreknowledge on the level of human opinion (5. p3. 7-19).

Boethius, having thus satisfied himself that the foreknowledge of God must be considered infallible as knowledge, next proceeds to examine whether foreknowledge must imply cause. Possibly, he argues, Providence remains passive in its observing of men. God foresees what will happen but does not necessitate it. Here he thinks, for a moment, that there may be a possible loophole which will enable him to refute the view that human affairs are in the grip of stern necessity, for instead of things coming to pass because God has foreseen them, the situation may be reversed and God may foresee things because they are to come to pass. Boethius runs this argument out to what he deems its logical conclusion, and satisfies himself by the following illustration that foreknowledge, even conceived as being determined by the fact that things will happen in the future, implies necessity in the occurrence of those things. The example which he chooses is a common one taken from daily life, but is comparable to God's observing of men. A sits down and B sees him sitting.

The fact that A sits down makes it necessary that B's opinion that he is sitting down be true. But also, if B's opinion is true that A sits, it is also of necessity equally true that B sits. There is necessity in each instance. Boethius is forced to admit that A does not sit down because B's opinion was true, but that the opinion was true because A sat down. Yet he reasserts, lamely, that there was a common necessity in each.[45] He does not stop to show how the necessity is common. Decidedly, and so we shall find later is the opinion of Dame Philosophy, there may be a distinction between the necessity which makes B sit, and the necessity which makes A's opinion true. This point is carefully to be noted. Boethius, as we remember all the time, is merely assuming the rôle of questioner, and is presently to answer his own questions through the symbolic fiction of Dame Philosophy. He has purposely left here a fallacy which, as we shall see, was the point about which he has Philosophy attack the validity of the arguments here assumed. But the point at which he is driving is plain: if men's acts are foreseen by God, the mere foreseeing implies necessity. Thus, in this last consideration, Boethius is again foiled in his effort to find an opportunity for the operation of man's free will; for even granting the extreme premise, which he professes to be very loath to grant, that the temporal things of earth occasion God's foreknowledge, he comes nowhere. Men cannot escape even then. Therefore he faces the same stone wall which originally confronted him—the impossibility of free will in men if God foresees long beforehand what men will do (5. p3. 19-71).

This long passage of the *Consolation* is taken over bodily by Chaucer in the passage of *Troilus* before referred to (4. 974-1078). It forms the speech of Troilus wherein he explains that it was due to destiny that Criseyde and he must be separated. Heaven had foreseen the separation, and therefore it must be. This is the longest passage from Boethius incorporated by Chaucer. It is virtually a verse translation, and is even closer to the original than the bond of Love pas-

[45] But therfore ne sitteth nat a wight, for that the opinioun of the sittinge is sooth; but the opinioun is rather sooth, for that a wight sitteth biforn. And thus, al-thogh that the cause of the sooth cometh of that other syde . . . , algates yit is ther comune necessitee in that oon and in that other (5. p3. 45-51).

sage just considered. The following lines of the poem are set down beside the corresponding lines of Chaucer's prose translation to show how close the correspondence is.[46]

For yif so be that god loketh alle thinges biforn, ne god ne may nat ben desseived in no manere,
than mot it nedes been, that alle thinges bityden the whiche that the purviaunce of god hath seyn biforn to comen.
For which,
yif that god knoweth biforn nat only the werkes of men, but also hir conseiles and hir willes, thanne ne shal ther be no libertee of arbitre;

For som men seyn, if god seth al biforn,
Ne god may not deceyved ben, pardee,
Than moot it fallen, though men hadde it sworn,
That purveyaunce hath seyn bifore to be.
Wherfor I seye, that from eterne if he
Hath wist biforn our thought eek as our dede,
We have no free chois, as these clerkes rede.   980

ne certes, ther ne may be noon other dede, ne no wil,
but thilke which that the divyne purviaunce,
that may nat ben desseived,
hath feled biforn.

For other thought nor other dede also
Might never be, but swich as purveyaunce,
Which may not been deceyved nevermo,
Hath feled biforn, with-outen ignoraunce.

For yif that they mighten wrythen awey in othre manere than they ben purveyed, than sholde ther be no stedefast prescience of thing to comen,

For if ther mighte been a variaunce
To wrythen out fro goddes purveyinge,
Ther nere no prescience of thing cominge;   987

but rather an uncertain opinioun. (5. p3. 7-18.)

But it were rather an opinioun
Uncerteyn [47]

The remainder of the two passages, *Troilus* 989-1078 and Chaucer's prose translation of the *Consolation* 18-71, shows an equally close parallelism. Throughout, the similarity in phrasing is as close, and the arrangement of ideas almost

[46] There is some ground for supposing that Chaucer used for the verse translation the Latin text rather than his own prose translation. In line 978 of *Troilus* occurs the phrase "from eterne". This translates "ab aeterno" of the Latin text (5. p3. 8). This phrase is omitted from Chaucer's prose translation. (Cf. line 11.) There exists, of course, the possibility that the prose translation did not exist when *Troilus* was written.

[47] The free will passage is not present in all the Mss. of *Troilus*. It is wholly omitted in Mss. Harl. 2392, Harl. 1239, and Gg. (all but the last stanza); it is added later in Phillipps. Professor Root has shown (*Textual Tradition of Chaucer's Troilus*, Chaucer Soc. 1st Ser., No. 99, pp. 216-221) that Chaucer added this passage in a second "edition" of the poem.

identical.[48] Skeat's remark (*Oxford Chaucer* II: 490), "a considerable portion of this passage is copied, more or less closely, from Boethius", is understated and misleading, for the entire passage, with the exception of the two lines quoted in the following paragraph, is copied directly from Boethius. The few changes made by Chaucer were slight, do not affect the subject matter, and were necessary to meet the requirements of the rhyme and the meter.[49]

The most extended passage added by Chaucer is a not altogether respectful allusion to the clerks:

> Eek this is an opinioun of somme
> That han hir top ful heighe and smothe y-shore; (995-6)

These two lines, embedded in the long discussion on free will, only echo, however, the sentiments of Troilus as stated more at length in the introduction of his speech:

> But nathelees, allas; whom shal I leve?
> For ther ben grete clerkes many oon,
> That destinee thorugh argumentes preve;
> And som men seyn that nedely ther is noon;
> But that free chois is yeven us everichoon.
> O, welaway! so sleye arn clerkes olde,
> That I not whos opinion I may holde. (967-73)

[48] Chaucer makes one slight change in the arrangement. He introduces in lines 990-2 these words:

> And certes, that were an abusioun,
> That god shuld han no parfit cleer witinge
> More than we men that han doutous weninge.

These words come from the same *prose* as the rest of the passage, but from ll. 96-9, which are a short space in advance of the lines upon which Chaucer makes so complete a draught.

[49] One of these minor changes involves Chaucer in an inconsistency of some interest. The italicized words in the following passage do not appear in the *Consolation:*

> And ferther-over now ayenward yit,
> Lo, right so it is of the part contrarie,
> As thus; *(now herkne, for I wol not tarie):*
> I seye, that if the opinioun of *thee*
> Be sooth etc. (1027-31)

Troilus is alone in a temple at the time of this soliloquy, and it is not to be expected, therefore, that he should thus address someone in the second person and solicit his attention. There are two possible explanations. Chaucer through interest in the subject may have forgotten that Troilus is the speaker and momentarily have assumed that position for himself. The inconsistency may also result from Chaucer's overlooking this point in a revision of the poem.

At the conclusion of the soliloquy, Troilus is just where he was when he began. He cannot reconcile foreknowledge and free will by his own reason, and the many decisions of the clerks in the matter serve only to confuse him the more.

The passage in the *Nun's Priest's Tale* (B 4420-40) is concerned altogether with the extent of the disputes of the clerks; a hundred thousand of them, says the Nun's Priest, have disputed on the matter. For this passage Chaucer derives his material from the explanation offered by Dame Philosophy in answer to the long argument of Boethius considered above. The wonder is that Chaucer got this answer at all, for it is deeply buried in a very elaborate proof by which Philosophy seeks to establish her point. To indicate how easy it is to miss the real answer of Philosophy, and to be misled by the steps used in its proof, we may say that neither Skeat (*Oxford Chaucer* II: xiv) nor Stewart (*Essay*, pp. 70-2) in their analyses of this discussion mention the real point. They, of course, convey the general idea of Book V of the *Consolation*, but they miss entirely the actual clash represented as existing between Boethius and Dame Philosophy. Chaucer, on the other hand, has the bare essentials and nothing else in the passage in the *Nun's Priest's Tale*.

The answer of Philosophy hinges on the argument that there exist two kinds of necessity, that which has a constraining influence on things and that which does not (5. p6. 125ff.). This distinction, Boethius did not recognize. In his discussion, as has been shown (p. 72), he considered the only possibility for reconciling Providence to free will to have been God's foreknowledge of events without His causing those events; i. e. foreknowledge without foreordination. After a careful consideration, however, he reaches the conclusion that even foreknowledge implies an inevitable necessity. He thus makes no distinction whatsoever between the necessity of foreknowledge and the necessity of foreordination; and we ourselves cannot but recognize that his argument rests upon mere assertion when he derives his conclusions from the illustration of the man who is sitting and is beheld by another man. He argues, as may be recalled, that it is equally necessary that the sitting cause the true opinion of the man who looks upon the act, and that the true opinion makes necessary the sitting. The true opinion did not cause the sitting and this, Boethius, in his question to Philosophy, did not see.

Dame Philosophy attacks the problem at identically the same point where Boethius atttacked it, considers foreknowledge without causation, but reaches entirely different conclusions. She substitutes for the illustration used by Boethius another illustration, but one exactly similar to it. A sees B driving a chariot. A, by the mere act of looking, in no way controls the rapid movements of the driver (5. p4. 60-6). Just so does God look upon the acts of men without causing them. But, it may be argued, this illustration is based upon human experience. It does not take into consideration that there may be a difference between seeing events which occur in present time before the eyes of men, and foreseeing events which will take place a thousand years from the present. Therefore Philosophy reduces, so to speak, the time element, as it is to God, to terms understandable by man (5. p4., p5., p6. to line 93). She establishes at length the idea that to God the infinity of time, past, present, and future, is an eternal present. The complete span of eternity to God is the same as the present moment to man. Thus, God's foreknowledge of men's acts is comparable to the opinion of A when he beholds the charioteer, and no more implies a constraining necessity than it does. The demonstration of the time element,[50] though it is elaborate, is really subordinated to the distinction brought out between two kinds of necessity for which it paves the way. Philosophy grants, as she must, that there is to a degree a necessity occasioned by the mere beholding of an act, that if A sees B sitting in a chair, it must be true that B sit in the chair. This necessity, however, is operative only in so far as the fact that the act is beheld makes necessary that the act be true. Such a limited necessity, she calls "conditional necessity", a necessity occasioned by the addition of the condition that the act is beheld. The actions in the daily life of men involve only "conditional necessity". But in contrast to this kind of necessity, is a stern and binding necessity from which there is no possible escape, and this is called "simple necessity". It involves natural and universal laws such as the laws that the sun must rise each morning or that

[50] Some intimation of this discussion on time may be contained in *Troilus* 5. 746-9. Cf. these lines with Boethius 5. m2. 8-9 and 5. p6. 10-16. That Chaucer had the *Consolation* in mind is perhaps more certainly shown by his use of "futur", a word which he seems to have derived from the *Consolation*.

all men must die (5. p6. 102-37). Universal occurrences, then, are the result of simple necessity, and the incidental occurrences of daily life involve only conditional necessity. This distinction is the contribution of Boethius on the question of free will which it is the purpose of Book V of the *Consolation* to develop, and it is this distinction which the Nun's Priest considers in his tale.

The discussion in the *Nun's Priest's Tale* is different from that in *Troilus* because it is humorous and because it is taken not from the question of Boethius to Dame Philosophy but from her answer to that question. It is similar in that the Nun's Priest like Troilus considers various possibilities of the relation between free will and foreknowledge and in that he leaves the question to the clerks to decide. The extent of the difference in opinion among the clerks is emphasized at the expense of a slight inconsistency. The question which confronts the Nun's Priest is to determine whether Chauntecleer flew down from the beams to where the fox is in hiding by free will or from destiny. It begins:

> "O Chauntecleer, acursed be that morwe,
> That thou into that yerd flough fro the bemes!
> Thou were ful wel y-warned by thy dremes,
> That thilke day was perilous to thee.
> But what that god forwoot mot nedes be,
> After the opinioun of certeyn clerkis.
> Witnesse on him, that any perfit clerk is, (B 4420-26)

We might naturally expect that what followed would be an expansion of the theme that the misfortune befell Chauntecleer by the stern decree of unyielding fate, and that it was to prove this point that the clerks were called upon for testimony; but not so:

> That in scole is gret altercacioun
> In this matere, and greet disputisoun,
> And hath ben of an hundred thousand men.
> But I ne can not bulte it to the bren,
> As can the holy doctour Augustyn,
> Or Boëce, or the bishop Bradwardyn, (B 4427-32)

Here three possibilities are offered:

> (1) Whether that goddes worthy forwiting
> Streyneth me nedely for to doon a thing,
> (Nedely clepe I simple necessitee);
> (2) Or elles, if free choys be graunted me

78

> To do that same thing, or do it noght,
> Though god forwoot it, er that it was wroght;
> (3) Or if his witing streyneth nevere a del
> But by necessitee condicionel.
> I wol not han to do of swich matere;
> My tale is of a cok, as ye may here, (B 4433-42)

It may be by accident, but the three different views presented in this passage are in accordance with the different positions held by the three philosophers mentioned in lines 4431-2. Bishop Brawardine ardently upheld foreordination and was opposed even bitterly to free will.[51] He thought it presumptuous for man to assume for himself the responsibility of freedom of action. He deemed all-sufficient for man the divine grace. The bishop Bradwardine, therefore, might be supposed to advocate "simple necessity", although he does not use this term himself; the Nun's Priest parenthetically assumes that responsibility. "(Nedely clepe I simple necessitee)." St. Augustine occupied the position presented in the second view.[52] He believed that free will was a *gift* from God to man and could be exercised by man only in so far as God permitted; hence the following line:

> Or elles if free choys be *graunted* me.

Boethius, as we have already seen, entertained as his belief the doctrine of "conditional necessity", mentioned here as the third possibility. Thus the Nun's Priest cannot decide to which of these three learned authorities to give most weight in accounting for Chauntecleer's flight from his beam on the eventful morning.

In conclusion of this section of the subject we may say (1) that Chaucer never expresses a complete acceptance of the Boethian doctrine of the reasons for the existence of evil or of his doctrine for free will, although he frequently dis-

[51] Milner's *Church History*, Vol. 4, pp. 89-101, contains a brief digest of the elaborate work of bishop Bradwardine on the question of free will, entitled *De causa Dei.*

[52] St. Augustine considers the subject of free will in the *City of God*, Book V, Chap. VIII-XII. He is particularly concerned in disproving the view of Cicero, who in the *De Divinatione* has argued that it is impossible for both the foreordination of God and the free will of man to exist and that, since a choice between the two is necessary, he prefers to believe in the latter (Teubner text, Vol. I. See in particular p. 207).

cusses the problems through his characters, (2) that he invariably leaves, sometimes humorously, these questions to the clerks, and (3) that he always bases these discussions on the *Consolation of Philosophy,* although he does not accept its conclusions. That Chaucer should have his characters persistently assume this attitude perhaps bespeaks his own point of view. And it would, indeed, be in accordance with his characteristic sanity of thought for him to see that these questions were beyond the sophistries of the philosophical schools. If the question of free will remains an open one in his mind, he is unique among the mediaeval writers who discussed this subject, and who might have had some weight with him. Boethius, Bradwardine, St. Augustine, Jean de Meun,[53] and Dante[54] all took sides one way or another on the problem.

[53] Jean de Meun accepts the explanation of Boethius in regard to necessity:

> C'est nécessité en regart,
> Et non pas nécessité simple;
> Si qui ce ne vaut une guimple;
> Et sa chose à venir est vaire,
> Donc est-ce chose nécessaire.   (R. R. 17917-21)

The entire discussion in the *Roman de la Rose* covers some five hundred lines (17789-18921), and, although the argument is an expansion of Boethian doctrine, yet it is changed almost beyond recognition by the introduction of extraneous matter and practical illustrations. (Cf. Langlois, *Origines et Sources du Roman de la Rose,* pp. 137-8). His discussion, for example, contains the practical suggestion that people often attribute to destiny the evils for which they are themselves responsible. His imagination leads him, further, to consider what a valuable thing it would be if human beings like God had foreknowledge. They could avoid flood, and famine; but at the same time it would be horrible if beasts like tigers and apes, and insects like flies and fleas, had the gift. His explanation of free will also includes an account of rainbows, comets, optic glasses, sleepwalking, dreams, and the hallucinations of fever.

[54] Dante's view of free will is in principle the same as that held by St. Augustine. Man has free will, but it springs from God. Cf. *Purg.* 16: 58-105.

CHAPTER III

INFLUENCE OF THE CONSOLATION ON CHAUCER'S THOUGHT: FELICITEE.

The *Consolation of Phliosophy* is essentially a picturesque and dramatic account, telling how Boethius was brought step by step from a condition of deep despair over the woes of life to a realization that, in his quest for happiness, he had been placing the emphasis on the wrong things, and that he should seek for this happiness elsewhere. What this true happiness is Dame Philosophy unfolds gradually, and reveals only after she has guided Boethius, somewhat as Vergil guided Dante, through many mazes of thought as intricate in its windings, so Boethius himself says, as was the Labyrinth of old (3. p12. 116-18). The explanation of true happiness, to be considered in detail later, is the crowning point of the treatise, the point which one, reading the *Consolation* really to find light, would await with concern. Let us now consider what Chaucer, interested in so many phases of the Boethian philosophy, has to say about this, its most essential phase. I wish in this chapter to show that Chaucer's whole conception of this fundamental question of the end of life or of "felicitee," as he commonly terms it, is unmistakably and to a large degree influenced by Boethius, that he discusses the problem in Boethian language, and that he reaches the same conclusions which Boethius reached.

Before discussing Chaucer's conception of the false felicity and of the true felicity, I shall try to show that Chaucer was interested in what constitutes "felicitee" as an abstract problem, just as, for example, he was interested in the problem of free will, and that with the use[1] of the word he probably associated the teaching of the *Consolation*.

The conception of Boethius on happiness, as it is explained in Book III, and particularly as it is outlined in 3. p2, runs somewhat as follows: Every human being seeks supreme

[1] According to the *New English Dictionary*, Chaucer was the first to use the word "felicity" in English. In the translation of the *Consolation*, he regularly translates *felicitas* by *blisfulnesse*. *Felicitee*, however, occurs in the translation.

happiness; it is the strongest instinct within him to do so. The difficulty, however, is that he becomes lost in the search, and staggers about blindly just as a drunken man seeking the house where he lives. He seeks for it in riches, in power, in fame, or in some other form of worldly prosperity; he may even seek for it as did Epicurus in the greatest pleasure and comfort that may be derived from life. The truth of the matter is that no one of these sources brings happiness, nor does any combination of them; each source is only a part of happiness. The real happiness is the sum total of all the imagined forms of happiness. It is, moreover, a thing which cannot possibly be divided into its parts. It must be taken whole or not at all. True happiness is, in fact, nothing less than the supreme good or God, and the impossibility of any division here will at once be seen. In the individual, therefore, true happiness is realized in goodness or virtue, or in being god-like. Chaucer, in different parts of his poetry, discusses different aspects of this theory, until, in the end, he has included all the phases of the question set forth by Boethius.

Arcite expresses the opinion that men seek, but seek blindly, after felicity:

> Som man desyreth for to han richesse,
> That cause is of his mordre or greet siknesse.
> And som[2] man wolde out of his prison fayn,
> That in his hous is of his meynee slayn.
> Infinite harmes been in this matere;
> We witen nat what thing we preyen here.
> *We faren as he that dronke is* as a mous;
> *A dronke man wot wel he hath an hous,*
> *But he noot which the righte wey is thider;*
> And to a dronke man the wey is slider.
> And certes, in this world so faren we;
> We seken faste after felicitee,
> *But we goon wrong ful often, trewely.*[3] A 1255-67.

Criseyde, as Arcite in the first five lines above, sees in worldly prosperity only false felicity. She enforces her point by a

[2] Cf. Boethius 3. p2. 17ff: Of the whiche men, *som of hem* wenen that *sovereyn good* be to liven withoute nede of any thing, and travaylen hem to be haboundant of *richesse. And som other men* demen that *sovereyn good be,* for to be right digne of reverence; . . . *And som folk* etc. Cf. also 2. p5. 64-7 for the allusion to the "meynee."

[3] The corage (of men) *alwey reherseth and seketh the sovereyn good,* al be it so that it be with a derked memorie; but he not by whiche *path, right as a dronken man not nat by whiche path he may retorne him to his hous.* 3. p2. 58-62.

subtle argument of fourteen lines which are not here quoted, but which are a direct quotation of the *Consolation,* 2. p4. 109-120:

> 'O god!' quod she, 'so worldly selinesse,
> Whiche *clerkes callen fals felicitee,*
> Y-medled is with many a bitternesse.[4]
> Ful anguisshous than is, god wot,' quod she,
> 'Condicioun of *veyn prosperitee;*[5] *Troilus* 3. 813-7.

The Franklin places felicity in pleasure:

> To liven in delyt was ever his wone,
> For he was *Epicurus* owne sone,
> *That heeld opinioun, that pleyn delyt*
> *Was verraily felicitee parfyt.*[6] A. 813-7.

Hypermnestra sees felicity only in goodness:

> conscience, trouthe, and dreed of shame,
> And of her wyfhood for to kepe her name,
> This, thoughte her, was *felicitee as here.*[7] *Leg.* 2586-88.

The aged and uxorious January is confronted by a deep philosophical problem. In his marriage with the youthful May he has found what seems to him the true felicity. There cannot, however, be two perfect goods; perhaps, therefore, he will be denied the bliss of heaven because he is enjoying his bliss on earth and attempting to part the true good:

> 'I have,' quod he, 'herd seyd, ful yore ago,
> *Ther may no man han parfite blisses two,*[8]
> This is to seye, in erthe and eek in hevene.
> For though he kepte him fro the sinnes sevene,
> And eek from every branche of thilke tree,
> Yet is ther so parfit felicitee,
> And so greet ese and lust in mariage,
> That ever I am agast, now in myn age, . . .
> That I shal have myn hevene in erthe here. E 1637-47.

[4] The swetnesse of *mannes welefulnesse is sprayned with many bitternesses;* 2. p4. 86-7

[5] For-why *ful anguissous* is the *condicioun* of mannes goodes; 2. p4. 56-7.

[6] Cf. 3. p2. 54-7. *Delyt only considered Epicurus,* and iuged and established that *delyt is the sovereyn good;* for as moche as alle othre thinges bi-rafte awey Ioye and mirthe fram the herte.

[7] It is the point of the first three books of the *Consolation* to prove that true happiness is in goodness.

[8] Cf. 3. p10. 85-89. *ther ne mowen nat ben two soverein goodes that ben dyverse amonge hem-self.* For certes, the goodes that ben dyverse amonges hem-self, that oon nis nat that that other is; thanne ne (may) neither of hem ben parfit, so as either of hem lakketh other. It is the chief point of p10 and p11 to prove the indivisibility of the good.

In this dreadful dilemma he goes to consult Justinus, who thus advises him:

> I hope to god, her-after shul ye knowe,
> That their nis so greet *felicitee*
> In mariage, ne never-mo shal be,
> That yow shal lette of your savacioun,   E 1674-77.

But January, too much consumed with passion, evidently does not follow this advice, for we learn later that he, like the Franklin, was a patron of Epicurus:

> *Somme clerkes holden that felicitee*
> *Stant in delyt,* and therfor certeyn he,
> This noble Januarie, . . .
> Shoop him to live ful deliciously.   E 2021-25.

The joy of Troilus and Criseyde at the climax of their love is thus described:

> *Felicitee, which that thise clerkes wyse*
> *Commenden so,* ne may not here suffyse. *Troilus.* 3. 1691-2.

Here again in these passages of Chaucer, as in his discussions of free will and the existence of evil, the "clerkes," so frequently alluded to, seem to mean only Boethius, or, at least, so the verbal and thought parallels indicate.

Now, having shown that Chaucer had an interest in felicity as an abstract problem, I shall attempt to consider certain passages in his poetry where he discusses definite phases of the question more fully. I shall discuss in Part I what he has to say of the false felicity, and in Part II what he has to say of the true felicity, and in each part the relation of Chaucer to Boethius.

Part I. False Felicity

Boethius in the *Consolation of Philosophy* analyzes false felicity twice, and each time at length: once in Book II where he discusses the gifts of Fortune—riches, dignities and powers, and fame, and again in Book III where Dame Philosophy explains to him what the false goods are before she ventures to explain the true goods. The second analysis is in part a needless repetition of the first, but is carried out to a finer point. Riches are discussed in 3. p3. and m3 much as in 2. p5 and m5. Dignities and powers, discussed in connection in 2. p6 and m6, receive a separate discussion in Book III, although little is contributed to the thought in the second discussion; dignities are discussed in 3. p4 and m4; and power, subdivided into kingly power and power obtained by having familiarity with kings, is discussed in p5. and m5. Fame is discussed in 3. p6. and m6 as in 2. p7 and m7. In the discussion of fame occurs the most important addition contributed in the second analysis. Here is explained the emptiness of pride in noble birth; and the nature of true gentility, translated as "gentilesse" by Chaucer, is described. In 3. p7 and m7 the insufficiency of bodily pleasures is discussed; this has no counterpart in Book II. Ignoring the more subtle and sometimes confusing distinctions and repetitions of Boethius in his analysis, we find most prominent and emphatic, discussions of riches, power, fame, gentility, and pleasures of the body. Chaucer considers all of these subjects in celebrated passages of his works. It now remains to see to what extent his consideration of these familiar themes is determined by Boethius. I dismiss at once the influence of Boethius on Chaucer's numerous sermons against voluptuous living and bodily pleasures as in the *Tale of the Man of Law,* or *The Pardoner's Tale,* or *The Parson's Tale,* for Boethius has relatively little to say on this theme so popular among mediaeval writers; for material of this kind Chaucer preferred to go to the copious storehouse afforded in the *De Contemptu Mundi* of Pope Innocent or *La Somme des Vices et des Vertus* of Frère Lorens. And in regard to the other sources of false felicity, riches, power, fame, and pride of birth, I do not wish to overemphasize the influence of Boethius. On the contrary, Chaucer seems to have been familiar with what many authors had to say on these subjects. It may well be that Boccaccio, Dante, or Jean de Meun had more influence on certain passages concerning these matters than did Boethius. The point which I wish to emphasize, however, is that the influence of Boethius is the one constant and unfailing influence, and, usually, the strongest influence running through Chaucer's discussions of these four phases of false felicity. I shall consider them in the following order: power, fame, riches, and gentilesse, the latter, however, under Part II for reasons obvious later.

1. *Power*

The *Monk's Tale* is nothing more nor less than a list of illustrations showing the fickleness and emptiness of power so emphasized by Boethius. The statement of Boethius in 3. p5. 3-5 might well serve as a text for the tale:

But certes, the olde age of tyme passed, and eek of present tyme now, is ful of ensaumples how that kinges ben chaunged in-to wrecchednesse out of hir welefulnesse.

The plan of grouping together a long list of stories, as Chaucer does, telling how great men and women had fallen from high to low estate of course resembles that of the *De Casibus Virorum Illustrium* of Boccaccio, but the point which both authors maintain is characteristically Boethian. Further, the influence of Boethius is more specific than in this general resemblance in purpose, as will be found by a comparison of certain passages of the *Monk's Tale,* particularly, with those parts of the *Consolation* which deal with the vanity of kingly power. In the first place, for three of his stories, those of Hercules, Nero, and Croesus, Chaucer was much indebted to Boethius. (Cf. pp. 144-5). In the second place, the tales of Nero and of Croesus are used in the *Consolation* to enforce the same point which Chaucer is making. (Cf. 2. m6, 3. m4, and 2. p2. 42-8). Nero is described in two different *meters* as an example of the undesirability of power, and in 3. p5. 34-41 an account is given of Seneca in connection with him, as in the *Monk's Tale* B 3685 ff. In connection with the account of Croesus 2. p2. 42-8, Boethius makes an allusion to tragedy to explain his downfall:

What other thing biwailen the cryinges of tragedies but only the dedes of Fortune, that with an unwar stroke overtorneth realmes of grete nobley? *Glose.* Tragedie is to seyn, a ditee of a prosperitee for a tyme, that endeth in wrecchednesse.

Chaucer brings in the same allusion in his account of Croesus. More than this, his entire list of disasters is to be a list of tragedies, as he announces at the outset of the tale in giving the Boethian definition of the word. Next, allusions to Fortune are frequent, prolonged, and are given the Boethian turn. Boethius holds that real power consists in having command over one's own self and not trusting to the possessions of Fortune. 2. p6. 29-57. Chaucer says in conclusion of his tale of Hercules:

Lo, who may truste on fortune any throwe?
For him that folweth al this world of prees,
Er he be war, is ofte y-leyd ful lowe.
ʹFul wys is he that can him-selven knowe. B 3326-29.

There are many other allusions to fortune.[9]   Lastly, after
the tale is interrupted by the knight, it is two of the Boethian
phrases which are recalled by the host in his ridicule of the
tale :

> 'Ye,' quod our hoste, 'by seint Poules belle,
> Ye seye right sooth; this monk, he clappeth loude,
> He spak how "fortune covered with a cloude"
> I noot never what, and als of a "Tragedie"
> Right now ye herde,   B 3970-74.

Thus it will be seen that the *Monk's Tale* is Boethian in spirit
and that Chaucer had the *Consolation* definitely in mind in
writing it.

2. *Fame*

Boethius, to prove the emptiness of fame, shows (2. p7 and
m7) that it can never spread far nor last long.   In the vast
infinity of space the fame of the most renowned individual
would spread relatively over only a pin point, and in the infinity of time would not continue so much as for a moment.
The fame of Rome in its palmiest days had not extended beyond the Caucasus mountains.   Fame, therefore, dwindles to
nothingness and is not worth the striving for.   Chaucer in
the *House of Fame* considers the subject.   In the first two
books his conception of Fame as a bearer of tidings and as
dwelling in a fixed abode is plainly influenced by Vergil and
Ovid (Cf. Professor Sypherd's *Studies in Chaucer's Hous of
Fame*, pp. 103-9), and so need not concern us here.   In Book
III, however, Chaucer presents an analysis of the abstract
question of fame which seems to have no close parallel either
in classical or in mediaeval literature.   In this discussion
Chaucer does not, like Boethius, argue primarily to prove the
insignificance of fame, but to prove the injustice of its be-
stowal.   Four classes of people approach the goddess of Fame.
The first class, of which there are three groups, all have
done good works, merit fame, and wish it.   Of these, the first
are sent away by the goddess empty handed, never to be remembered by men; the second group fare even worse, for
slanderous reports are noised about in the world concerning
them although they deserved good reports; the third group,

[9] In B 3431ff. we learn that Fortune takes away a man's friends; in
B 3586 and 3635 are allusions to her wheel; in 3712 she is represented
as explaining her conduct; in 3956 her face is said to be covered with
a cloud.

more fortunate than the other two, get more fame than their works merit. The second class, approaching in two separate groups, are composed of those pious folk who have done good works simply for the love of it and who desire no fame at all. The first group are granted their request, but the second receive fame whether they want it or not. The third class are the idlers, who acknowledge that they deserve no fame, but who yet wish it. Part of these are granted their request. The last class are composed of evil doers who desire fame. Part of them receive it. Thus, Boethius argues the littleness of fame, and Chaucer its injustice. But, notwithstanding this difference, the inference in each case is, that fame is not to be counted on for happiness. Chaucer, himself, somewhat indeed in the spirit of the Boethian admonition of self reliance, has no business with the goddess when someone asks him whether he is present to beseech the goddess for fame:

> 'Nay, for-sothe, frend!' quod I;
> 'I cam noght hider, graunt mercy!
> For no swich cause, by my heed!
> Suffyceth me, as I were deed,
> That no wight have my name in honde.
> I woot my-self best how I stonde;
> For what I drye or what I thinke,
> I wol my-selven al hit drinke,
> Certeyn, for the more part,
> As ferforth as I can myn art.' 1873-82.

This is precisely what Boethius would have said under similar circumstances.

Further than the general resemblance, there is a more tangible evidence of the Boethian influence. It is my intention in another place (Cf. pp. 140-1) to take up the influence of Boethius on the *House of Fame* as a whole; there are strong marks of this influence throughout. At this place it will be sufficient to indicate how Chaucer may be indebted to Boethius for his conception of the goddess of Fame. First, her stature ever changing, like that of Dame Philosophy (1. pr. 8-13), she sometimes pierces the clouds, and sometimes shrinks to the height of common mortals (Cf. ll. 1368-75). Secondly, Fame is given one of the chief attributes of Fortune—injustice. She bestows her gifts absolutely without rhyme or reason. In the *Consolation,* fame is only one of the gifts of Fortune. Chaucer raises the conception to the rank of Fortune and to kinship

with her as he specifically states in the following lines of the
House of Fame:

> And somme of hem she graunted sone,
> And somme she werned wel and faire;
> And somme she graunted the contraire
> Of hir axing utterly.
> But thus I seye yow trewely,
> What hir cause was, I niste.
> For this folk, ful wel I wiste,
> They hadde good fame ech deserved,
> Althogh they were diversly served;
> *Right as hir suster, dame Fortune,*
> *Is wont to serven in comune.*[10] 1538-48.

Thus, Chaucer's discussion of the fickleness of fame, included
with the rest that he has to say about fame, of itself is significant in indicating the influence of the discussion of fame which
he found in the *Consolation,* especially since he is interested
in the other forms of false felicity therein described; and the
unmistakable instances of Boethian influence in his description
of the goddess of Fame help to confirm this view. Moreover,
the original use to which he puts the Boethian material shows
a complete assimilation and mastery of it.

3. Riches

One of the best known *meters* of Boethius is the *meter* on
the "former age." This *meter* (2. m5) is a part of his argument against riches. In it he contrasts the turmoils of his own
times with the peace of primitive days. His point is to show
how primitive man was content with little things. The men
of the "former age" were content to eat what grew naturally,
fruits and acorns. They did not drink wine, but drank water

[10] Professor Sypherd in his *Studies in Chaucer's Hous of Fame,* pp.
122-6, makes a point of the probable influence of Boethius on Chaucer
in his discussion of Fame in the abstract, and quotes these lines. I
cannot quite agree with his statement (124n) that the discussion of
fame in Boethius is much nearer to Chaucer's conception than is the
somewhat similar treatment in the *Somnium Scipionis.* The treatment in the *Consolation* and in the *Somnium Scipionis* are closely related, as Boethius was influenced by the latter. He specifically alludes
to it in his discussion of fame in 2. p7. 40-45. The chief argument
of both is, the smallness of earth in comparison to the vastness of
heaven and the consequent uselessness of attempting to secure fame
on earth. Each alludes to the earth as a mere point *(punctum).* Compare this use with Chaucer's similar use in line 907 of the *House of
Fame.* Chaucer was entirely familiar with both works.

from the running streams. They did not have houses, but slept in the shadows of the lofty pines. They did not sail the seas in quest of merchandise. They did not go to war, and they did not mine gold. Boethius longs for such simplicity in his own day.

That Chaucer's poem, *The Former Age,* was suggested to him by this *meter* of the *Consolation,* and adapted from it is shown by the facts that Chaucer uses for the title of his poem the title suggested by Boethius *(prior aetas)* in preference to the more usual classical title, the "golden age"; that the first five lines are a free verse translation of the first three lines of the corresponding Boethian passage; that the length and nature of the poem more nearly resemble that of the *meter* of Boethius than that of any of the numerous sources to be mentioned below; and that the general outline of the poem is almost precisely the same as that in the *Consolation,* although this similarity is likely to be lost sight of because of the difference in details.[11]

We, today, would regard a poem which dealt with the golden age as a literary convention to be considered lightly; but to Chaucer without the classical background that we have, I think the poem would make a more powerful appeal. His interest is shown in a number of ways. In the first place, the outline of the *Former Age,* derived from the *Consolation* as I have explained, is filled in with details gathered from a surprisingly large number of sources, some of them also describing the primitive age. In addition to the *Consolation of Philosophy,* these sources were Ovid's description of the four ages of the world (*Metamorphoses* 1. 89-162) and the long description of the golden age in the *Roman de la Rose,* 8671-8772; besides these main sources, he incorporated a passage from another *meter* of Boethius which deals with the

[11] I think that the closeness with which Chaucer follows the sequence of thought in the Latin *meter* has not previously been noted. Each poem makes the same general points in practically the same order: Lines 1-5 of Chaucer's poem on the simplicity of foods in the former age are an expansion of 2. m5. 1-3; lines 6-14 on the lack of agricultural pursuits are suggested by lines 3-5; lines 15-18 on the dearth of wine and dyes correspond to lines 5-11; lines 21-6 on the evils of mercenary voyages and of war, to lines 13-20; lines 26-40 on the strenuous and accursed efforts to acquire riches are an expansion of lines 24-8; lines 40-46 on the luxury of human abodes, of lines 11-13; lines 46-64 on the lack of faith and the disorders of the present age are suggested by the *Consolation* but have no direct counterpart in it.

insatiable greed of men for riches, and a passage from the *Policraticus* of John of Salisbury, or if not from this, from St. Jerome's *Epistle against Jovinian;* and there is a strong hint that Chaucer used the Fourth *Eclogue* of Vergil on the return of the golden age.[12]

The next evidence of Chaucer's interest in the poem is in his attempt to modernize it by his various additions, and hence to make it more applicable in his own day; although the additions may seem old-fashioned enough to us now. For example, instead of the classical allusion of Boethius to mixing the gift of Bacchus with honey, Chaucer alludes to grinding spices in mortars, and to mixing them with *clare* and galantine sauce; instead of the remote allusion to the effects of Tyrian purple dyes on Syrian wool, he speaks of the dye plants, madder, weld, and woad. He tells of counterfeiting money, of palace chambers where beds are soft with down of feathers and white with bleached sheets, and of armed hosts storming cities with round or square towers to find fat bags of gold and rich booty.

Most important in indicating Chaucer's genuine interest in the thought of the poem is the fact that the point most emphasized, the lack of faith in men, corresponds to the chief point of a very serious poem of Chaucer, *Lack of Steadfastness,* a poem of counsel addressed to King Richard II. The insistence upon the lack of faith in men appears most strongly in the closing lines of the *Former Age:*

> Everich of hem his feith to other kepte . . .
> The lambish peple, voyd of alle vyce,
> Hadden no fantasye to debate,
> But ech of hem wolde other wel cheryce;
> No pryde, non envye, non avaryce,
> No lord, no taylage by no tyrannye;
> Humblesse and pees, good feith, the emperice,
> [Fulfilled erthe of olde curtesye.] . . .

> Allas, allas! now may men wepe and crye!
> For in our dayes nis but covetyse
> Doubleness, and tresoun and envye,
> Poysoun, manslauhtre, and mordre in sondry wyse. 48-64.

[12] The extent of Chaucer's indebtedness to each one of these sources is considered elsewhere (p. 134). The influence of the *Consolation* 3. m10. 9-14 on line 30, of certain lines of Ovid, and the probable influence of the Fourth *Eclogue* of Vergil have not been considered before.

Lack of Steadfastness is an expansion of just this theme. It deplores the lack of faith between men, their striving against each other for gain, and the consequent confusion in the world. It also suggests a contrast with previous times, although this aspect is not emphasized. The first two stanzas are quoted below:

> *Som tyme* this world was so stedfast and stable
> That mannes word was obligacioun,
> But *now* hit is so fals and deceivable,
> That word and deed, as in conclusioun,
> Ben no-thing lyk, for turned up so doun
> Is al this world for mede and wilfulnesse,
> That al is lost for lak of stedfastnesse.
>
> What maketh this world to be so variable
> But lust that folk have in dissensioun?
> Among us *now* a man is holde unable,
> But-if he can, by som collusioun,
> Don his neighbour wrong or oppressioun.
> What causeth this, but wilful wrecchednesse,
> That al is lost, for lak of stedfastnesse?

Chaucer's two minor poems, the *Former Age* and *Lack of Steadfastness,* are, therefore, the same in spirit, and, as will presently be shown, these poems are to be closely associated with other of the minor poems of Chaucer, and all are to be closely associated with Boethius.

The *meter* of Boethius on the "former age" is only a small part of his discussion of riches. In 2. p5 and 3. p3, m3, he directs many arguments against them. In the first place, the care of them in itself leads to trouble and even to danger. In the second place, riches in themselves, the mere fact of possession, does not make a man any happier. He may own fine clothes and precious gems, but they in no way add to *his* merit. He shines from his own virtue, and his possessions do not confer their properties upon him. He is one thing; they are another. The accident of possession counts for nothing. One should be content with little things such as are sufficient to satisfy the demands of nature, and should know and appreciate himself. Inner worth is what counts most. That Chaucer insists upon this point of view is shown by lines 1255-9 of the *Knight's Tale* where Arcite in Boethian language proves that riches bring only trouble; by the essay on gentilesse in the *Wyf of Bath's Tale* and in the minor poem *Gentilesse* where Chaucer argues that not "olde richesse" but virtue constitutes true nobility; and by the minor poem *Truth* where he admonishes contentment in little things. All of these passages, as will soon be shown, are of the very essence of Boethian philosophy.

From the foregoing it will appear that Chaucer has considered at length power, fame, and riches, the three phases of false felicity most emphasized in the analysis of Boethius. That he was truly disappointed in the selfishness of human pursuits, and in the vain quest of men for false and transitory felicity, we have the evidence afforded by a sincere poem like *Lack of Steadfastness* and by other passages equally sincere to be considered later. His point of view is well shown by lines which come in the conclusion of the *Man of Law's Tale*. They are the more unusual because they are suggested by the joyful union of King Alla and his wife Constance after their long years of separation. Even deserved human joys of the most noble kind will not last:

> But litel whyl it lasteth, I yow hete,
> Joye of this world, for tyme wol nat abyde;
> Fro day to night it changeth as the tyde. B 1132-34.

PART II. TRUE FELICITY

I shall discuss this part of the subject under the two headings: Gentilesse and Truth.[13] Gentilesse, it is true, in the *Consolation* is discussed under false felicity, for the reason that Boethius considers pride of birth to be one of the mistaken sources of happiness. He does not, however, emphasize the baseness and falseness of would-be nobles, but, rather, defines true nobility and shows who possess it. This discussion occupies only the last part of 3. p6 and the short *meter* following it, but, in spirit, has an intimate connection with all the foregoing analysis of false felicity in Books II and III. In analyzing power, fame, and riches, Boethius is bent not only on showing the insufficiency of these, but on pointing the way to what is really sufficient; namely, a steadfast spirit and *virtue*. For example, under riches he says:

Richesses, ben they precious by the nature of hem-self, or elles by the *nature of thee?* 2. p5. 6-7.

[13] Chaucer frequently associates the ideas of Truth and Gentilesse as in the statement "in honour of trouthe and gentilesse". (*Troilus* 3. 163). See also other examples in *Troilus:* 2. 159-60; 3. 963; 5. 1616.

Again he says:

Is it thanne so, that ye men ne han no *proper good y-set in you,* for which ye moten seken outward youre goodes in foreine and subgit thinges? 2. p5. 88-9.

Under "dignitees" he says:

And yit more-over, yif it so were that thise dignitees or powers hadden any propre or natural *goodnesse in hem-self,* never nolden they comen to shrewes. 2. p6. 54-7. Dignitees apertienen proprely to *vertu.* 3. p4. 25-6.

Likewise in 3. p6 under the discussion of noble birth, one of the subdivisions of fame or glory, he shows that it, too, really depends on virtue. This belief, running through the argument as an undercurrent before, here breaks forth in full force. After all, power, fame, riches, noble birth are very closely allied. With noble birth frequently go the other attributes, and what applies to one applies to all; indeed, as I shall discuss more fully presently, Dante, in his discussion of *gentilezza,* associates both riches and noble birth in his phrase *antica ricchezza.* Boethius, by all this preliminary discussion of virtue in the analysis of false felicity, is merely paving the way to what he considers of greater importance, the true felicity which is to be found in the *supremum bonum.* From the considerations of this paragraph it may be seen that the discussions of gentilesse and of truth, which Boethius closely links with the *supremum bonum,* logically fall together.

1. *Gentilesse*

The subject of true nobility, so often alluded to as "gentilesse" by Chaucer, was frequently discussed by mediaeval writers. The starting place for this discussion seems to have been the *Consolation of Philosophy;* for not only do later writers follow the particular turn which Boethius gave the discussion by bringing in the element of heredity, as we shall see, but they repeatedly refer to him as an authority. Dante in the fourth Tractate of the *Convivio,* the theme of which is *gentilezza,* alludes to the *Consolation* four times (Cf. ch. 12 and 13). Chaucer in the *Wife of Bath's Tale* in a long discourse on *gentilesse* (D 1109-76) not only borrows passages from Boethius, but refers to him by name as an authority (D 1168). And Machault in the *Confort d' Ami* says, if his friends wish to know whence come *richesse* and *noblesse,* they should read the book of Boece. (Cf. Professor Sypherd's *Studies in Chaucer's Hous of Fame,* p. 123.)

The importance of this passage of the *Consolation* admits of its being quoted in full:

But now, of this name of gentilesse, what man is it that ne may wel seen how veyn and how flittinge a thing it is? For yif the name of gentilesse be referred to renoun and cleernesse of linage, thanne is gentil name but a foreine thing, *that is to seyn, to hem that glorifyen hem of hir linage.* For it semeth that gentilesse be a maner preysinge that comth of the deserte of ancestres. And yif preysinge maketh gentilesse, thanne moten they nedes be gentil that be preysed. For which thing it folweth, that yif thou ne have no gentilesse of thy-self, *that is to seyn, preyse that comth of thy deserte,* foreine gentilesse ne maketh thee nat gentil. But certes, yif ther be any good in gentilesse, I trowe it be al-only this, that it semeth as that a maner necessitee be imposed to gentil men, for that they ne sholden nat outrayen or for-liven fro the virtues of hir noble kinrede. 3. p6. 24-38.

Al the linage of men that ben in erthe ben of semblable birthe. On allone is fader of thinges. On allone ministreth alle thinges. He yaf to the sonne hise bemes; he yaf to the mone hir hornes. He yaf the men to the erthe; he yaf the sterres to the hevene. He encloseth with membres the soules that comen fro his hye sete. Thanne comen alle mortal folk of noble sede; why noisen ye or bosten of youre eldres? For yif thou loke your beginninge, and god your auctor and your maker, thanne nis ther no forlived wight, but-yif he norisshe his corage un-to vyces, and forlete his propre burthe. 3. m6.

The views of Boethius, here expressed, may be summed up as follows: (1) Virtue constitutes true gentility. (2) Gentility cannot be transmitted by inheritance from father to son, for virtue depends on the individual. (3) Gentility proceeds from God alone, the common father of all.

For the purpose of comparing the general ideas of Chaucer and Boethius on this question, I cite the following passages, one from the *Wife of Bath's Tale* and the other the *balade, Gentilesse*. The subject is brought up in the former, it will be recalled, by the heroine, the loathly lady, in persuading her reluctant husband, the knight, that he should think of her intrinsic merits rather than her ugly body, poverty, and low estate:

> But for ye speken of swich gentillesse
> As is descended out of old richesse,
> That therfore sholden ye be gentil men,
> Swich arrogance is nat worth an hen.
> Loke who that is most vertuous alway,
> Privee and apert, and most entendeth ay
> To do the gentil dedes that he can,
> And tak him for the grettest gentil man.
> Crist wol we clayme of him our gentillesse,
> Nat of our eldres for hir old richesse. . . .
> Thy gentillesse cometh fro god allone. D 1109-62.

95

The parts of the passage not quoted here contain a detailed proof showing that virtue is not inherited, and this phase of the argument is carried out to a much greater length than by Boethius. The balade *Gentilesse* contains much the same general idea, although the divine aspect of nobility is more emphasized in it:

> The firste stok, fader of gentilesse—
> What man that claymeth gentil for to be,
> Must folowe his trace, and alle his wittes dresse
> Vertu to sewe, and vyces for to flee.
> For unto vertu longeth dignitee,
> And noght the revers, saufly dar I deme,
> Al were he mytre, croune, or diademe.
>
> This firste stok was ful of rightwisnesse,
> Trewe of his word, sobre, pitous, and free,
> Clene of his goste, and loved besinesse,
> Ageinst the vyce of slouthe, in honestee;
> And, but his heir love vertu, as dide he,
> He is noght gentil, thogh he riche seme,
> Al were he mytre, croune, or diademe.
>
> Vyce may wel be heir to old richesse;
> But ther may no man, as men may wel see,
> Bequethe his heir his vertuous noblesse
> That is appropred unto no degree,
> But to the firste fader in magestee,
> That maketh him his heir, that can him queme,
> Al were he mytre, croune, or diademe.

It becomes obvious upon comparison that the general idea in the passages of the two authors is the same. Chaucer defines nobility as dependent on virtue and not on lineage, and shows that true nobility comes from God alone. And now comes the question, to what extent was Boethius responsible for Chaucer's conception. Here once more, as several times before, we are face to face with the problem of the blending of the influence of Boethius and of Dante, and the separation of the two is made all the more difficult, and in part impossible, because Dante himself was unquestionably influenced by Boethius, as I trust will become apparent before this chapter is finished. The separate influence of each in the two passages of Chaucer, however, can be shown. Professor Lowes (*Modern Philology*, Vol. XIII, pp. 19-27, May 1915) has proved clearly that Chaucer was indebted to Dante's discussion of *gentilezza* in the fourth Tractate of the *Convivio* and in the canzone prefixed to it. He has left, however, the influence of Boethius completely in the background save for the briefest possible mention, apparently giving Jean de Meun a more prominent place in his discussion than he gives Boethius. After devoting half a page (p. 20) to Chaucer and his sources, Dante and Jean de Meun in particular, he thus concludes: "And in the present instance (Chaucer's passages on gentility) the fine democracy of Jean de Meun's conception of true nobility has been merged with Dante's loftier idealism, and both have been tempered by Chaucer's own broad humanity".[14] Although the influence of Jean de Meun is undoubtedly felt in the poems, it seems to me that the fusion of ideas primarily concerns Boethius and Dante. Professor Lowes, moreover, attributes to Dante's influence passages which could equally well be attributed to Boethius; and to a surprising degree ignores him. That he should not have done so is the purpose of the following paragraphs to show.

Professor Lowes points out the division of Dante's argument on the nature of *gentilezza* into two parts, a negative argument devoted to the refutation of the view that *gentilezza* depends on ancestral riches or descent and a positive argument tracing *gentilezza* to its ultimate and only source in God. He shows that Chaucer, mainly under the influence of Dante, as he thinks, is interested in just these things, and supports his view by pointing out verbal parallels between Chaucer's passages and the *Convivio*. And now let us examine the negative and positive arguments in Chaucer's passages in relation to both Dante and Boethius, for the two sets of arguments are also present in the *Consolation,* as becomes at once apparent.

Concerning the negative argument, the passage to which Professor Lowes first calls attention is the first four lines of

[14] The two chief passages in the *Roman de la Rose* where Jean de Meun discusses nobility are ll. 6863-76 and ll. 19297-19590. The French author was interested most of all in the practical side of nobility for different kinds of men, as kings, knights, and clerks. The idea that virtue does not come through a man's lineage is asserted (Cf. l. 19297), but Jean de Meun is content with the mere assertion and does not attempt anywhere to prove the point in detail as does Chaucer in the *Wife of Bath's Tale.* And never, in these discussions of virtue does he allude to its divine origin. Consequently the influence of Jean de Meun in the passages of Chaucer under discussion is aside from the main trend of the argument. For the specific lines influenced by Jean de Meun, see Dr. Fansler's *Chaucer and the Roman de la Rose,* p. 221.

the *Wife of Bath,* quoted above (D 1109-12). He shows that Dante's phrase *antica richezza,* repeated numerous times in the *Convivio* and pointed out long ago by Koeppel in connection with Chaucer, has a deeper significance than being a mere verbal parallel to Chaucer's *old richesse,* used in lines 1110 and 1118 of the *Wife of Bath* and in line 15 of the *balade;* that, indeed, *antica richezza* is the essential point on which Dante's whole discussion turns. He further finds a similarity of expression between these opening lines of Chaucer and lines 21-37 of Dante's canzone. His evidence, on this point, is convincing. It is very significant that Chaucer should discuss true nobility particularly in relation to riches, although they are ancestral riches, instead of in relation to lineage alone as Boethius discussed it in the *Consolation,* and it is further significant that Chaucer should emphasize, to such an extent, as he does through the long discussion in the *Wife of Bath,* the argument that virtue is not a matter of inheritance. Boethius certainly suggests the point, but he does not go into it with nearly Dante's completeness.[15] But now let us pass to the contribution of Boethius in the negative argument.

Professor Lowes quotes D 1133-38 as being especially influenced by Dante. Chaucer follows them by an illustration drawn from the *Consolation* 3. p4. 44-8. The purpose of the illustration is to prove that true gentility does not naturally pass down the family line from father to son:

> Tak fyr, and ber it in the derkeste hous
> Bitwix this and the mount of Caucasus,
> And lat men shette the dores and go thenne;
> Yet wol the fyr as faire lye and brenne,
> As twenty thousand men mighte it biholde;
> His office naturel ay wol it holde,
> Up peril of my lyf, til that it dye.
> Heer may ye see wel, how that genterye
> Is nat annexed to possessioun,
> Sith folk ne doon hir operacioun
> Alwey, as dooth the fyr,   D 1139-49.

[15] Dante shows, for example, that, if virtue or baseness were inherited, all men would have to be like Adam. If Adam were base, all men must be base; if Adam were noble, all men must be noble. This similarity in men does not exist. Therefore virtue and baseness are not inherited. But suppose that Adam was not the common father. This supposition is impossible, as it is against the teaching of the Bible and of Aristotle. See chapters 14 and 15 of the fourth Tractate.

Boethius uses the illustration to prove that true dignity does not go naturally with the mere holding of offices, for the dignity of the office holder no longer shines when it passes among strange people; in this it is unlike fire which by its own nature shines everywhere. Further, Chaucer's allusion to the Caucasus mountains in line 1140 may have been suggested by its use in the *Consolation* 2. p7. 43. Here Boethius, in discussing the emptiness of fame, alludes to these mountains as the most distant limit of the glory of Rome. Such evidence indicates that Chaucer is associating the parts in the Boethian analysis of false felicity as they logically are associated. Again, Professor Lowes (p. 26) quotes lines D 1152-58 as influenced by lines 34-37 of the canzone, and especially by the commentary upon them in the Tractate. These lines also are supported by a passage from the *Consolation,* this time a definition straight from the discussion of Boethius on gentility. The corresponding passages follow:

> For *gentilesse* nis but *renomee*
> Of *thyne auncestres,* for hir heigh bountee,
> Which is a *straunge thing* to thy persone. D 1159-61.

For yif the name of *gentilesse* be referred to *renoun* and cleernesse of linage, thanne is gentil name but a *foreine thing,* . . . For it semeth that gentilesse be a maner preysinge that comth of the *deserte of ancestres.* . . . *foreine* gentilesse ne maketh thee nat gentil. 3. p6. 26-34.

Next, Mr. Lowes quotes a passage containing a proverb of Juvenal which is found in chapter 13 of the Tractate:[16]

> Verray povert, it singeth proprely;
> Juvenal seith of povert merily:
> "The povre man, whan he goth by the weye,
> Bifore the theves he may singe and pleye." D 1191-94.

The *Consolation of Philosophy* also contains this proverb, and in Chaucer's translation there is a gloss concerning it, supplied from the commentary of Nicholas Trivet. This occurs at the conclusion of the discussion of riches in 2. p5 and leads up to the *meter* on the former age:

A povre man, that berth no richesse on him by the weye, may boldely singe biforn theves, for he hath nat wherof to ben robbed. 2. p5. 129-30.

In discussing the positive argument, Professor Lowes points

[16] This passage is not included in the discussion of the negative side of the argument on nobility by Professor Lowes, but is quoted later as an additional parallel. Dante attributes the proverb to "il Savio". Neither he nor Boethius mentions Juvenal as its author.

to lines 19-20 of the balade *Gentilesse,* line 1117 in the *Wife of Bath,* and quotes the following:

> Thy gentilesse cometh fro *god allone;*
> Than comth our verray gentillesse of *grace.* D 1162-3.

It would be futile to argue whether Dante or Boethius influenced Chaucer the more in the conception that true gentility comes from God alone. He evidently was perfectly familiar with what both authors had to say on the subject, and was no doubt strengthened in his opinion by the fact that both of these learned authorities said the same thing. Professor Lowes (p. 25) shows close parallels to Chaucer's lines in the canzone and in the commentary, the latter of which states:

> Dice adunque che *Iddio solo* porge *questa grazia* all' anima di quello, etc.

The *Consolation* in its statement of this idea contains no allusion to *grace* except by inference in the repetition of the verb *yaf;* otherwise Dante and Boethius agree. Boethius says in part:

> *On allone* is fader of thinges. *On allone ministreth* alle thinges. *He yaf* to the sone hise bemes; *he yaf* to the mone hir hornes. *He yaf* etc. . . . *He encloseth* with membres the soules that comen fro his hye sete. 3. m6. 2-6.[17]

One of the most striking verbal parallels pointed out by Professor Lowes is between lines five and six of the balade on *Gentilesse* and lines 101-4 of Dante's canzone:

> *For unto vertu longeth dignitee,*
> *And noght the revers,* saufly dar I deme.
> *È Gentilezza dovunque è virtute,*
> *Ma non virtute ov' ella;*
> Siccome è 'l cielo dovunque è la stella,
> *Ma ciò non e converso.*

In the *Consolation* there are the following parallels:

> And therfor it is thus, that *honour ne comth nat to vertu for cause of dignitee, but ayeinward honour comth to dignitee for cause of vertu.* 2. p6. 17-19. 'Certes, *dignitees,'* quod she, *'apertienen proprely to vertu;'* 3. p4. 25-6.

The decision here, if one is to decide whether Boethius or Dante had more influence in determining Chaucer's conception of gentilesse, seems to rest on whether to give more weight

---

[17] These quotations from both Dante and Chaucer come in passages where the subject is gentility.

to *revers,* corresponding to Dante's *converso,* or to *dignitee,* corresponding to the *dignitee* of Chaucer's translation of Boethius. As a matter of fact, the influence of the two authors seems to be fused almost beyond separation. Chaucer must, indeed, have had a tenacious memory and a keen analytical faculty to have merged the essential points of these two discussions on gentility with accompanying illustrations, definitions, and striking phrases drawn from each, and from Jean de Meun besides. Certainly, Boethius had a very important part in determining Chaucer's conception of gentilesse.

The two passages concerning gentilesse just discussed are by no means the only ones devoted to the subject. It is brought up again and again, sometimes manifesting itself in single lines and sometimes in much longer passages, as there are numerous examples to show. The Manciple deplores the fact that an unfaithful wench is regarded as more guilty in a breach of faith than an unfaithful gentlewoman (H 205-37). In the legend of Lucretia (1819-24) the evil deed of Tarquin calls forth a lament that he, who was heir to a king, who by lineage should have conducted himself as a true knight, had done a churl's deed. The young lord Walter in the *Clerk's Tale* defends his quest for a wife of lowly origin on the ground that true goodness comes from God and is not engendered in the strain to which the individual may belong (E 155-161), although what he has to say is based largely on Petrarch's version of the tale. The Parson also discusses gentility (I 460-70).

Several of the Canterbury tales are avowedly tales of gentilesse, and several are avowedly tales of churls. Chaucer in the well known lines of the Miller's Prologue (A 3176-84) invites the reader to turn over the leaves and take his pick. The *Reve's Tale* and the *Miller's Tale* are conspicuously tales of churls; they are churls and tell churls' tales. Just as these two tales are companion tales of churls, so the *Squire's Tale* and the *Franklin's Tale* may be regarded as companion tales of gentilesse. The *Squire's Tale* might well have for a text Chaucer's familiar line, "pitee renneth sone in gentil herte."[18]

[18] Pity and gentility were frequently associated together in Chaucer's mind. Cf. *The Compleynte Unto Pite,* where gentilesse has made an unnatural alliance with cruelty; Prologue to *Legend of Good Women,* B 161, A 491; *Legend* 1018; *Canterbury Tales,* A 920, B 660, E 96-7, E 1987, F 479. The manifestations of gentility especially mentioned in the balade on *Gentilesse* (ll. 9-11) are truth to promises, sobriety,.

Both Canacee and the gentle falcon, so sympathetically comforted by her, exemplify this theme in word and action. The falcon thus speaks after awakening from the swoon into which her grief has caused her to fall:

'That pitee renneth sone in gentil herte,
Feling his similitude in peynes smerte,
Is preved al-day, as men may it see,
As wel by werk as by auctoritee;
For gentil herte kytheth gentillesse. F 479-83.

After the tale was finished, everyone apparently at once recognized it as a tale of gentillesse, as well they might, for the chivalric and enthusiastic young squire had simply piled up his allusions to gentleness one after the other;[19] the understanding of it was one of his accomplishments, as he seems to have wished the humbler members of the pilgrimage distinctly to understand. The Franklin evidently is duly impressed, for he wishes that his own son were similarly versed. His speech is colored somewhat by the influence of Boethius and Dante:

I have a sone, and, by the Trinitee,
I hadde lever than twenty pound worth lond, . . .
He were a man of swich discrecioun
As that ye been! fy on *possessioun*[20]
But-if a man be *vertuous* with-al.
I have my sone snibbed, and yet shal,
For he to *vertu* listeth nat entende;
But for to pleye at dees, and to despende,
And lese al that he hath, is his usage.
And he hath lever talken with a page
Than to comune with any gentil wight
Ther he mighte lerne *gentillesse* aright.' F 682-94.

pity, generosity, purity, and honest and active work. See also the *Parson's Tale* (I 464-70) for "signes of gentilesse." It may be interesting in this connection to point out that the manifestations of virtue mentioned by Dante in the *Convivio* (ch. 17 of the fourth Tractate) were the eleven qualities approved by Aristotle in the *Ethics:* courage, temperance, generosity, munificence, consciousness of greatness, proper pride, serenity, affability, frankness, moderation in sports, and justice.

[19] Cf. F 452, 472, 483, 505, 517, 546, 620, 622. It will be noted that all of these allusions come after the story of Canacee and the falcon has begun and within the space of something under two hundred lines.

[20] Cf. *Wife of Bath's Tale* D 1146-47:
Heer may ye see wel, how that *genterye*
Is nat annexed to possessioun.

Professor Lowes shows in his article (p. 21) that in Dante's canzone

But the host breaks in on this sermon on gentilesse just as the Knight broke in on the Monk's sermon on the adversities of Fortune:

> 'Straw for your gentillesse,' quod our host;   F 695.

The Franklin, no doubt spurred on by this retort, tells a tale in which, before he is finished, he heaps on the gentilesse almost as thickly as the Squire had done. The *denouement* of his tale turns on three gentle deeds, so called by Chaucer. The Knight Arveragus was gentle in compelling his wife Dorigen to keep her love-compact with the squire Aurelius. Aurleius was gentle in not making Dorigen live up to her promise, and the philosopher was gentle in not exacting from Aurelius the gold promised him for the successful operation of his magic arts.[21] Arveragus thus bids Dorigen go to Aurelius to keep her pledge:

> Ye shul your trouthe holden, by my fay! . . .
> Trouthe is the hyeste thing that man may kepe:'—
> But with that word he brast anon to wepe,   F 1474-80.

Aurelius, however, cannot think of such a thing as to force her to keep her promise under the circumstances:

> 'Madame, seyth to your lord Arveragus,
> That sith I see his grete gentillesse
> To yow, and eek I see wel your distresse, . . .
> I have wel lever ever to suffre wo
> Than I departe the love bitwix yow two. . . .
> Thus can a squyer doon a gentil dede,
> As wel as can a knight, with-outen drede.'   F 1526-44.

When Aurelius goes to the philosopher to pay him the gold promised him for having made it possible to secure the compact with Dorigen, the philosopher is not to be outdone in gentility by either a squire or a knight:

prefixed to the fourth Tractate he uses (l. 23) the phrase *antica possession* instead of the *antica richezza* which appears later in the commentary.

> Tale impero che Gentilezza volse,
> Secondo 'l suo parere,
> *Che fosse antica possession d'avere,*
> Con reggimenti belli.

[21] Since the above was written, I find that Professor Kittredge makes the same point. *Chaucer and his Poetry*, pp. 204-6.

> This philosophre answerde, 'leve brother,
> Everich of yow dide gentilly til other.
> Thou art a squyer, and he is a knight;
> But god forbede, for his blisful might,
> But-if a clerk coude doon a gentil dede
> As wel as any of yow, it is no drede! F 1607-12.

If the instances where Chaucer discusses gentilesse in the *Canterbury Tales* be considered collectively, it will be seen that he discusses the question from several different angles along with the marriage problem. The Wife of Bath proves by a lengthy argument that a veritable hag may be worthy of a belted knight, if she be virtuous. The Clerk tells of a common country girl who showed herself worthy of the most gentle lord of Lumbardy who came from a long line of illustrious ancestors. The Squire tells of a tercelet, a "welle of gentilesse," who so far forgot his gentleness of birth as to desert his true love, the gentle falcon, for an obscure kyte. The Franklin tells first of a husband and wife, both noble by birth, who showed themselves truly noble in their deeds, and then of a squire and a common clerk who acquitted themselves as nobly as this lord and lady.[22]

Throughout all the above discussion it has been emphasized that gentilesse consists in goodness, and this brings us to the next division of the subject.

2. *Truth*

Among the most sincere passages in Chaucer's poetry are those which concern "trouthe" or "sothfastnesse". His characters in speaking of it always regard it as the one thing above all else sacred; and to be "trewe" is the highest quality which his characters can possess. The following lines from the *Canon's Yeoman's Tale* are a good example. The deceitful canon thus boasts to the priest whom he wishes to rob:

> 'What!' quod this chanoun, 'sholde I be untrewe?
> Nay, that were thing y-fallen al of-newe.
> Trouthe is a thing that I wol ever kepe
> Un-to that day in which that I shal crepe
> In-to my grave, and elles god forbede;[23] G 1042-46.

[22] For the possibility that Chaucer in these four tales was deliberately considering phases of the question of gentilesse, I am indebted to a suggestion of Professor Root.

[23] Cf. the similar sentiment in lines 110-12 of the *Compleynte unto Pite*. It is well here also to recall the high praise which Arveragus bestows on truth in lines F 1474-80, in part quoted above: "Trouthe is the hyeste thing that man may kepe."

Criseyde values, especially, in Troilus the truth which he had:

> For trusteth wel, that your estat royal
> Ne veyn delyt, nor only worthinesse
> Of yow in werre, or torney marcial,
> Ne pompe, array, nobley, or eek richesse,
> Ne made me to rewe on your distresse;
> But moral vertue, grounded upon *trouthe,*
> That was the cause I first hadde on yow routhe!
> Eek gentil herte and monhod that ye hadde,
>
> *Troilus* 4. 1667-74.

There are many other instances in Chaucer's poetry to be cited later which indicate the high esteem in which truth was held by him. The two passages, however, where the idea is discussed most specifically are Chaucer's two minor poems, *Truth* and *Lack of Stedfastness,* or, as it might be called, lack of truth; these two poems stand at opposite poles from each other and represent the positive and negative phase of the same subject. Presently, by an examination particularly of the former poem, it is my intention to attempt to show what Chaucer meant by truth, and to what extent his conception of it may be determined by the conception of truth found in the Boethian philosophy. First, however, it may be well to enter upon some preliminary considerations.

At the outset, it is important to know not only that Chaucer recognized truth in its philosophical and religious sense as a universal principle as well as in its every day sense of good faith in human relations, but that he closely associates these two applications of the word, just as, for instance, they were associated by Francis Bacon in his essay *of Truth.* Mention of the falseness of man suggests to Chaucer by contrast the abiding faith of God, as a great exemplar of truth. For example, Anelida in *Anelida and Arcite* thus laments the lack of truth in her lover who has broken his vows to her:

> Almighty *god, of trouthe sovereyn,*
> Wher is the *trouthe of man?* who hath hit sleyn?
> Who that hem loveth shal hem fynde as faste
> As in a tempest is a roten mast. 311-14.

Again, in the *Envoy* to Bukton a lie which Chaucer is about to tell brings up the question, "what is truth," asked by Pilate of Christ, himself "the way, the truth, and the life." The answer which Chaucer thinks[24] Christ intended for this question may seem on a different plane from the question:

[24] Actually, Pilate did not give Christ time to reply (John 18:38).

My maister Bukton, whan of Criste our kinge
Was axed, *what is trouthe or sothfastnesse,*
He nat a word answerde to that axinge,
As who saith: *'no man is al trewe,'* I gesse.
And therfor, thogh I *highte* to expresse
The sorwe and wo that is in mariage,
I *dar nat* wryte of hit no wikkednesse,
Lest I my-self falle eft in swich dotage.   1-8.

Here again a broken promise of man is associated with divine truth.   Finally, *Lack of Stedfastness* deals with the falseness of men to each other, whereas *Truth* deals with a lofty abstract conception.

Chaucer's association of the two kinds of truth may be explained, I think, by a comparison with a similar association in the *Consolation of Philosophy.*   According to the latter (2. m8, the *meter* on the "bond of love"), an important attribute of the deity is that he establishes faith in the universe.   By "stable faith" the stars, the seasons, the ocean, and the land are controlled in harmony, and it is by precisely the same faith that human relations between man and man, husband and wife, friend and friend should be controlled that they may proceed harmoniously as external nature.   A lack of faith in any way means becoming separated from the control of God, from the harmony of the divine system; and such a separation can only mean confusion and ruin.   Of the results of lack of faith between men, Chaucer gives an impressive description in *Lack of Stedfastness,* quoted in part below:

Som tyme this world was so stedfast and stable
That mannes word was obligacioun,
And now it is so fals and deceivable,
That word and deed, as in conclusioun,
Ben nothing lyk, *for turned up so doun*
Is al this world for mede and wilfulnesse,
That al is lost,[25] for lak of stedfastnesse.—

Bacon, in beginning his essay *of Truth,* says on this point: *"What is truth?* said jesting Pilate, and would not stay for an answer." Chaucer may have had in mind the corresponding passages in *Matthew* and *Mark* where Christ does answer by silence, although in these the question of truth does not enter.

[25] These words should be compared with *Troilus* 3. 1762-4:
And if that Love ought lete his brydel go,
Al that now loveth a-sonder sholde lepe,
And lost were al, that Love halt now to-hepe.
These lines in *Troilus* come from the *Consolation* 2. m8, the *meter* on the "bond of love" discussed above, although the italicized

Trouthe is put doun, resoun is holden fable;
Vertu hath now no dominacioun,
Pitee exyled, no man is merciable.
Through covetyse is blent discrecioun:
The world hath mad a permutacioun
Fro right to wrong, fro *trouthe* to fikelnesse,
That al is lost, for lak of stedfastnesse. 1-21.

That Chaucer, in thus lamenting the deceitfulness of men
and the widespread ruin that it brings, had a lofty conception
of truth, it is my hope to show by an analysis of his poem
Truth, and by a comparison of it with the *Consolation.* The
poem is here quoted in full:

Flee fro the prees, and dwelle with sothfastnesse,
Suffyce unto thy good, though hit be smal;
For hord hath hate, and climbing tikelnesse,
Prees hath envye, and wele blent overal;
5 Savour no more than thee bihove shal;
Werk wel thy-self, that other folk canst rede;
And trouthe shal delivere, hit is no drede.

Tempest thee noght al croked to redresse,
In trust of hir that turneth as a bal:
10 Gret reste stant in litel besinesse;
And eek be war to sporne ageyn an al;
Stryve noght, as doth the crokke with the wal.
Daunte thy-self, that dauntest otheres dede;
And trouthe shal delivere, hit is no drede.

15 That thee is sent, receyve in buxumnesse,
The wrastling for this worlde axeth a fal.
Her nis non hoom, her nis but wildernesse:
Forth, pilgrim, forth! Forth, beste, out of thy stal!
Know thy contree, look up, thank God of al;
20 Hold the hye wey, and lat thy gost thee lede:
And the trouthe shal delivere, hit is no drede.

ENVOY.

Therfore thou Vache, leve thyn old wrecchednesse
Unto the worlde; leve now to be thral;
Crye him mercy, that of his hy goodnesse
25 Made thee of noght, and in especial
Draw unto him, and pray in general
For thee, and eek for other, hevenlich mede;
And trouthe shal delivere, hit is no drede.

words are a free rendering of the corresponding Latin. Again in
Troilus 3. 1266 Chaucer, alluding to the bond of love, makes use of
the same clause.

An examination of the poem reveals that it was addressed to a would-be reformer.[26] Chaucer counsels this reformer not to assume the impossible task of redressing certain evils unmentioned in the poem, but perhaps arising out of the troubled conditions of the court of Richard II; for if he does attempt to redress them, he will only be vainly kicking against the pricks. An unswerving and never failing force, the truth, is eternally at work making straight all the crookedness of the world. The reformer will do his part if he reforms himself. There are three essential points in the advice which Chaucer gives: (1) to flee from the press, an expressive word implying the hoarding, hating, envy, vain struggle for position, failure, lack of steadfastness—in brief all the false felicity which enthralls men and makes them beasts; (2) to dwell with truth, attained through contentment with little things, virtue, a contemplation of the highest things, and a realization that heaven, and not the wretched wilderness of this world is man's true country; (3) truth shall deliver. The inspiring refrain is the most significant part of the poem and raises it above the level of any ordinary exhortation to monastic asceticism. It is a philosophy in itself and expresses an attitude toward life— an aloofness, an interest, a bigness of view, and a hope which would be almost necessary for the writer of a *Canterbury Tales* to have. The poem has always been regarded as unusual. Shirley, with no other evidence apparently than its unusualness, decided that it must have been written by Chaucer on his death bed, and in this conclusion he was followed by no less a scholar than ten Brink. Miss Rickert's discovery that it was addressed to Sir Philip la Vache, however, discredits this view. But whatever the occasion of the poem, it stands out as one of the most sincere and noble of Chaucer's utterances.

No stronger evidence of the lasting influence of the *Consolation of Philosophy* upon Chaucer could be shown than that it is the dominating influence of this poem. It shows that the *Consolation* had entered into the very fibre of his thought. The *Consolation* is not a source of the poem in the usual sense. Chaucer went to no particular passage or passages of the

---

[26] Sir Philip la Vache. See the article of Miss Rickert, *Modern Philology*, Vol. XI, pp. 209-225. The *Envoy*, where his name is mentioned, occurs in but one Ms. (Addit. 10340). There is a possibility that it may have been added after the original composition.

Consolation for the immediate purpose of its composition. In this supposition lie the mistakes which Koch and Skeat have made when they point out Boethius as a source,[27] and which Professor Manly has made when he brushes aside the influence of Boethius so easily as a consequence of the discovery of Miss Rickert.[28] *Truth* sums up in a nut shell the teaching of the first three books of the *Consolation*. There might be pointed out in the latter any number of passages which dimly or even closely resemble some portion of the poem.[29] But the teaching of the poem and the *Consolation* coincide, as I shall now attempt to show.

The first thing which brings the poem *Truth* into connection with the *Consolation* is that it brings into juxtaposition the two ideas: (1) of universal truth, and (2) of man's relation to the world in attempting to reform its evils.[30] This is a discussion of truth in an advanced form. To flee from the press and dwell with truth is precisely the theme of the sixth book of Plato's *Republic* and of the entire *Consolation*. Although Chaucer could not have known the teaching of the former of these except indirectly through Boethius (Cf. I. p4. 18-39), it may be well to consider briefly the attitude of Plato in this matter. Plato discusses the question how a true philosopher should conduct himself in recognition of the evils which he knows to exist in the state where he lives. The truth, the universal model for all things, the philosopher knows better than anyone else. Should he not apply his knowledge of it to the affairs of his own country? No, says Plato, he should not do so at once. He should hold himself aloof and perfect

[27] See the notes in the *Oxford Chaucer*. Koch cites 3. m11. 1-9 which contains the idea that truth is in one's self. Skeat says that 2. p5 has more general likeness to the poem than this passage cited by Koch. This *prose,* directed against riches, contains nothing about the idea of truth so essential to the poem. Skeat also points out other minor verbal resemblances. The Boethian influence in the poem transcends verbal borrowing.

[28] *Modern Philology, op. cit.,* p. 226.

[29] Cf. I. m2. 19-22; p3. 51-6; p5. 6-25; m7. 10-15; 2. p4. 96-101; p7. 106-111; m7. 1-7; 3. p1. 26-9; m1. 8-12; m8. 14-18; m9. 28-35; m10. 1-8; m11; 3. p12. 37-9; m12. 1-2; 4. p1. 46-50; m1; m5. 22-7; p6. 33-5; m7. 44-50; 5. m2; m3. 34-8; m4; m5. Other citations may be easily found.

[30] In this respect, Chaucer's poem may well be compared with the essentially Christian idea of truth in *Piers Plowman* at the beginning of Passus I, and in lines 12-14 of Passus II (C version). It has no resemblance to Chaucer's poem.

himself in the knowing of the truth. If he leaps rashly into the turmoil and corruption of the state, he himself will be tainted. Instead of his reforming the state, his knowledge of the truth will be debased. He will be forced to concede points to the multitude, not prepared to receive his advanced teachings. But there will come a time, perhaps, when the hour is ripe for the counsel of a philosopher. The multitude itself will some day feel the need of a leader who knows the truth. Then is the time for a philosopher to allow himself to be placed at the head of the state, and then the ways of the truth will prevail.

The *Consolation of Philosophy,* written by Boethius in consciousness of this discussion of Plato after he had tried in vain to put its teaching into practice, departs from it in supposing that the only end of the philosophical life is in contemplation of the divine truth. The symbolic emblem woven on the garment of Dame Philosophy is indicative of the general attitude of Boethius:

> In the nethereste hem or bordure of thise clothes men redden, y-woven in, a Grekissh P, that signifyeth the lyf Actif; and aboven that lettre, in the heyeste bordure, a Grekissh T, that signifyeth the lyf Contemplatif. And bitwixen these two lettres ther weren seyn degrees, nobly y-wroght in manere of laddres; by which degrees men mighten climben fro the nethereste lettre to the uppereste. (1. p1. 20-26).

The discussion of Boethius, an elaborate plea for the contemplative life, has definite characteristics which make it possible to detect its influence in Chaucer's poem. It consists of an attractive account written in figurative language, telling how Boethius was led by Philosophy from the bestial and enthralled condition of worldly life back to his own *country,* the supreme good, the *middel soothfastnesse.* The situation described in the *Consolation* is as follows. Boethius, acting upon the advice which Plato gives that a philosopher should take a part in the administration of public affairs (1. p4. 24ff.), has tried to reform the state. He has met with false accusations and injustice. For his pains he has been thrown into prison by the very persons whom he tried to protect. There Dame Philosophy finds him weeping, and crying out against the injustice of god and man. His neck is weighed down as if with heavy chains, and he seems constrained as if by some great weight to look "adoun" on the foul earth, forgetful of the heavens above. (1. m2. See *Truth* l. 19.) She asks him his trouble (1. p4. 1-4), and hereupon Boethius launches forth on an impassioned expostulation in which he questions even the divine justice of God (1. p4. m5). Dame Philosophy in reply to this fervid speech expresses her disappointment that he has allowed himself to fall into so wretched a state, that he has so far lost the vision of a philosopher, and offers to guide him back to his true *country* from which he has been exiled (1. p5. 3-16). Then changing the figure somewhat, she represents herself in the light of a physician (1. p5. 46-54; 3. p1. 10-13), and promises to cure the feebleness of will to which Boethius has fallen a prey. She suggests two remedies, a light one and a strong one. Through these she finally effects his cure. I believe that Chaucer was influenced by the discussion of the *Consolation* in the central ideas of his poem: (1) "flee fro the prees"; (2) "dwelle with sothfastnesse"; (3) "trouthe shal delivere."

(1) "Flee fro the prees."—The light remedy of Philosophy, which she terms the *"poynt* of sovereyne blisfulnesse" (2. p4. 96), is the equivalent of Chaucer's "flee fro the prees."

I shal shewe thee shortely the *poynt* of sovereyne blisfulnesse. Is there any-thing more precious to thee than *thyself?* Thou wolt answere, "nay." Thanne, yif it so be that thou art *mighty over thy-self* (Cf. *Truth,* lines 6 and 13), that is to seyn, by *tranquillitee of thy sowle,* than hast thou thing in thy power that thou noldest never lesen, ne Fortune ne may nat beneme it thee (2. p4. 96-101). And forthy, if thou wolt *fleen* the perilous aventure, that is to seyn, of the worlde; have minde certeinly to ficchen thyn hous of a merye sete in a lowe stoon. For al-though the wind, troubling the see, thondre with over-throwinges, thou that art put in quiete, and weleful by strengthe of thy palis, shalt leden a cleer age, scorninge the woodnesses and ires of the eyr (2. m4. 8-13).

That Chaucer recognized the significance of this passage is indicated by the following lines from *Troilus:*

> For certeinly, the *firste poynt* is this
> Of noble corage and wel ordeyne,
> A man to have *pees with him-self,* y-wis; 1. 891-3.

The whole of Book II of the *Consolation,* of which the passages just quoted are the central teaching, is devoted to showing how unsatisfactory are the avarice, the ambition, and the general turmoil of the world, and how necessary it is to escape from them. If Chaucer were trying to sum up the substance of Book II, he could not do it in more complete and yet compressed form than he does in the first two stanzas of *Truth.*

I have shown elsewhere how he has emphasized in his poetry the false felicity of the world, and how, as in the poem *Fortune,* he advocated self-mastery as a means to evade the subtle wiles of Fortune—all in the Boethian manner. These ideas, therefore, are very general throughout his writings. The three following passages are additional confirmation of his opinion of the "prees":

> Lo, who may truste on fortune any throwe?
> For him that folweth *al this world of prees,*
> Er he be war, is ofte y-leyd ful lowe.
> Ful wys is he *that can him-selven knowe.* B. 3326-29.

The following stanza from the *Clerk's Tale* is among the few lines added by Chaucer to his original, Petrarch's version of the Griselda story:

> *Auctor.* 'O stormy peple! unsad and ever *untrewe!*
> Ay undiscreet and chaunging as a vane,
> Delyting ever in rumbel that is newe,
> For lyk the mone ay wexe ye and wane;
> Ay ful of clapping, dere y-nogh a jane;
> Your doom is fals, your constance yvel preveth,
> A ful greet fool is he that on yow leveth!' E 995-1001.

Chaucer in the *House of Fame* thus laments the sad fate of those good people, who seek of the goddess Fame distinction for their good works, who, quite to the contrary, are refused it, and who are stigmatized among men:
be-times to escape from the press and his busy life among men.

> 'Alas,' thoughte I, 'what aventures
> Han these sory creatures!
> For they, amonges *al the pres,*
> Shul thus be shamed gilteles!
> But what! hit moste nedes be.' 1631-35.

From what we know of Chaucer's life, and from what he has told us in well-known passages, we know that he himself liked to escape from the press and his busy life among men.

(2) "Dwelle with sothfastnesse."—The strong remedy of Philosophy, the equivalent of Chaucer's "dwelle with sothfastnesse," is to conduct Boethius to the "supremum bonum," the "mediae *veritatis* notam," or, as Chaucer translates it, the "middel *sothfastnesse,* that is to seyn, the prikke." The way is long and arduous. Boethius is guided by Dame Philosophy, as has been explained before, much as Dante is guided by Vergil, or as Scipio is guided in his dream by Africanus, or

as Chaucer himself is guided by Africanus in the *Parliament of Fowls,* or by the eagle in the *House of Fame.* At the outset, when Dame Philosophy discovers the lamentable state of mind into which he has fallen, she promises to conduct him back to his own *country.* (Cf. *Truth,* "know *thy contree,*" line 19.) The following are her words:

'Whan I say thee,' quod she, 'sorweful and wepinge, I wiste anon that thou were a wrecche and exiled; but I wiste never how fer thyne exile was, . . . But certes, al be thou fer fro *thy contree,* thou nart nat put out of it; but thou hast failed of thy weye and gon amis. . . . For yif thou remembre of what *contree* thou art born, it nis nat governed by emperours, ne by governement of multitude, as weren the *contrees* of hem of Athenes; but oo lord and oo king, and that is god, that is lord of *thy contree,* whiche that reioyseth him of the *dwelling* of hise citezenes, and nat for to putte hem in exil; (1. p5. 3-16)

In passing, it may be well for me to point out that the figurative conception of heaven as man's true "country" was evidently recognized in Chaucer's time as being thoroughly Boethian, as is shown by the following passage from the English translation of the *Roman de la Rose.* I quote from the translation because the translator has taken the pains to add to the original the lines, italicized below, pertaining to this matter:

> He is a fool, withouten were,
> That trowith have his countre here.
> "In erthe is not our countree,"
> That may these clerkis seyn and see
> In Boece of Consolacioun,
> *Where it is maked mencioun*
> *Of our countree pleyn at the eye,*
> *By teching of philosophye,*
> Where lewid men might lere wit,
> Who-so that wolde translaten it.[31]   5659-67 (B)

We now turn to the progress of Boethius toward his country, and it is well to remember in following Boethius that we are treading ground which was very familiar to Chaucer, and from which he took something at almost every point in the journey. The first step (Bk. II), as we have seen, is in the explanation of the mutability of fortune, and of the necessity of escape from worldly pursuits. Boethius, when this explanation is concluded impressively with the "bond of love" *meter,*

[31] Skeat considers it possible that these lines may have suggested to Chaucer that he undertake the translation of the *Consolation. Oxford Chaucer,* Vol. II: x.

marvels at the sweetness of the consolation thus far received, but expresses a longing for the further revelations which have been promised him. Dame Philosophy intimates that he little realizes the transcendent joy in store for him; but she cannot bring him to the goal, the "verray welefulnesse," without further preparation (3. p1). She must first describe the false felicity; how minutely she does so will be recalled from the previous discussion. Even after this description, the conduct of Boethius to the true felicity cannot be achieved. Before the final step, God must be invoked in prayer. This Philosophy does most fervently in 3. m9, a *meter* which is a repetition of the "bond of love" *meter,* although it is more advanced in thought in accordance with the more advanced stage of the argument. All through the first part of Book III hints are thrown out as to what is coming; repetitions emphasize particular points, and additions are made to them; parts are carefully interrelated—the whole argument, in brief, is constructed to focus finally on one point. In proses 10 and 12 Boethius must be imagined on the mountain peaks of philosophical disquisition. Here, Dame Philosophy by an intricate argument succeeds in showing him that the "verray welefulnesse" is the same as the supreme good, and that the supreme good is the same as God. Happiness, then, consists in goodness or in communion with God, who is goodness, and from whom all goodness springs (Cf. "clere welle of good" 3. m12. 1). "Good is the fyn of alle thinges" (3. p11. 170). Boethius has at last been brought to the "middel *sothfastnesse,*" the consolation of philosophy. And now, at the very climax, in exultant vein Dame Philosophy sings her song in praise of *truth* (3. m11). Truth is not far away, nor hard to find. It is implanted within *one's self:*

Who-so wole seken the deep grounde of sooth in his thought, . . . lat him techen his sowle that it hath, *by natural principles kindeliche y-hid with-in it-self, alle the trouthe* the whiche he imagineth to be in thinges with-oute (3. m11. 10-17).[32]

[32] The first nine lines of Chaucer's translation are paraphrased in a gloss, the longest gloss in the entire translation. The long paraphrase may indicate the importance in which the *meter* was regarded. The quotation above is taken from the gloss. This *meter* is based on the Platonic doctrine that ideas exist by nature in the soul and receive confirmation by comparison with things outside. In 5. m4 Boethius refutes the belief of the Stoics that all conceptions are received passively by the soul through the senses, just as a mirror receives reflections. Chaucer was much interested in this *meter.* Cf. p. ——.

The end of life is to be in communion (to "dwelle," Chaucer would say) with the good, or the truth, or the God within one's self. Here, in passing, we may see with greater clearness the validity of points made earlier by Dame Philosophy in her discussion of gentility, first that virtue is a very essential quality to possess, because, as we may see here, in it alone lies happiness, and secondly that only the good are truly noble, because goodness is the very essence of God, the common ancestor of all, and because those who sin have, in sinning, lost all of their divine ancestry. Thus, the close relation between Chaucer's minor poems, *Gentilesse* and *Truth,* will be seen.

In the first *meter* of Book IV, Philosophy, again resorting to figurative language, gives the subject a different turn. Truth is in one's self, but it is in the heavens too; it is wherever God or goodness is. She now describes in triumphant song how she bears the mind aloft on her wings to its *country* in the heavens, where its *dwelling* is, where she promised long before to conduct it. This flight must have been of considerable interest to Chaucer, because many of his favorite authors describe similar flights, and because he himself, under the influence of these various sources, describes similar flights in no less than three of his poems; in the *House of Fame,* where he himself is carried aloft to the skies, he makes specific reference (lines 972-78) to this passage, and performs exploits very similar to those described here.[33] The following lines are taken from the latter part of this *meter:*

And yif thy wey ledeth thee ayein so that thou be brought thider, thanne wolt thou seye now that that is the *contree* that thou requerest, of which thou ne haddest no minde: "but now it remembreth me wel, heer was I born, heer wol I fastne my degree, heer wol I *dwelle."* 4. mI. 23-7.

From this lofty vantage place, the mind may look back and scorn the dull earth in which it once was so much engrossed. It will be recalled that Troilus after his tragic death ascends

[33] Chaucer in *The Parliament of Fowls* (36-84) summarizes Cicero's *Dream of Scipio* as preserved in the *Commentary* of Macrobius. In *Troilus* (5. 1807-27), Chaucer in describing the flight of the hero translates a passage from Boccaccio's *Teseide* (XI, first three stanzas). He also must have known the account of a flight in the *Divine Comedy* (*Par.,* 22, 128-154); it is sometimes thought that from here he gets the idea of the eagle to conduct him through the skies in the *House of Fame.* Chaucer's friendly visit among the stars, described in Book II of the *House of Fame,* is very reminiscent of the *Consolation.*

to heaven and looks back on the wretched earth just as is here described (5. 1807-27). The situation inspires in Chaucer sentiments akin to those in *Truth,* and he incorporates them in the conclusion of the poem as the moral to be drawn from it :[34]

> O yonge fresshe folkes, he or she,
> In whiche that love up groweth with your age,
> *Repeyreth hoom* from worldly vanitee,
> And of your herte *up-casteth the visage*[35]
> To thilke god that after his image
> Yow made, and thinketh al nis but a fayre
> This world, that passeth sone as floures fayre. 5. 1835-41.

(3) "Trouthe shal delivere."—After the goal, the "middel sothfastnesse," is reached, Dame Philosophy takes up a point which arises from the conclusion thus arrived at; namely, the relation between God, or the supreme good, and evil in the world. After a careful and difficult argument in which she attempts to reconcile the existence of a benevolent God and evil, an argument, moreover, the like of which many of Chaucer's characters find too deep for their comprehension (Cf. pp 69-71), she reaches a conclusion with which Chaucer expresses agreement in the words, "trouthe shal delivere." Dame Philosophy, having shown in the third book what goodness is, in the fourth book shows what it will do when it is pitted against the contrary force, evil. According to her teaching, the power of good, the equivalent of God, is absolute and is the supreme power of the universe. She gives it an extremely benevolent turn by her figure of the chain of love, the operation of which is described in no less than four poetic *meters,* one in each of the last four books (2. m8; 3. m9; 4. m6; 5. m3). Her theory of the harmonizing power of good or love, gathering force as the discussion advances, breaks out in full in the discussion of evil. In 4. p6, she unfolds her famous description of the concentric circles at the center of which is the divine intelligence, whence in all directions ema-

[34] Lines 1807-27 mentioned are from the *Teseide* (XI, first three stanzas), but the lines here quoted are Chaucer's own idea.

[35] Cf. line 19 of *Truth,* "*Know thy contree, lok up,* thank god of al;" see also *Consolation* 5. m5, the injunction of which is that man should look upward and not downward as beasts, "this figure amonesteth thee, that axest the hevene with thy righte *visage,* and hast areysed thy fore-heved, to beren up a-heigh thy corage;" See p. 136 for several traces of Boethian influence not considered above.

nates the ordinance of destiny binding all things beyond external control, and with increasing intensity outward from the center. This force, as is explained in 4. p6 and m6, moves the stars through the heavens; it prevents them from crashing together. It controls the elemental forces of nature, the hot, the cold, the moist, and the dry. It affects living things. It causes life and death. It controls the events of human life. It gives to some prosperity, and to others adversity. It may even grant to the wicked their evil desires. It is responsible for everything that happens, that which is apparently good and that which is apparently bad. I say "apparently," because man, with his limited intelligence, is not able to distinguish the good from the bad and to see that all things are moving to a good end. A good man may be given adversity that his character may be strengthened or that he may be an example of fortitude to others; a bad man may be given prosperity that good folk may see the very incongruity which appears in such a man's having riches. Dame Philosophy cites many examples to enforce this point. With such a force in operation, the inference is easy that man's feeble power avails nothing either in resisting good or in attempting to cope with that which he considers to be evil. He needs only to look out for himself; and, if he is unhappy, help is near at hand. The force of good operating everywhere and in all things, is operating also in him, however benighted, blinded, and engrossed in worldly pleasures he may be, and is prompting him to good (3. m2).[36] What he needs to do is to become conscious of the particular strand of the divine chain within himself, the principle of truth implanted within him by nature, and then he will be in harmony with the rest of the universe, he will feel the "olde pees" which governs the stars. On the other hand, if he is evil, false, discordant, he simply vanishes, is lost, is nothing at all; for what obstacle will his puny strength be against the overwhelming tide of goodness which flows through the universe, bringing back all things to God whence they sprang. Therefore the cause of love, of truth, of God, of goodness, whatever it may be called, is certain ultimately to triumph, although evil men, outside the bounds of good, for

[36] This *meter*, the purpose of which is to show that just as all things follow the promptings of their own nature, so man must follow *his* strongest instinct, the quest for supreme happiness, made a strong impression on Chaucer. See *Squire's Tale,* 608 ff., and the *Manciples Tale,* 160 ff.

a time may seem to throw the world into an uproar. Evil is
destined to be dispersed: "he (God) chaseth out yvel fro
the boundes of his comunalitee by the ordre of necessitee
destinable" (4. p6. 251-2).

Chaucer makes use of the passages under discussion (4. p6
and m6)[37] especially in the *Knight's Tale* (A 2987-3015; 3035-
40) in the long speech where Theseus proves that the death
of Arcite is part of a divine plan which does all for the best.
Skeat is mistaken in assigning 2. m8 as the source of Chaucer's
lines on the bond of love. 4. m6 also describes its operation.
It is, moreover, introduced by Boethius for the express purpose of showing that God does all for the best, the point which
Theseus is maintaining. It states (lines 25-6) the particular
point of Theseus that God ordains death. It states also that
love binds the hot, the cold, the moist, and the dry as the
Knight's Tale does (A 2991-3); 2. m8 does not make this point.
It further contains lines corresponding to lines A 3055-40:

> For yif that he ne *clepede ayein* the right goinge of thinges, . . . they
> sholden departen from hir *welle,* . . . and faylen, . . . For elles ne
> mighten they nat lasten, yif they ne come nat eft-sones ayein, *by Love
> retorned, to the cause that hath yeven hem beinge,* 4. m6. 31-40.
> to the cause that hath yeven hem beinge, 4. m6. 31-40.

> What maketh this but Jupiter the King?
> The which is prince and *cause* of alle thing,
> *Converting al* un-to his propre *welle,*
> *From which it is deryved,* sooth to telle.
> And here-agayns no creature on lyve
> Of no degree availleth for to stryve.

These lines sum up very well at once the benevolence and
might of the Providence described in the *Consolation.*

The Boethian conception of the divine control contained
especially in 4. p6 had a strong hold on Chaucer, particularly
when he wrote *Troilus* and the *Knight's Tale.* The chief attribute of the very absolute deity described by Boethius is
goodness, a goodness so mighty and irresistible as to make it
possible for a man unselfishly to leave the world to its own
good fate and to make it advisable that he improve himself.
Just as "flee fro the prees" concisely and accurately sums up

[37] For a complete account of the influence of these passages on the
Knight's Tale see p. 143; 4. p6 of the *Consolation* gives expression to
the fatalistic conception of Boethius which had so pronounced an influence on Chaucer, especially in *Troilus* and in the *Knight's Tale.*
Chaucer is far more indebted to this *prose* than to all the rest of the
fourth Book.

the second book of the *Consolation* and as "dwelle with sothfastnesse" concisely and accurately sums up the third book,
so "trouthe shal delivere, hit is no drede" sums up the fourth.
Chaucer in *Truth* the *Balade de bon conseyl* was giving to
Sir Philip la Vache as counsel the *Consolation of Philosophy*
in epitome!

Here we may bring into consideration the Biblical influence
in the poem. It is undoubtedly present. But it is necessary
to remember that Chaucer would not distinguish between the
Biblical truth and the Boethian truth. He doubtless thought
what Boethius had to say on the subject was a learned clerk's
interpretation of the Biblical truth, no connected and detailed
account of which is to be found in holy writ. *Truth* thus becomes a good example of the fusion of the Boethian philosophy
and Christianity which must have existed in the minds of
mediaeval readers. To Chaucer, the truth which Boethius so
warmly praises in 3. m11 is the same as the truth of which
St. John speaks in his Gospel. Chaucer's allusion to fortune
(line 9) in the midst of his discussion of the divine truth
seems fitting to him, just as the wheel of Fortune in the rose
window of the cathedral of Amiens seemed fitting to the
monks or craftsmen who designed it.[38] The "country" discussed by Boethius is to him the kingdom of heaven; the
principle of truth inherent within things which is described
in 3. m11 is identical with the "gost" which should lead one,
as is explained in line 20 of *Truth*. The identification, in the
Consolation, of the supreme good, God, and the truth might
easily be construed by him to be of somewhat the same import
as the well known verse, "I am the way, the truth, and the
life." In the refrain, "the trouthe shal delivere," Chaucer may
well have had in mind the Biblical passage, "ye shall know
the truth, and the truth shall make you free"; but the conclusion which he draws therefrom, if he does have it in mind,
is different from that arrived at in the Bible. The truth of
which Christ speaks to the Pharisees is to free them individ-
ually from the bondage of their sins, if they will permit it;
there is no reference to a great world force, which under any
condition, independently of the actions of men will deliver
the world and redress its evils. Nowhere in the Bible is set
forth the particular combination of central points common to
Truth and the *Consolation of Philosophy.*

[38] For a description of rose windows containing the wheel of fortune, see the *Revue de l'Art Chrétien,* 889, p. 283, and *Annales Archéologiques,* Vol. I, p. 241.

CHAPTER IV

INFLUENCE OF THE CONSOLATION ON TROILUS AND THE KNIGHT'S TALE

It has long been recognized that the *Consolation* had more influence on *Troilus* and the *Knight's Tale* than on any other of the longer poems of Chaucer. I have, therefore, found it advisable to consider these poems specially in relation to the *Consolation*. Such a study at once reveals that Chaucer did not use the Boethian material haphazardly for the interest that might be attached to particular lines in themselves, but that, as might be expected from the foregoing chapters, he brings its consideration of the fundamental questions of human existence to bear in a large way on the lives of his characters. Chaucer's thoughts must have been afire with the Boethian philosophy when he worked over these tales from their Italian originals, for always looming up in their background, as he worked them over, are the fundamental Boethian conceptions of fate and human felicity, determining his mental attitude toward the subject matter. *Troilus,* especially, offered Chaucer opportunity for a practical study in real life of the working out of the Boethian teaching. In the tale, as it was presented to him in the *Filostrato* of Boccaccio, he saw a capital example of the sudden reversal of Fortune's wheel, and an unusually interesting example of human falseness or lack of steadfastness, of worldly felicity, and of human affairs directed to a predetermined end by a relentless fate; and it will be found that most of the extended passages gathered by Chaucer from sources outside the immediate original, itself influenced somewhat by the *Consolation,* concern these very things.[1] I shall now consider the two conceptions of fate and

[1] See complaint of Troilus against Fortune and the reply of Pandarus, I. 837-853, from various passages in the first part of Book II of the *Consolation;* Criseyde's account of false felicity, 3. 813-36, from the *Consolation,* 2. p4. 109-20 and other Boethian passages; hymn of Troilus on the "bond of love," 3. 1744-64, from the *Consolation* 2. m8; free will soliloquy of Troilus, 4. 958-1078, from the *Consolation,* 5. p3.

felicity as they are discussed in *Troilus* and in the *Knight's Tale*.

The fatalistic tendency in *Troilus* has often been commented upon, but Professor Kittredge, in his recent discussion of the poem,[2] for the first time reveals how important is an understanding of Chaucer's emphasis on fate for a full appreciation of the poem. Not only are the hero and heroine borne irresistibly to an inevitable doom, but their doom is linked inseparably with the larger doom of Troy; all are swept headlong to certain ruin. Chaucer heightens the effect by assuming an attitude of reluctance at being the narrator of events so tragic; but, having once begun, he must not draw back from his thankless task; it is almost as if he too, by the mere act of narration, is drawn relentlessly into the course of destiny. The fate of Troilus and Criseyde is the more terrible, because they themselves, aside from human frailties, do nothing to bring on the catastrophe. Even Criseyde commits no overt act, but is led on from step to step by Pandarus, by circumstances, and by her own spirit of curiosity, succumbing throughout to a tenderness of heart which she retains to the end and to her weakness in character, her "slydinge corage." Her final unfaith, as a tragedy in character, as her part in the "double sorrow" which Chaucer is describing, I shall discuss more at length presently. Troilus and Criseyde, thus, are the victims of a concatenation of circumstances largely outside of their own control. Pandarus, of course, attempts to manage their affairs, but he is only a link in the chain of fate, a "fly on the chariot wheel." Nothing may stem the tide on which they are driven by "necessitee."

The machinery by which fate operates in *Troilus* is entirely Boethian. It is true that the gods must be the gods of classical mythology as the tale concerns ancient Troy, but the attributes which they possess are the attributes of the Boethian deity, and what is said about them to a great extent will be found in the *Consolation*. Almost every phase of the Boethian discussion of Providence is repre-

7-71; lines on fate, 5. 1-7, from *Teseide*, the first stanza of the ninth book and from the *Consolation*, 4. p6. 29-56; Cassandra in her prophecy to Troilus, 5. 1457-1519, shows him by examples, drawn chiefly from the *Thebaid* of Statius, that many lords have been overthrown by Fortune; attainment by Troilus of the true felicity in heaven, 5. 1807-27, from the first three stanzas of the eleventh book of the *Teseide*.

[2] *Chaucer and his Poetry*, pp. 108-145.

sented.[3] His scheme of the hierarchy of providential agencies
is recognized. Jove, of his wise "purveyaunce," grants to the
Parcae or Fates, and to the goddess Fortune the execution of
the destinal ordinances, just as described in the *Consolation*.
Fortune is given a very high rank among the gods, and is
honored by Troilus above all the others. Chance is regarded
by the characters as of great significance. Events happen by
"necessitee." There are also brought up in *Troilus* the two
questions which lead respectively to the discussions of the
fourth and fifth books of the *Consolation:* namely, how may
a just god permit evil and how is free will in man possible
in the face of so unescapable a destinal control. The most
remarkable departure from classical mythology, perhaps, is
in the case of the god of love. This god in *Troilus,* not at all
the mischievous young archer of conventional love poetry, is
given all the qualities of the celestial love described so at length
by Boethius; and to the description of the might of this god
throughout all the universe Chaucer devotes almost one hundred lines. The "bond of love" in the *Consolation* is a poetic
conception, and, accordingly, belongs mainly to the *meters* and
not to the more matter of fact *proses* where pure reason rather
than poetic inspiration is the guide. Chaucer apparently recognized this distinction; accordingly, in a poem like *Troilus*
he may express himself in terms of the "bond of love," a liberty which he does not take in a more genuinely philosophical
poem like *Truth* or *Lack of Stedfastness.* And throughout
Troilus it is necessary to remember that he is using the
Boethian material poetically and artistically and that, as a
complete master of it, he is adapting it to the purposes of the
poem.[4]

[3] See Chapter II of this dissertation.

[4] Following are the passages which contribute most to the fatalistic
conception in *Troilus:* Fortune's wheel bears up and under, in turn,
both Greeks and Trojans, 1. 138-40; the might of celestial love is described, 1. 232-59; Troilus considers that he must love through his
destiny, 1. 520; Troilus suspects that "cas or aventure" has guided
Pandarus to him, 1. 568; Troilus blames Fortune for his woe, 1. 837-
40; Troilus begins a prayer with a statement that god in his wise
"purveyaunce" directs the life of every man to the "fyn," 2. 526-8;
by "necessitee" Troilus passes by the window of Criseyde at the
psychological moment, 2. 622-3; the might of the love celestial is again
described, 3. 1-42; Troilus swears by the god who may govern all the
world, 3. 372-3; Fortune, executrix of wierds under god, although the

Chaucer, further, in his interest in the question of fate, makes one of his characters a fatalist, and this is Troilus, imaginative and fanciful as Richard II of Shakespeare's play. More than this, Troilus is conceived to be the kind of fatalist that Boethius was in the *Consolation,* and by Boethius I mean Boethius in the rôle which he assumes for himself in contrast to his consoler, Dame Philosophy, the man who cries out against Fortune, who cannot reconcile to his misfortune the irrevocable decrees of destiny, in the grasp of which he feels himself bound by stern necessity and to which he attributes his misfortunes. In brief, Troilus, intellectually, resembles Boethius in the rôle which the latter assumes for himself in the *Consolation.*

If the poem be examined, it will be found that Troilus alone of the characters[5] imparts the fatalistic spirit evident in the poem, that he alone makes the speeches which tell of the inexorable might of god. His prayers, especially, are prefaced or concluded with tributes to the greatness of heavenly law as in the following instance:

> O fatal sustren, which, er any clooth
> Me shapen was, my destenè me sponne,
> So helpeth to this werk that is bi-gonne!' 3. 733-5.

Pandarus and Criseyde are not nearly so conscious of the higher powers which operate in human life. Their oaths and allusions to the gods are more casual. Indeed, Professor

causes are not known to men, brings on the rain which detains Criseyde at the house of Pandarus, 3. 617-20; Criseyde complains that the gods permit the innocent to suffer, 3. 1016-1020; Troilus praises the might of love, 3. 1261-6; Fortune wills that the blissful time of Troilus shall come, 3. 1667; Troilus once more sings of the might of the love celestial, 3. 1744-64; Fortune turns her face from Troilus to Diomede and the former loses Criseyde, 4. 1-14; Troilus laments that Fortune, whom he has always honored above all the gods, has snatched Criseyde from him, 4. 260-87; Troilus argues that men cannot have free will, 4. 958-1078; the fatal destiny approaches, 5. 1-7; Cassandra cites examples which show how lords fall from their high estates through Fortune, 5. 1457-1512; to Fortune is committed the permutation of things, and, therefore, Troy must fall, 5. 1541-48.

[5] The extent of the interest of Troilus in fate may be better understood by glancing through the foot-note just preceding. He is concerned with some phase of it in a great many of his speeches. Chaucer himself is the spokesman in several passages as in 3. 617-20, 5. 1-7, 5. 1541-48. The other characters besides Troilus are not greatly concerned with the question.

Kittredge sees possible traces of religious scepticism in Criseyde. But Troilus is acutely sensitive to divine operation. Any happening, no matter how trivial, is significant, for it may mean the moving of the hand of fate. Upon the occasion of Pandarus' first visit Troilus asks with some suspicion (1. 568-9): *"What cas or what aventure hath gyded* thee to see my languisshinge?"* This statement is consistent with his general attitude. I shall now consider some specific points of resemblance between Troilus and Boethius.

The first visit of Pandarus to Troilus lying grief-stricken on his bed seems to recall to Chaucer the similar visit of Dame Philosophy to Boethius on his bed in prison. Pandarus has aptly been compared by Dr. Fansler to Amis of the *Roman de la Rose,* but here, in the consolation which he offers Troilus, he has strong points of resemblance to Dame Philosophy in the consolation which she gives Boethius. Troilus, like Boethius, cries out against Fortune; then Pandarus in a passage of eighteen lines comforts him in the words of Dame Philosophy. Also in the words of Dame Philosophy, he bids Troilus arouse from his lethargy, to cease longer to be like the ass to the harp; he offers to be the leech who will cure his woe and recalls to him that the first point of happiness is to have inner peace, that he must be self contained, whole not divided. But Pandarus is able to administer to Troilus only the "lighter remedies" of Dame Philosophy; he does not administer the "stronger remedies" of which Troilus on his higher intellectual plane stands in need, but which Chaucer himself reserves to state in the conclusion as we shall see. This brings us to another resemblance. The mistake of Troilus is the mistake of Boethius. Recognizing the might of heaven, he expects heaven to give permanence to a worldly joy, and complains, accordingly, when that joy is snatched away, or is jubilant in his praises when he thinks that the joy is vouchsafed. A conception of Troilus as having an attitude toward the deity such as Boethius had gives consistency to the passages which Chaucer gathers from sources outside the *Filostrato* to put into his lips. It explains why Troilus should sing the paean in praise of heavenly love derived from 2. m8 of the *Consolation;* why he should attempt to prove in a long passage, a translation of the similar lament of Boethius, that men do not have free will; and why Chaucer should borrow from the *Teseide* the passage wherein he describes how Troilus, as Boethius, finally journeys through the stars to experience the true felicity. Further, this conception, taken in connection with Criseyde's views on false felicity, explains Chaucer's conclusion and moral in stanzas 262-5 of Book V, to be discussed below.

Now let us pass from Chaucer's consideration of fate in the poem to his consideration of felicitee, two considerations which are necessarily related as is illustrated in chapters II and III of the present study. At the outset of *Troilus* Chaucer announces that his tale is to relate how Troilus passed "fro wo to wele, and after out of joye," and in the conclusion he calls the tale a "tragedie." "Tragedies," it will be recalled, is what he terms the series of tales recounted by the Monk where he quotes the definition of tragedy from Boethius; and by tragedy, Chaucer seems to have meant principally[6] a sudden reversal from prosperity to adversity, a turn of Fortune's wheel, although it is interesting to note that he refers twice in *Troilus* to Oedipus, the typical tragic figure in classical literature.[7] *Troilus and Criseyde,* then, may be considered a Monk's tale, told with minute attention to human psychology and wrought into infinitely better poetry. Cassandra in *Troilus,* moreover, somewhat as the Monk, recounts a series of catastrophies derived from Statius, and by these she prophesies to Troilus that his misfortune will be comparable to the misfortunes of many other lords who have been overthrown by Fortune in the old time.[8] The entire poem abounds in allusions to the transitory

[6] The Monk in the prologue to his tale (B3163-67) defines tragedy as the kind of tale which concerns those who stand in high degree and who fall miserably to a wretched end; he adds that they are commonly versified in a meter of six feet, called "exametron." In the conclusion of his tale he defines the word again:

Tragedie is noon other thing,
Ne can in singing crye ne biwaille,
But for that fortune alwey wol assaille
With unwar strook the regnes that ben proude;
For when men trusteth hir, than wol she faille,
And covere hir brighte face with a cloude. B 3951-56.

Chaucer seems to have regarded it as a mark of wisdom to be able to recount such tales as this. Cassandra in *Troilus* recounts them to the despairing Troilus, and in the *Knight's Tale* the aged Egeus (A 2842) recounts examples of changes from joy to woe to the despairing Theseus and Emily.

[7] *Troilus* 2. 102 and 4. 300.

[8] The speech of Cassandra (5. 1464-1512) consists chiefly of the argument of the twelve books of Statius' *Thebaid* in abridged form.

nature of worldly joys, now brightening, now darkening, but ever fading entirely away in the end. The variety of figures by which Chaucer illustrates this idea is, to say the least, unusual.[9] Although there are thus to be heard intimations of the turning of Fortune's wheel throughout the poem, the decided turn comes between Books III and IV, and it comes with startling suddenness. At the close of Book III, both Troilus and Criseyde are intoxicated with passion; they think that they are supremely happy; Troilus sings the song in praise of celestial love. In the first part of Book IV, Troilus is complaining against heaven, Criseyde is bewailing the bitterness of worldly joys, and neither ever enjoys a moment of even imagined happiness again. They have descended abruptly from the stars to earth, a spectacular example of the abruptness with which Dame Fortune turns her wheel and snatches away joys of the troubled world.

Just as Troilus displays an intellectual interest in fate, so Criseyde displays an intellectual interest in felicity. Above all things she desires the highest happiness possible of attainment. At the same time, perhaps because she has had the experience of being a daughter of Calcas, the traitor, she understands the falseness of the world, and shudders at it because it is what may take her joy away. Worldly happiness, she reasons, is transitory, is subject to fickle human relations; and constantly, she is confronted with the fear that now has come the dreaded, but expected moment, when her happiness will disappear, just as Troilus was constantly confronted with the fear of the intervention of the gods in his happiness. Criseyde must have been in some such mood as that just described, when Pandarus, after craftily laying his plans, has announced to her the love of Troilus for herself:

> And she bigan to breste a-wepe anoon!
> And seyde, 'allas, for wo; why nere I deed?
> *For of this world the feith is al agoon!*
> Allas! what sholden straunge to me doon,
> When he, that for my beste freend I wende,
> Ret me to love, and sholde it me defende? . . .
> *This false world, allas! who may it leve?* 2. 410-20.

But one of the foremost traits of Criseyde is curiosity. After the first moment of hesitation and rejection she becomes in-

[9] For instances, see 1. 138-40; 215-17; 946-52; 2. 764-70; 3. 351-57; 1058-64; 1221; 1625-28; 1635; 1714; 4. 1-11; 269-72; 323-26; 384-92; 421-24; 834-40; 5. 731-2; 1432-5; 1457-1519; 1541-47.

terested in that which she is spurning so hastily. Perhaps love contains some great happiness that she does not know. She debates with herself the *pros* and *cons*. At one moment she is decided for love:

> What shal I doon? to what *fyn* live I thus?
> Shal I nat loven, in cas 'f that me leste? 2. 757-8.

After she has decided for love, a cloudy thought passes through her mind. If she yields to love, she may be surrendering her own liberty:

> That thought was this, 'allas! sin I am free,
> Sholde I now love, and putte in jupartye
> My *sikernesse,* and thrallen libertee? . . .
> For love is yet the moste stormy lyf, 2. 771-78.

While she is debating this question, at the psychological moment she hears the enraptured love song of her niece Antigone. In this song (2. 827-75), Antigone lauds to the skies the bliss which true lovers enjoy, and, by chance, touches on the express point which Criseyde is debating. Those who say that love is thraldom, so her song runs, have simply lost the power to love or have never actually experienced the power. This song of the "fresh Antigone the whyte" resembles the songs of Pippa in Browning's poem. It helps Criseyde to decide her debate. She says:

> *Is there* swich blisse among
> These loveres, as they conne faire endyte?' 2. 885-6.

Later, after her first meeting with Troilus at the house of Deiphebus, so delilghtful are her feelings that she decides that she is at last realizing a genuine love:

> But thilke litel that they speke or wroughte,
> His wyse goost took ay of al swich hede,
> It semed hir, he wiste that she thoughte
> With-outen word, so that it was no nede
> To bidde him ought to done, or ought forbede;
> For which *she thoughte that love, al come it late,*
> *Of alle joye hadde opned hir the yate.* 3. 463-69.

Her joy, however, soon suffers a shock. Pandarus announces to her that Troilus is jealous. Jealousy is a thing which she despises. She is too big-minded for jealousy; she does not like to be bothered by so useless a thing. Now, her worst fears are realized; a worldly imperfection has arisen to mar her joy, and love is not what she was beginning to dare to hope. The idea contained in the following lines, and especially in the italicized lines, all based on Boethius,[10] I think materially determined Chaucer's conception of Criseyde. He conceived her as representative of the class of people described by Boethius who are constantly beset by the fear that joys will fade, and in this passage he has her give expression to the idea herself:

> 'O god!' quod she, 'so worldly selinesse,
> Which clerkes callen fals felicitee,
> Y-medled is with many a bitternesse.
> Ful anguisshous than is, god woot,' quod she,
> 'Condicioun of veyn prosperitee;
> For either joyes comen nought y-fere,
> Or elles no wight hath hem alwey here.
>
> O brotel wele of mannes joye unstable!
> With what wight so thou be, or how thou pleye,
> Either he woot that thou, joye, art muable,
> Or woot it not, it moot ben oon of tweye;
> Now if he woot it not, how may he seye
> That he hath verray joye and selinesse,
> That is of ignoraunce ay in derknesse?
>
> *Now if he woot that joye is transitorie,*
> *As every joye of worldly thing mot flee,*
> *Than every tyme he that hath in memorie,*
> *The drede of lesing maketh him that he*
> *May in no parfit selinesse be.*
> And if to lese his joye he set a myte,
> Than semeth it that joye is worth ful lyte.
>
> Wherfore I wol deffyne in this matere,
> That trewely, *for ought I can espye,*
> *Ther is no verray wele in this world here.* 3. 813-36.

Once more, however, her doubts are allayed, and she is carried away by the passion of love. She and Troilus are enjoying the very essence of bliss. Chaucer says:

> Felicitee, which that thise clerkes wyse
> Commenden so, ne may not here suffyse.
> This joye may not writen been with inke,
> This passeth al that herte may bithinke. 3. 1691-94.

[10] Lines 820-33 of Criseyde's speech should be compared with 2. p4. 109-20 of the *Consolation:* what man that this toumbling welefulnesse ledeth, either he woot that it is chaungeable, or elles he woot it nat. And yif he woot it nat, what blisful fortune may ther be in the blindnesse of ignoraunce? *And yif he woot that it is chaungeable, he moot alwey ben adrad that he ne lese that thing that he ne doubteth nat but that he may lesen it;* ... *For which, the continuel dreed that he hath ne suffreth him nat to ben weleful. Of yif he lese it, he weneth to be dispysed and forleten. Certes eek, that is ful litel good that is born with evene herte whan it is lost.*

In the beginning of Book IV, however, the crash comes and the joy fades with startling suddenness. Hero and heroine lament in characteristic fashion. Troilus in protracted laments blames Fortune and Providence. Criseyde blames the fickleness of worldly joys:

> *Endeth than love in wo?* Ye, or men lyeth!
> *And alle worldly blisse, as thinketh me,*
> *The ende of blisse ay sorwe it occupyeth;*
> And who-so troweth not that it so be,
> Lat him upon me, woful wrecche, y-see,
> That my self hate, and ay my birthe acorse,
> *Felinge alwey, fro wikke I go to worse.* 4. 834-40.

Finally, Criseyde, who is thus so keenly conscious of the falseness of worldly hopes, by a kind of auto-suggestion becomes false herself. Nothing of the world (and she knows nothing else) is abiding. How could she be expected to be abiding! Her faith is overcome at the first barrier with amazing swiftness. In lines 731-65 of Book V, in soliloquy she is insisting on her faith to Troilus, on her intention to return to Troy against the counsel of her friends, come what come may; "felicitee," she says, is in her own "suffisaunce." And then a few lines later, she has denied Troilus to Diomede as strangely as St. Peter denied Christ. Her tragedy was, that she, beautiful, tender-hearted, womanly in every instinct, had so earnestly sought happiness, and instead of finding it, had, because she knew the world only too well, plunged headlong into an act of unfaith of the very kind that she herself most abhorred and feared, to be the eternal example of unfaithfulness in love. And no one is more conscious of her tragedy than Criseyde herself, as she shows in the plaintive words which mark her last appearance in the poem. In her tragic downfall Chaucer's promise of the outset has its fulfillment. Criseyde is to have her tragedy as well as Troilus:

> Now herkeneth with a gode entencioun,
> For now wol I gon streight to my matere,
> In whiche ye may the *double* sorwes here
> Of Troilus, in loving of Criseyde,
> *And how that she forsook him er she deyde.* 1. 52-6.

There are probably no more sincere words in the poem than those with which Chaucer conducts her from the scenes for the last time:

> Ne me ne list this sely womman chyde
> Ferther than the story wol devyse.
> Hir name, allas! is publisshed so wyde.
> That for hir gilt it oughte y-now suffyse.
> And if I mighte excuse hir any wyse,
> For she so sory was for hir untrouthe,
> Y-wis, I wolde excuse hir yet for routhe. 5. 1093-99.

Furthermore, Criseyde's view that the felicity which Troilus and she enjoy may be false felicity is correct, and she is the only character of the poem who has the intellectual discrimination to discern it. The end of earthly joy *is* woe. There is only one true felicity, and but one spark of this might have made Criseyde, with all her truly splendid qualities, an Alcestis. Chaucer himself announces what felicity is in stanzas 262-5 in the conclusion of the poem. It is *truth* of the kind which is described in Chaucer's poem of that name.[11] It was unfortunate that Chaucer could not have sent to both Troilus and Criseyde the counsel which he sent to Sir Philip la Vache.

It was fitting that such a poem should be dedicated, as it is, to the philosophical Strode and the moral Gower. The poem, moreover, seems to have been regarded as a philosophical one by Chaucer's contemporaries. Thomas Usk,[12] in alluding to the free will passage, so criticized on artistic grounds by modern authors, calls Chaucer "the noble philosophical poete in Englissh." Deschamps, too, probably had *Troilus* in mind, among other works of Chaucer, when he styles Chaucer as the Socrates who was enlightening England with his philosophy.[13] Indeed so philosophical a poem is *Troilus,* so much does it abound in Boethian passages, so much does it illustrate the truth of the Boethian teaching, that it is possible even to suppose that Chaucer translated the *Consolation* for the express purpose that *Troilus* might be the better interpreted; at any rate, the two works go hand in hand.

In the *Knight's Tale,* which is less a psychological study than *Troilus,* there is less contrast between the characters; but even here there is evidence of a careful selection of the Boethian material. It is commonly known that the *Knight's Tale* is full of the influence of the *Consolation,* but it may not be realized that the greater part of this influence is concen-

---

[11] For the discussion of *Truth* see pp. 104 ff. of this dissertation.
[12] *Testament of Love,* III, ch. 4, p. 249.
[13] *Oeuvres. Société des anciens Textes Français.* Vol. IX, pp. 139-40.

trated into three long speeches,[14] one allotted to Arcite, one to Palamon, and one to Theseus; that each one of these speeches is on a common theme; and that this theme is the relation of Providence to man's happiness, a point which it is the prime object of the *Consolation* to discuss, and a point which Chaucer made much of in *Troilus,* as we have just seen. Arcite, ill satisfied with events, wonders why he cannot understand the wise purveyance of god, who does all things for the best; but he blames himself for stumbling around so blindly for false happiness—such stumbling as Dame Philosophy describes in 3. p2. Palamon, on the other hand, does not blame himself, but takes the benighted position in which Boethius describes himself at the outset of the *Consolation;* he, like Boethius in 1. m5, cries out against the cruel gods who permit innocent men to suffer. Theseus blames neither god nor himself, but, by explaining the origin of the universe and the divine plan, shows, as Dame Philosophy does in 4. p6, m6, that there is an established order to which men must submit and which turns all things to good; his speech might be summed up in Chaucer's line, "trouthe shal delivere, hit is no drede," as has been explained elsewhere (pp. 116 ff). That the distinctions between the three speeches were not calculated by Chaucer, it is difficult to believe. Palamon's speech follows immediately after that of Arcite, and the proximity of the two intensifies the contrast between them. Impressions of the characters are given which extend throughout the poem. More pity is aroused for Arcite, that he who acknowledges that God's ways are always just meets in the moment of his greatest triumph a sudden and tragic death, whereas Palamon who complains against heaven receives the high reward. The speech of Theseus, to be sure, softens down the tragic end of Arcite, but at the same time it points back to the speeches of the two younger and less wise men and is made to appear more noble and dignified by a contrast with theirs.

From the preceding it will appear that Chaucer's indebtedness to the *Consolation* in the poems under consideration was large. In each Boccaccio furnished the tale, but Boethius, in *Troilus* especially, gave an impetus of thought, which, among other things perhaps, prompted Chaucer to mould Boccaccio's

[14] Speech of Arcite A1251-1272; speech of Palamon A 1303-1333; speech of Theseus A2987-3040.

tales into something different and to recast the characters. The explanation why Boethius had so profound an influence may well be due to the fact that the *Consolation of Philosophy* contained a solution for the end or "fyn" of life. So masterly a philosophical treatise, one so highly thought of by Chaucer, so frequently used in his poetry, may be considered to have determined his attitude toward everything, at least for a period of his life.

CHAPTER V

THE BOETHIAN INFLUENCE IN DETAIL

This chapter consists of two parts: (1) a list of the passages in Chaucer's poetry showing Boethian influence, (2) a list of the passages in the *Consolation* influencing Chaucer.

PART I. PASSAGES SHOWING BOETHIAN INFLUENCE

A list of the passages in Chaucer's poetry showing Boethian influence has been made by both Stewart and Skeat.[1] The

[1] See the essay of Stewart, Appendix B, and *Oxford Chaucer*, Vol. II, pp. xxviii-xxxvi.

present list is intended to be a revision and expansion of theirs. The newly found passages are indicated by a star. There are also frequent changes from the older lists. The influence of Boethius on the individual poems follows.

Book of the Duchess

The influence of Boethius is only indirect through the *Roman de la Rose* and the *Remède de Fortune*. The reference to Sesiphus, line 589, to Tantale, line 708, to the mind as a parchment, lines 779-84, and to Alcipyades, lines 1056-7, and the long discussion of Fortune, lines 617-719, by peculiarities in spelling and figures of speech all show the influence of the poems mentioned rather than of the *Consolation*. For a consideration of the sources of the long discussion of Fortune see pp. 55-7 of this dissertation.

Parliament of Fowls

The influence of Boethius in this poem is of a general nature or doubtful. The influence of Dante, Macrobius, and Alanus de Insulis is more in evidence.

*90-91. I had what I did not want, and I wanted what I did not have. 3. p3. 24-26.

380-81. Nature knits the hot and cold, the heavy and light, the moist and dry. The idea is very common in mediaeval literature. It occurs, however, several times in Boethius, 3. m9. 12-6, p11. 98-111, and in 4. m6. 15-20.

599-600. The duck fares in love as the owl in the day-light. 4. p4. 132-3.

The Complaint to Pity

*99-105. I have what I do not want, and I want what I do not have. 3. p3. 24-6. This idea occurs frequently, especially in the complaints.

The Complaint to Mars

*218-26. How may a just and powerful god permit sorrow? 1. m5. 22-35.

A Complaint to His Lady

*47-8. I have what I do not want, and I want what I do not have. 3. p3. 24-6.

Anelida and Arcite

*Frequent allusions to destiny, characteristic of the period when the influence of Boethius was highest are found in this poem. See lines 243, 339, 348.

*203. Man wants what he may not have. 3. p3. 24-6.

The Former Age

As explained before (p. 90) the order in which the ideas of the poem are presented conforms almost exactly to that of the *Consolation, 2. m5,* and the outline thus obtained is filled in with details from other sources as follows: Lines 1-5 of Chaucer's poem correspond to lines 1-3 of the *Consolation,* and are taken directly from it. Lines 6-14 correspond to 3-5; 9-10 to Ovid's *Metamorphosis,* I, 102; 11 to the *Roman* 8689; 12 to the Fourth *Eclogue* of Vergil, "quae iubeant telluri infindere sulcos." Lines 15-18 to the *Cons.* 5-11; 15-16 to the *Roman* 8694-5; 17-18 to *Roman* 8703-4. Lines 21-6 to *Cons.* 13-20; 24 to Fourth *Eclogue* of Vergil, "quae (iubeant) cingere muris oppida." Lines 26-40 to *Cons.* 24-8; 28-9 to *Metam.* I, 139; 30 to *Cons.* 3. m10. 9-14; 33-40 from the *Policraticus* of John of Salisbury or from the *Epistle against Jovinian* of St. Jerome (*Oxford Chaucer,* I, 539). Lines 40-46 to *Cons.* 11-13 and are based on *Roman* 8717-26. Lines 48-64 seem to be an expansion of Chaucer's, from Ovid chiefly; cf. allusions to lack of faith to *Metam.* I, 129-31; allusion to Jupiter to *Metam.* I, 113-15; allusion to towers of Nembrot, *Metam.* 151-3.

Fortune

Fortune, discussed at length pp. 57-60, is a summary of all that Boethius has to say of Fortune throughout the *Consola-*

tion. Verbal resemblances imperfectly represent Chaucer's indebtedness, and many of them, moreover, may be paralleled in other sources, as the *Roman de la Rose,* or the *Remède de Fortune.* Boethius, however, is the ultimate source of all, and Chaucer's discussion contains, in compact form, all the essential phases of the Boethian discussion, as has been shown elsewhere.

1-4. The "transmutacion" of the world is governed by Fortune. Skeat cites 2. m1. 5-7, but the idea is general and it would be difficult to show that Chaucer had any specific passage in mind.

10-12. Fortune teaches men their true friends. 2. p8. 22-5.

14-15. To be master of one's self is to be master of Fortune. 2. p4. 98-101.

17-22. Socrates was a champion against Fortune. Boethius mentions Socrates in 1. p3. 20, but not in the relation under consideration. Socrates as a champion against Fortune was a convention in art and literature.

25-48. Fortune defends herself. 2. p2.

25-26. No man is wretched unless he think so. 2. p4. 79-80.

29-30. No man is wretched unless he thinks so. 2. p4. 79-80.

31. Fortune may advance one as well as harm him. 2. p2. 59-60.

33-34. Fortune teaches the distinction between "frend of effect and frend of countenaunce." Stewart and Skeat refer to 2. p8. 25-28. The phrasing, however, is almost identical with the English version of the *Roman,* 5486.

38. Let your anchor hold. 2. p4. 40.

43-44. Fortune is queen. 2. p1. 69-72, 78-80.

45-46. The realm of Fortune is common. 2. p2. 60-62.

50-52. Fortune teaches men their true friends. 2. p8. 25-8.

57-60. Fortune lends her riches. 2. p2. 4-19.

61-63. The sea ebbs and flows, the sky is bright and again is dark with rain; why may not Fortune change also? 2. p2. 27-33.

65-69. There are powers higher than Fortune. 5. m1. 13-15 and 4. p6. 42-6.

71. The rule of Fortune ends when a man dies. 2. p3. 58-61.

Gentilesse

This poem depends upon 3. p6. 24-38, and upon 3. m6. It also shows the influence of Dante. For the general discussion see pp. 94 ff.

5. Virtue makes real dignity. 2. p6. 17-19 and 3. p4. 25-6.

Lack of Steadfastness

For the resemblance between this poem and Chaucer's *Former Age* see pp. 91-2. For its dependence on 2. m8, the "bond of love" *meter,* see pp. 106-7.

*4. Word and deed are not alike. 3. p12. 152-3. Cf. *Prologue* A 742.

*5. The world is "turned up so doun." 2. p5. 91-92.

*7, 14, 21. "al is lost." Cf. Chaucer's translation of 2. m8 in 3. 1764 of *Troilus* and his allusion to the bond of love in 3. 1265 of the same poem.

Truth

The influence of Boethius in the poem is great, but is an influence of thought rather than one of words. See pp. 104 ff. The passages which have most influence are 2. p4. 96-101 and 2. m4, the first "point" of happiness, 3. p11. 161-170 and 3. m11, the second "point" of happiness, and 4. p6 and m6 which explain the refrain of the poem.

2, 5, 10. Be content with little things. 2. p5. 56-60 and 3. p3. 72.

3. Hoarding causes hatred. 2. p5. 11-12.

9. Do not trust in Fortune. 2. p4. 49-51; cf. "tempest" with *Truth,* line 8.

15. Receive in happiness what is sent thee. 2. p1. 66-9.

19. Know thy country. 1. p5. 6-25 and 4. m1.

18-19. "Forth beste—look up." Boethius emphasizes the bestial condition of men: In 4. p3. 73-88 he compares different kinds of evil-doers to different kinds of beasts, the wolf, the hound, the fox, etc. 4. m3 is devoted to a long simile showing that vices turn men to beasts even more surely than Circe turned the companions of Ulysses to beasts. 5. m5 is devoted to showing that men should not look down like the beasts, but should bear "up a-heigh" their heads.

These resemblances, although general, are of increased significance if one recalls the influence of Boethius on the thought of the poem as discussed previously. Boethius in 4. p3. 1-37 has a discussion of the heavenly meed and in 5. p3. 133-148 tells of the necessity of prayer as Chaucer in lines 26-7.

Troilus and Criseyde

Book I

*4. Chaucer considers *Troilus* a tragedy. Cf. this line with 5. 1786 and with the definition of tragedy in the *Consolation* 2. p2. 51-2; cf. also with the *Monk's Tale* B 3163-7, 3181-4, 3951-4, 3973.

*295-8. A deep impression of Criseyde sticks in the depths of Troilus' heart. 5. m4. 1-15, 29-32. Cf. also with reference just below.

365-7. Troilus makes a mirror of his mind in which he sees the figure of Criseyde. 5. m4. 7-10.

*637-46. Pandarus to Troilus. Things are declared by their contraries; therefore Pandarus who has been unfortunate in love will be able to tell Troilus how to conduct a fortunate love affair. 4. p2. 9-10.

638-9. Pandarus to Troilus. To know sweetness it is necessary to have tasted bitterness. 3. m1. 4-5. A general resemblance.

730. Pandarus to Troilus. What? slombrestow as in a lytargye. 1. p2. 14.

731-35. Pandarus to Troilus. Artow lyk an asse to the harpe? 1. p4. 2. Chaucer explains the proverb in lines 732-5. In the Bodleian Ms. Rawlinson. Poet. 163 at these lines appear the words, "Baicius de consolacione philosophie."

786-8. Pandarus to Troilus. Pandarus grants that he may suffer with pangs of love as Tityus suffered in hell. 3. m12. 28-30. Cf. allusion to Tantalus 3. 592 and to Orpheus and Eurydice 4. 791. All of the allusions appear together in 3. m12.

837-40. Troilus, as Boethius, complains against Fortune. Cf. 837 with 1. p4. 8; 838-9 with 2. p1. 80-82; 840 with 2. m1. 10.

841-53. Pandarus comforts Troilus in this matter as Dame Philosophy comforts Boethius. Cf. 841 with 2. p2. 19-20; 843-4 with 2. p2. 60-2; 846-7 with 2. p3. 52-4.; 848-9 with 2. p1. 82-4; 850 with 2. p2. 59-60.

857-8. Pandarus to Troilus. If one will have help from a leech, he must first disclose his wounds. 1. p4. 3-4. Philosophy thus speaks to Boethius. Cf. 2. 571.

*891-3. Pandarus to Troilus. The first point is for a man to have peace with himself. 2. p4. 96-101.

*960-1. Pandarus to Troilus. He that is parted is not whole. 3. p11. 46-51.

1065-71. Pandarus carefully thinks out a way to help Troilus, as a man who has a house to build plans beforehand. 4. p6. 57-60.

Book II

42. Every country has its own laws. 2. p7. 49-51. Doubtful.

526-8. Prayer of Troilus. God leads the "fyn" by just "purveyaunce." 4. p6. 49-51. See also 1. p5. 22.

*622-3. What betides of necessity may not be disturbed. 5. p6. 115-18.

764-770. A cloud is driven over Criseyde's thoughts. 1. m3. Cf. 781 in the following speech of Criseyde where the figure is used again.

*981. Criseyde prints in her heart every word of Antigone's song. 5. m4. 6.

*1065. Troilus calls Criseyde his sorrow's leech. 1. p4. 3-4.

Book III

617-22. Fortune and fate, the executors of god, bring the rainfall which detains Criseyde at the house of Pandarus. 4. p6. 35-54 and 5. m1. 13-16.

624. The bent moon with his hornes pale. 1. m5. 6-7. Doubtful.

813-36. Criseyde to Pandarus. Speech on false felicity. 2. p4. 56-130. Cf. 813-5 with 2. p4. 86-87; 816-9 with 2. p4. 56-58; 820-33 with 2. p4. 109-120.

*1016-19. Criseyde to Troilus. The innocent suffer; the guilty prosper. 1. m5. 26-30.

*1060-64. Similes to show that joys succeed sorrows. Cf. 2. m3.

1254-, 1261. Troilus to Criseyde on divine love. Cf. "O, love, O, Charitee" with 3. p11. 128. Cf. 1261 with 2. m8. 9-11.

1625-28. Pandarus to Troilus warning him of the necessity of caution when he is at the height of his bliss. The greatest misfortune is, in adversity, to remember past happiness. 2. p4. 4-7.

1691-2. Felicity of which the clerks tell may not be compared to the bliss of Troilus and Criseyde. 3. p2. 6-8.

1745-64. Song of Troilus on celestial love, a translation of 2. m8.

Book IV

1-7. Deceit and scorn of Fortune. Cf. 3 with 2. p1. 12-13; 6-7 with 2. p2. 38-30 and 2. m1. 9. Cf. 1-3 with *Filostrato* 3. st. 94 and 6-7 with the *Roman* 8076-9 (Skeat). The allusions are conventional, and it is not necessary to suppose that Chaucer had definite sources in mind.

200. The cloud of error prevents people from seeing what is best. 3. m11. 7.

391-2. Pandarus to Troilus. The gifts of Fortune are common. 2. p2. 7-9; 61-2.

481-2. Troilus recalls the speech of Pandarus, 3. 1625-8, where he says that the greatest misfortune is to remember past happiness in adversity. 2. p4. 4-7.

503-4. Troilus to Pandarus. Death is happy as it ends pain. 1. m1. 12-4.

*791. Orpheus and Eurydice. 3. m12. 41. Cf. allusions to the suffering of Tityus in 1. 786-8 and to Tantalus 3. 592. All are mentioned in 3. m12.

*767-8. A plant cannot live without the nourishment natural to its kind. 3. p11. 75-90.

835-6. Criseyde to Pandarus. The end of worldly bliss is woe. This is the teaching of the *Consolation*. Cf. 2. p4. 90-1. Skeat cites *Proverbs* 14: 13.

958-9. Troilus. All that comes, comes by necessity. 5. p2. 30-34.

961-6. God of his purveyaunce sees everything as it will come by destiny. 5. p2. 30-34.

974-1078. Free will debate of Troilus, a translation of 5. p3. 7-71.

*989-92. The divine prescience is no better than the opinion of man, if it is uncertain. 5. p3. 16-7. This point is alluded to again in the *Consolation* at lines 5. p3. 96-9.

1587-9. Men may be lords of Fortune. This is one of the central teachings of the *Consolation*. Cf. 2. p4. 96-

101 and 4. p7. 55-76. For line 1589 Skeat cites the *Filostrato* 4. st. 154.

*1654. Troilus. "Now god, to whom ther nis no cause y. wrye. 4. p6. 106-17.

Book V

*1-3. The idea that god commits to fate the execution of his decrees is from the *Consolation* 4. p6. 29-56.

278. The rosy cart of Phoebus. 2. m3. 1-2.

*746-9. Criseyde may remember time passed; she may see the present; but she may not see future time. This sounds reminiscent of the discussion in the *Consolation* of man's limited powers of embracing time. Cf. 5. p6. 12-17. Chaucer appears to have been first, in his translation of the *Consolation*, to use the word *future* in English.

762. Criseyde calls her suffisaunce her felicity. 2. p4. 96-101; 3. p2. 63-66.

1541-4. To Fortune is committed the permutation of things. 5. m1. 13-16.

*1818. Troilus is brought to "pleyn felicitee." These words do not occur in the *Teseide* 11. st. 1 on which the stanza of *Troilus* in which they occur is otherwise based. Boethius closely associates true felicity and man's real "country," whither Troilus has been brought. See pp. 112-6 of this dissertation.

Verbal resemblances inadequately represent Chaucer's indebtedness to Boethius in this poem. Chaucer may have the *Consolation* very much in mind where there is not a word to show for it. The influence of the *Consolation,* indeed, led him to borrow passages from other sources. For the influence of Boethius on Chaucer's thought in the poem see pp. 120 ff.

The House of Fame

The *House of Fame,* also, may be indebted to the *Consolation* more than the verbal resemblances indicate. Chaucer's conception of the goddess of Fame seems to have been influenced by the Boethian conception of Fortune; his discussion of fame in the abstract may have been influenced by the similar discussion of Boethius (cf. pp 87-89). Furthermore, his flight through the heavens described in Book II is much in the spirit of that described in 4. m1 of the *Consolation* (cf. pp. 115-16).

Book I

*81-2. God, mover of all things. 3. m9. 18-19.

Book II

534-6. Thunder which smites towers to powder. Skeat shows
that these lines are derived from Machault. "Tour"
may be from Boethius, 1. m4. 7-9.

730-756. Chaucer explains why sound arises to the house of
Fame. It is on the principle that every element, every
plant, and every animal by nature seeks its proper
place. As Chaucer says in lines 759-60, many clerks
know the truth of this. It is one of the central points
in the *Consolation*. Boethius uses it to show that just
as every thing by nature seeks its place, so man by
nature seeks the highest possible happiness, the supreme good, his true "country." Cf. lines 738-46 concerning inanimate things with 3. m9. 12-16; 3. p11.
98-111; 4. m6. 15-20. Cf. lines 750-755 concerning
animate objects with 3. p11. 71-90.

907. To Chaucer in his flight the world seems no more
than a "prikke." 2. p7. 18. Here the word is used to
show the vastness of heaven in relation to the earth.
The word "prikke" occurs in the *Dream of Scipio* in
the same connection.

972-8. A reminiscence of the flight of "Thought" described
in 4. m1, lines 1-5 especially. Line 973 is to be noted,
'a *thought* may flee so hye.' It may be of some significance that Chaucer invokes "Thought" to assist
him in describing his flight (line 523).

Book III

1368-75. The goddess of Fame is described as Boethius describes Dame Philosophy. Her feet touch earth; her
head reaches to heaven. 1. p1. 8-12. Philosophy was
thus sometimes symbolically depicted in mediaeval
art. She was so sculptured at Laon. See the description by Emile Male in *Religious Art in France*,
translated by Dora Nussey, pp. 90-92.

1545-8. The goddess serves people diversely, just as her sis-
ter Fortune serves her gifts in common, without pay-
ing attention to their deserts. 1. p5. 43-4; 2. p2. 60-1.

1920-1. Chaucer sees the *domus Dedali*, that is called
Laborintus. 3. p12. 117-8. *Laborintus* does not

occur in the Latin text. If Chaucer is indebted to Boethius for the allusion, he must have received part of his information from a gloss.

Legend of Good Women

195. Chaucer's tale is to be of another "tonne" than that of the flower and the leaf *balades*. 2. p2. 53-5.

*1819-24. Tarquin, though heir of a king, has done a churl's deed; his lack of true gentility is lamented. 3. p6. 24-38; m6.

2228-9. An invocation to the giver of the forms, who has wrought the fair world. 3. m9. 1-10.

*2231-5. How may a powerful god permit the evil which Tereus did? The general plan of lines 2228-35 is the same as that of 1. m5. The greatness of God is recognized, and then the query is raised, how may He suffer evil to exist.

*2586-88. Hypermnestra thinks that felicity is in virtues. 3. p11. 166-70.

Canterbury Tales

Prologue

336-8. The Franklin, "Epicurus owne sone," held that plain delight was perfect felicity. 3. p2. 54-6.

*490. The Parson "coude in litel thing han suffisaunce." 3. p3. 72, "litel thing suffiseth to nature."

741-2. Plato says that the word must be cousin to the deed; therefore Chaucer must tell each tale as the narrator told it. 3. p12. 152-3.

The Knight's Tale

925-6. An allusion to Fortune's wheel. Skeat and Stewart both cite 2. p2. 37-9. The figure was so common that a specific source seems improbable.

1164-6. An argument of Arcite for loving Emily. Who may give a lover any law? Love is a greater law than any man may give. 3. m12. 37-9.

1251-67. Lament of Arcite after escaping from prison so that he may no longer see Emily. Taken chiefly from 3. p2. 17-30; 57-87. Specific resemblances follow.

1251-4. God gives men better than they themselves can devise. This is the point that 4. p6 establishes; see especially 161-4 and 243-5.

1255-58. Forms of false felicity pursued by men. 3. p2. 17-27.

*1258-9. A man may think he is well off, and be slain in his house by his "meynee." 2. p5. 64-7.

1260-65. We seek blindly after felicity as a drunken man seeking his house. 3. p2. 60-62.

1266-7. We seek after felicity, but we go wrong. 3. p2. 58-60.

1303-15. Lament of Palamon when he is left in prison; if he were out like Arcite, he might win Emily. How may a mighty God cruelly permit the innocent to suffer. 1. m5. 22-6; 4. p1. 19-26.

1663-65. Destiny, the minister of Providence. 4. p6. 35-54.

*1670-3. Our desires are ruled by the sight above; therefore Theseus desires to hunt and so meets Arcite and Palamon. 4. p6. 164-236. Lines 1663-73 might be considered as a summary of 4. p6.

1946. The rich Croesus in captivity, the subject of one of the paintings in the temple of Venus. 2. p2. 44. Croesus is also described in the *Roman*.

2987-3015; 3034-3940. Speech of Theseus. God, in his wisdom, brings about all things, even death; therefore the death of Arcite should not be lamented. This is taken chiefly from 4. p6 and m6. Specific resemblances follow.

2987-93. The first mover, by the fair chain of love, binds the fire, the air, the water, and the land. 3. m9. 1-19; 4. m6. 13-19. The influence of the *Teseide* (Bk. 2, st. 52), pointed out by Skeat for the whole passage, is limited to lines 2989-90.

2994-99; 3011-15. The same mover causes birth and death in progressions. 4. p6. 101-106.

3004-09. Everything, even the corruptible, is derived from God, the whole and absolute, and does not take its beginning from any part. 3. p10. 18-22.

*3035-40. God converts all things back to the good from which they are derived. 4. m6. 31-40. (Cf. pp. 117-8.)

Man of Law's Tale

127. Merchants seek land and sea for winnings. 2. m5. 13-16. Doubtful.

295-99. The moving firmament. 1. m5. 1-3; 3. p8. 22; p12. 145-7; 4. m1. 6.

422. "Worldly blisse, spreynd with bitternesse." Skeat

points to the *De Contemptu Mundi* as the source of lines 421-7. For the words quoted, however, compare 2. p4. 86-7, "the swetnesse of mannes weleful-nesse is *sprayned* with many bitternesses."

481-3. God does things for good ends, although the ends may seem dark to men. 4. p6. 114-17; 152-54.

813-16. How may a mighty God permit innocent people to suffer. 1. m5. 22-30; 4. p1. 19-26.

Melibeus

2321. Avarice is insatiable. 2. m2. 7-16. Doubtful.

2479. Good and evil are contraries. 4. p6. 9-10.

*2802-4. A man may not take riches with him out of the world, for death ends the present life; everyone knows he must die. These lines do not come from Albertano of Brescia. 2. p3. 54-61. Doubtful.

The Monk's Tale

For discussion of this tale see pp. 85-7.

3163-67; 3181-84. A definition of tragedy. 2. p2. 51.

*3185-6. No one may withhold the course of Fortune. 2. p1. 80-84.

3285-3300. Exploits of Hercules from the similar account of his exploits in 4. m7. 20-43. The only deviation is in line 3294 where Chaucer substitutes Busirus for Diomedes.

3326-29. Self knowledge is better than trust in Fortune. 2. p4. 96-101; 2. p5. 106-9.

*3429-36. The tragic fate of Balthasar is an example showing that there is no security in lordship, because Fortune takes away the riches and friends of lords. This is the main point of 3. p5.

3653-80. Account of Nero. Chaucer drew from Boethius, Suetonius, and Boccaccio. The following lines are from Boethius: 3656-7 from 2. m6. 14-17; 3658-60 in part from 3. m4. 1-3 ("perles whyte"); 3669-80, except 3671 and the last half of 3672, are directly from 2. m6. 2-9. Boethius in 3. p5. 34-41 discusses Seneca as the master of Nero, but not in detail as Chaucer does, 3685ff.

*3711. Fortune is stronger than Nero. 2. m1. 11.

*3739-40. Fortune laughs and has a game. 2. m1. 11-12.

3917-22. These beginning lines of the long account of Croesus are directly from Boethius 2. p2. 42-6.

3951-54. Second definition of tragedy. 2. p2. 51-2. It will be noted that both in 2. p2 of the *Consolation* and here in the *Monk's Tale* the definition of tragedy follows the account of Croesus. Cf. also with B3973.

3956. Fortune covers her face with a cloud. 2. p1. 42. See also the long simile of Boethius 1. m3 and 1. p3. 1. Cf. B3972.

The poem contains many conventional allusions to Fortune not taken account of above.

Nun's Priest's Tale

*4029. The poor widow had "hertes suffisaunce." 2. p4. 96. 101 ; p5. 56-60.

4190. Fortune governs all in common. 2. p2. 61.

4424-44. Debate on free will. For a discussion of this passage see pp. 78-79. Cf. 4424 and 4. p6. 101-117 ; 4433-4, 4436-8 and 5. p2. 2-5, p3. 5-7 ; 4435, 4439-40 and 5. p6. 126-152.

4484. An allusion to Boethius as a singer, based probably on his reputation as author of *De Musica*.

*4528. Destiny that may not be "eschewed." 5. p3. 70-71.

*4560. An allusion to Nero's burning Rome and killing the senators ; their wives did not weep more wildly than did Pertelote. 2. m6. 2-3.

Physician's Tale

*294-96. The gifts of Fortune are often cause of death ; so Virginia's beauty was cause of her death. 3. p8. 35-39. The fairness of Alcibiades is discussed in this connection. See also 3. p8. 10-12 and 2. p5. 64-67. Cf. also *Knight's Tale* B 1235-8 ; *Parson's Tale* I 471-74.

Wife of Bath's Tale

100. He hath not every vessel all of gold. 4. p1. 30-3. Doubtful. Skeat also cites 2 *Tim.* 2 : 20.

170. The Wife of Bath's tale is to be of another "tonne" than the Prologue. 2. p2. 53.

1109-1176. Discussion of gentilesse by the loathly lady. See pp. 98-99. The passage upholds the view of Boethius and Dante that true gentility is not inherited from ancestors, that it depends on virtue, and that it proceeds from God alone, the source of all good. 3. p6. 24-38 and 3. m6. Boethius is mentioned in 1168. The argument is built up by passages from several sources. Chaucer was indebted to Boethius for the two specific passages indicated just below.

1139-49. Fire burns everywhere between here and the Caucasus mountains. Those of high birth often do evil deeds; if they had an innate quality of nobility, they would always do virtuous deeds just as the fire always burns. 3. p4. 44-48. Boethius uses the illustration much in the same way to show that "dignitees" are not innate. Boethius also uses the Caucasus mountains as an extreme limit of distance in 2. p7. 43. The allusion occurs in the *Dream of Scipio* in the same connection.

*1159-61. Gentilesse, in the usual sense, is but renown of ancestors, and such renown is foreign to the descendant. 3. p6. 26-8; 31-3.

1187. A covetous person is in a pitiful condition, because he wishes what he may not have. 3. p5. 23-5. Doubtful.

*1192-4. A poor man may sing before thieves. A proverb of Juvenal, quoted in 2. p5. 127. Chaucer probably knew Juvenal second hand. He quotes another proverb of Juvenal in *Troilus* 4. 197, and this is the extent of Juvenal's influence. (Cf. Lounsbury's *Studies,* II: 260-1.)

1203. Poverty shows a man his true friends. 2. p8. 23-5, 31-3.

The Friar's Tale

1483. Sometimes fiends are god's instruments. 4. p6. 62-64, 69.

The Summoner's Tale

1968-9. A thing is stronger when it is one than when it is scattered. 3. p11. 37-40.

*2214. "To parte that wol nat departed be." 3. p9. 66-70.

The Clerk's Tale

The *Clerk's Tale,* although it is based on Petrarch's tale of Griselda, contains several passages of the Boethian flavor. The following all have parallels in the Italian version; but I cite them for comparison with the *Consolation:* 155-161 with 3. p6.

24-38 and m6, true gentility comes from god and not from family; 424-5, another allusion to true gentility; 810-12 with 2. p1. 66-69, "suffren with evene wille in pacience" all that Fortune does—the resemblance in phrasing is here very close to the *Consolation;* 1155-62 with 4. p6. 180-6 and 245-7, God scourges men with adversity to improve them, doing all for the best.

The Merchant's Tale

1579-82. January's mind, receiving impressions of May, compared to a mirror receiving images from without. 5. m4. 7-10.

*1638. "Ther may no man han parfite blisses two." 3. p10. 85-6. The opinion of January expressed in the line is the starting point for lines 1637-1681.

*1671-3. May, the instrument for bringing about the salvation of January. 4. p6. 62-71. Cf. lines 1967-9 below.

1784. Familiar foe. 3. p5. 51.

1849. The "slakke skin" shakes on the neck of January as he sings, just as on the neck of Boethius when he is inspired by the woeful muses in 1. m1. 12.

1967-9. Through one or another of the instruments of Providence, May becomes favorable to Damian. 4. p6. 62-71. Cf. lines 1671-3 above.

*1972. All things have their times. 4. p6. 49-50. See also 5. p1. 65-9 and 1. m6.

*1975. No act is causeless. 4. p6. 101-117. It will be noted that many of the passages in the tale show the influence of 4. p6.

2021-3. January held to the Epicurean doctrine that felicity stood in delight. 3. p2. 54-6. Cf. 1637-81 above. The emphasis on felicity in the tale will be noted.

2026. Fortune, the monster. 2. p1. 10-14.

*2178. May is deeply imprinted in January's thought. 5. p4. 7-10. Cf. 1578-82 above.

The Squire's Tale

258. Some men wonder on the cause of thunder. 4. m5. 6. Doubtful.

608-17. All things act in accordance with their natural instincts; for example, the bird will fly from his life of ease in the cage to the forest. It is in the same way the instinct for men to love "newfangelnesse";

therefore the tercelet deserted the falcon. 3. m2. 27-9; 15-22.

*684-94. Gentility, according to the Franklin, depends on virtue and not on possession. 3. p6. 24-38, m6. See pp. 102-3.

The Franklin's Tale

*829-34. Consolation is imprinted in Dorigene just as a figure is graven on stone. 5. m4. 10-13. Chaucer changes the figure somewhat, but the idea is Boethian.

865-87. Lament of Dorigen that God permits evil. 1. m5 and 4. p1. 13-26. For a discussion see pp. 69-70. Specific borrowings follow.

865-7. Invocation to god, the mighty governor. 1. m5. 22; 3. m9. 1-2.

*872. "Why han ye wroght this werk unresonable." 1. m5. 24-26.

879. Mankind is a fair part of God's work. 1. m5. 37-8.

886-7. All things are for the best, although Dorigen cannot understand the causes. 4. p6. 110-117.

1031-34. God gives the plants their times and seasons. 1. m6.

The Second Nun's Tale

114. Heaven is swift, round, and burning. 1. m5. 1-3; 3. p8. 21-2; 4. m1. 5-6. Skeat's citation from Isidorus, however, is closely parallel to Chaucer's lines.

*327. God has created with a skillful thought. 3. m9. 8-10.

The Canon's Yeoman's Tale

958. Men do not have what they wish. 3. p3. 24-6. Doubtful.

The Manciple's Tale

160-174. All things act in accordance with their natural instincts, as the bird which will flee from the gilded cage to the cold forest. Chaucer cites other examples. 3. m2. 27-9; 15-22. The passage is also influenced by the *Roman de la Rose,* which itself is influenced by the *Consolation.* As in the *Squire's Tale,* the discussion is to prove that men, by instinct, follow their "likerous appetyt." The *Consolation,* in the corresponding discussion, attempts to prove just the opposite, that men, by nature, seek the highest good.

*207-10. The word must be cousin to the deed. 3. p12. 151-3.

212. A shadow is not the same thing of which it is a shadow. 5. p4. 45-6. Doubtful.

*460-70. A discussion of the signs of true gentility. 4. p6. 24-38 and m6.

471-74. Fortune's gifts are not to be trusted; power, riches, pleasures of the body, fame or glory are taken up in order. A summary of 3. p8, where a similar analysis occers.

The above list considers 1041 lines of Chaucer. Of these 1041 lines, some 562 show direct verbal indebtedness to the *Consolation*. The remaining 479 lines embrace passages which are original expansions by Chaucer of Boethian material, as, for instance, January's discussion of the idea that no man may enjoy two perfect blisses (E1637-81), and passages in which the Boethian influence is mixed with that of other sources, in the development, however, of an idea characteristically Boethian, as the discussion of gentilesse in the *Wife of Bath's Tale*. The table below traces, numerically, the influence of the *Consolation* through Chaucer's poetry. The figures indicate the number of lines affected.

	General Influence.	Verbal Influence.	Total.
Parliament of Fowls	2	4	6
Complaint to Pity	7	0	7
Complaint to Mars	9	0	9
Complaint to his Lady	0	2	2
Anelida and Arcite	3	1	4
Former Age	60	4	64
Fortune	46	26	72
Gentilesse	20	1	21
Lack of Steadfastness	25	3	28
Truth	20	8	28
Troilus and Criseyde	21	268	289
House of Fame	26	25	51
Legend of Good Women	8	9	17
Prologue of C. T.	0	8	8
Knight's Tale	18	48	66
Man of Law	10	4	14
Melibeus	1	4	5
Monk	7	61	68
Nun's Priest	13	11	24
Physician	3	0	3
Wife of Bath	54	21	75
Friar	0	1	1
Summoner	0	3	3
Clerk	20	0	20
Merchant	44	20	64
Squire	12	10	22
Franklin	22	11	33
Second Nun	1	1	2
Canon's Yeoman	1	0	1
Manciple	15	4	19
Parson	11	4	15
	479	562	1041

It might be possible to obtain results a little different from these, as it is difficult sometimes to draw the line between general resemblances and verbal resemblances, but the above figures, I trust, will hold in the main. More passages might have been included under general resemblances than have been included, as many of the allusions to the fickleness of worldly joy in *Troilus* and the discussion of abstract fame in the *House of Fame*.

Further, the influence of Boethius on Chaucer may be divided into three periods: the first, when he knew the *Consolation* indirectly through other sources or superficially; the second, coming after the translation, when he was fired with the thought of the *Consolation;* the third, when his interest became more quiescent, breaking out only at intervals as it was suggested from time to time in the subject matter of his later poetry. What follows has no pretensions of being the final word on the complicated subject of the chronology of the poems discussed; but, as the influence of Boethius on Chaucer was great, it is of weight in determining the chronology of his poems.

In the first period came chiefly the *Book of the Duchess* and the *Parliament of Fowls.* The former poem, as has been shown, was influenced by Boethius indirectly through outside sources. The latter poem shows no vital Boethian influence; at the best, the influence of Boethius in it is vague and uncertain. Instead, the influence of Alanus de Insulis, of the *Dream of Scipio* as it is preserved in the *Commentary* of Macrobius, and especially of Dante is predominant. All of these authors write of the celestial and philosophical subjects with which the *Consolation* deals. It may possibly have been that Dante turned Chaucer's mind to serious writers and ultimately to Boethius.[2] As has been observed in the previous chapters, the influence of Dante and of Boethius frequently coalesce in Chaucer's poetry. But, however this may be, the *Parliament of Fowls* shows little Boethian influence.

The translation of the *Consolation,* I think, marked the beginning of the second period of Boethian influence. The next work undertaken after the translation, almost simultaneously with it perhaps, must have been *Troilus.* All the direct evidence obtainable indicates that these two works were written about the same time. As explained in Chapter IV, Chaucer's mental attitude, his conception and disposition of the characters in *Troilus,* in a large degree, are determined by the *Consolation of Philosophy.* It is even possible to suppose, as was suggested before (p. 130), that Chaucer translated the work of Boethius so that the philosophical side of his poem might

[2] It is possible that Chaucer gradually passed out of the influence of Dante and into the influence of Boethius. The following consideration supports this view. Dante's influence is predominant in the *Parliament of Fowls.* Both Chaucer and Dante have a marked influence on *Troilus* although the influence of Boethius is very much greater. In the *House of Fame* both authors have an influence, the precise extent of which is difficult to determine in either case. In the *Knight's Tale* and in the *Canterbury Tales* generally the influence of Boethius is predominant.

be the better understood. More than this, some of the manuscripts of *Troilus* contain important Boethian passages which others do not, as if Chaucer, in revision, were considering the extent to which the *Consolation* should enter into his poem. Lastly, he himself in the well known lines to Adam, his scrivener, mentions the two works in the same breath, as if he associated them closely in his own mind. In view of these facts it seems impossible to suppose, as has been supposed,[3] that the date of the translation should be far removed from that of the poem. Rather, they should be placed in the same year or years, and this would probably be after 1381, the date of the *Parliament of Fowls,* the poem which by all odds shows the least Boethian influence of all the longer poems of Chaucer's middle period. And now let us pass to a consideration of these poems. The *Knight's Tale,* although in a somewhat lesser degree, continues the discussion of *Troilus* concerning fate and felicity in the Boethian manner. If we may believe that the *Consolation* had so firm a grip for a time on Chaucer's mind that no poem could fail to be decidedly affected by it, we must place this tale before the *Legend of Good Women,* a poem which shows considerably less the imprint of the Boethian philosophy; and, if this view of the early date of the *Knight's Tale* be entertained, the allusion in the Prologue of the *Legend* to the "love of Palamon and Arcyte of Thebes, thogh the story is knowen lyte" (B 420-1) may be held to refer to the *Knight's Tale* practically as we now know it. The *House of Fame,* in which the Boethian material is put to very original use, may have been written either before the *Knight's Tale* or after it, but close to it. The *Monk's Tale,* with its strong flavor of the *Consolation,* may likewise have been composed in this period, and later converted into a Canterbury tale. Here also belongs *Anelida and Arcite,* as is shown by its allusions to destiny, allusions, along with the allusions to "cas or aventure," common to the period when the Boethian influence was strongest.[4] This period would lie between the years 1381 and 1385-6.

[3] The dates assigned to the translation are various: about 1381, ten Brink; about 1377, Koch; 1377-81, Skeat; about 1376, Furnivall; 1373-8, Mather; 1380-3, Pollard; "one of the earliest of his longer works," Liddell; about 1370-2, Tatlock; about 1380, Root; 1382-3, Lowes.

[4] Allusions to destiny are most frequent in *Troilus, Knight's Tale, Anelida and Arcite, House of Fame* (cf. lines 145 and 188) and the *Legend of Good Women* (cf. lines 952 and 1299). In the first three

The *Legend of Good Women* and the *Canterbury Tales* show a decrease in the influence of Boethius, although this influence never ceases to manifest itself abundantly. This decrease is shown not only by a less frequent use of the Boethian material, but by a less serious tone in its use. There is noticeable in certain of the *Canterbury Tales* a tendency to give the passages taken from the *Consolation* a humorous turn, as in the discussion of free will in the *Nun's Priest's Tale* and in the discussion of felicity in the *Merchant's Tale;* it is given even a coarse turn in the few lines where it appears in the *Summoner's Tale.* It is also of interest to note that in the *Squire's Tale* and in the *Manciple's Tale* Chaucer draws the pessimistic deduction from his use of 3. m2 that by the promptings of nature men are untrue to their loves, and must always be seeking after "newfanglenesse." Boethius uses similar arguments and illustrations to prove quite the opposite point, that men by nature seek the supreme good. On the other hand, we find serious discussions of gentilesse in the tales of the Wife of Bath, of the Clerk, of the Squire, and of the Franklin. This varied use of the Boethian material indicates that Chaucer was adopting it to the mood of particular poems, and no longer considering it for its own sake as in *Troilus.*

PART II. PASSAGES IN THE CONSOLATION INFLUENCING CHAUCER

Part II of this chapter considers, book by book, the specific passages of the *Consolation* which influenced Chaucer. A list of such passages shows, almost without exception, that he did not take the *Consolation* at a dead level, dipping down here and there for attractive passages without regard for their significance as a part of a larger whole, but that he was most interested in those passages which, structurally, are the turning point in the argument, that he was primarily concerned with the thought of the *Consolation.*

poems a frequent allusion is a statement that destiny is "shaped." Cf. *Anelida and Arcite* 243, *Troilus* 2. 1091 and 3. 734, A1108, 1465-6, 1842, 2323-4. In the *Canterbury Tales* after the *Knight's Tale* the use of the word "destiny" is infrequent. Cf. use in B4528 and E1967. The use of "cas or aventure" occurs in *Troilus* 1. 568, 4. 388; in *House of Fame* 1052; in the Prologue A844; in the *Knight's Tale* A1074.

Book I

m1. Introduces Boethius in his lamentable state of mind, weeping in prison, calling on the woeful muses. Cf. line 12 and E 1849, the "slakke skin" trembles on his body and on January's; 12-14 and *Troi.* 4. 503-4, death is sweet which comes to wretched men, often called.

p1. Introduces and describes Dame Philosophy who disperses the woful muses. Cf. 8-12 and HF. 3. 1368-75, Philosophy and the goddess of Fame have ever changing statures.

m2. Dame Philosophy laments the fallen state of Boethius who has forgotten to reflect on universal wonders.

p2. She bids him awaken from his lethargy. Cf. 14 and *Troi.* 1. 730.

m3. Simile of the cloud which disappears before the beams of the sun; so the cloud is lifted from Boethius' mind. *Troi.* 2. 764-70, 781; B 3956, 3972.

p3. Philosophy tells Boethius that his is the common lot of philosophers.

m4. He should stand firm amid the wildest convulsions of nature and the madness of tyrants. Chaucer has based no passages upon this *meter* immediately; it is, however, an expression of the stoicism which is one of the central points in the Boethian teaching, which is made much of later, and which especially appealed to Chaucer. Boethius, at this point, does not understand Philosophy, as may be gathered from the next *prose*.

p4. Dame Philosophy asks Boethius whether he has forgotten the true spirit of a philosopher. Is he like the ass to the harp, and heeds not her inspiring message? If she is to be his leech, he must uncover his wounds. Boethius, given this opportunity, begins a long and tiresome expostulation against his false accusation by the senate, and his imprisonment, in which Chaucer does not appear to have been interested. The first four lines of the *prose* are used in *Troilus,* 1. 731-5, 857-8. Pandarus, it will be recalled, arouses Troilus from his lethargy in the words of Dame Philosophy.

m5. Boethius now discloses the grievance which causes his mental anguish. He has received torments in return for his good deeds. Why does the omnipotent God, the governor of all things permit the innocent to suffer and the guilty to be honored? This is the initial impulse, the question which starts the discussion; in it Boethius discloses his "wound." Chaucer is concerned with the question brought up in this *meter* more than in all the rest of the first book together. See *Complaint to Mars* 218-26, *Troilus* 3. 1016-19, *Legend of Good Women* 2231-5, *Knight's Tale* A 1303-15, *Man of Law's Tale* B 813-16, and the *Franklin's Tale* F 865-87.

p5. Dame Philosophy offers to bring Boethius back to his real "country," a realm not ruled over by tyrants like Theodoric, and to effect his cure by administering two remedies, a light one and a strong one. Cf. *Truth* 19, and see pp. 113-15 of the dissertation.

m6. God assigns the times. E1972, F1031-34. In this *meter* Philosophy is preparing for the following prose.

p6. Philosophy asks Boethius whether he believes that the world is governed by chance or by divine reason. Boethius answers that he believes fully in divine control; what he is complaining of is the injustice of divine control. From this "little spark" of belief, Philosophy offers to save him. Nowhere in Chaucer's poetry, likewise, may be found a questioning of divine power, although the injustice of that power is frequently discussed.

m7. Dame Philosophy, before beginning her argument, first exhorts Boethius to drive from his mind joy, dread, hope, and sorrow, if he will look upon "sooth with cleer light."

Book II

This book teaches straight stoical doctrine. On one side, under the allegory of Fortune and her gifts, is pictured the tumult and vanity of the world; on the other is shown the necessity of stoical fortitude and self-reliance.

p1. Lady Fortune, also called a monster, is irresistibly fickle; if she were not fickle, she would not be Fortune. Cf. 11 and E2026; 69-72 and *Fortune* 43-4; 80-2 and *Troi.* 1. 838-9, B3185-6; 82-4 and *Troi.* 1. 848-9.

m1. The account of her wiles continued. Cf. 10 and *Troi.* 1. 840; 11 and B3711; 11-2 and B3739-40.

p2. Account of Fortune continued under the guise of her defending herself. Chaucer has used almost the entire *prose*. In the poem *Fortune* he has Fortune defend herself, 25-48. Cf. also 4-19 and *Fortune* 57-60; 19-20 and *Troi.* 1. 841;

17-8 and *Fortune* 29-30; 27-33 and *Fortune* 61-3; 36-41, the description of Fortune's wheel, so frequently referred to in all mediaeval literature; 42-6, account of Croesus, and A 1946, B3951-54; 48-52, definition of tragedy, and B3163-7, 3181-4, 3951-4, 3973, *Troi.* 1. 4, 5. 1786; 53-5 and *Leg. G. W.* 195, D170; 59-60 and *Fortune* 31, *Troi.* 1. 850; 60-62, the realm of Fortune is common, *Fortune* 45-6, *Troi.* 1. 843-4, 4. 391-2, *HF.* 1545-8, B4190.

m2. No matter how much Fortune would give men, they would never be satisfied.

p3. Boethius still has blessings left. Here again private affairs of Boethius are discussed, except in the last few lines. Cf. 52-4, joys succeed sorrows just as sorrows succeed joys, and *Troi.* 1. 846-7; 55-61 and B28off.

m3. Similes to show that joys succeed sorrows and sorrows joys. *Troi.* 3. 1058-64.

p4. Philosophy, having shown Boethius that Fortune is not to be relied upon for happiness, states the first "point" of happiness, 93-109. It is to have peace of soul and to be master of self amid all the tumult of Fortune. Two of Chaucer's poems *Fortune* and *Truth* emphasize this point. See also *Troi.* 1. 891-3, 4. 1587-9, 5. 757-63, A490, B3326-9, B4029. For resemblances to other parts of the *prose* cf. 4-7 and *Troi.* 3. 1625-8, 4. 481-2; 40 and *Fortune* 38; 56-8 and *Troi.* 3. 816-9; 79-80 and *Fortune* 25-6; 86-7 and *Troi.* 3. 813-5, B422; 90-1 and *Troi.* 4. 835-6; 109-20 and *Troi.* 820-33. The prose is very important in considering the influence of Boethius on Chaucer. With *prose* 2 above, it forms the chief source of the poem *Fortune;* it is also the source of Criseyde's long speech on false felicity; as has been seen, it is one of the chief influences on *Truth.*

m4. Flee from the perilous adventures of the world. Cf. "flee fro the prees" of *Truth.*

p5. Philosophy begins the discussion of the specific gifts of Fortune, first of riches. Cf. 11-2 and *Truth* 3; 56-60 and *Truth* 2, 5, 10; 64-7 and A1258-9, C294-6; 91-2 and *Lack of Steadfastness* 5; 106-9 and B3326-9; 127 and D1192-4.

m5. The former age, the *meter* which becomes the basis for Chaucer's poem of that name. For resemblance between it and *Lack of Steadfastness* see pp. 91-2.

p6. Dignities do not bring happiness. 17-19 and *Gentilesse* 5. "Unto vertu longeth dignitee."

m6. Nero, an example of the uselessness of dignity, used in the *Monk's Tale*. Cf. 14-7 and B3656-7; 2-9 and B3669-80; 2-3 and B4560-2.

p7. Fame does not bring happiness. For Chaucer's discussion of fame in the abstract see pp. 87-89. Cf. also 18 and *HF*907; 43 and D1140; 49-51 and *Troi.* 2. 42.

m7. If any one thinks that fame is the greatest happiness, let him consider the heavens, and earthly fame passes to nothingness.

p8. The false gifts of Fortune having been discussed, Philosophy says a good word for Fortune, lest it be thought that she bear "untretable battle" against her. Fortune, especially "contrarious fortune," makes men wise through adversity; above all she shows them their true friends. Cf. *Fortune*, 10-12, 32, 33-4, 40, 48, 50-2, and D1203.

m8. The "bond of love." Philosophy, in closing the book, indicates that there is something far greater than the gifts of Fortune, and points forward to what is coming. The *meter* is translated in *Troilus* 1746-64. See also *Troi.* 3. 1261 and A2987-94. For the relation between this *meter* and *Lack of Steadfastness* see pp. 106-7.

Book III

After unfolding the doctrine of stoicism in Book II, Dame Philosophy, in Book III, unfolds a Platonic conception of the ideal good. This is her second "point," her "stronger remedy."

p1. Transitional. Boethius announces that he is now able to suffer all the assaults of Fortune patiently. Philosophy promises to lead him to the "verray welefulnesse."

m1. Simile to show that the false felicity must be described before the true felicity. To have sweetness it is necessary to have tasted bitterness. *Troi.* 1. 638-9.

p2. An important *prose;* in it Philosophy defines all the conceptions of felicity, for which men, by nature, strive though it may be blindly. See pp. 81-84 of this dissertation. Cf. 17-30, 60-2, 58-60 and A1255-58, 1260-65, 1266-7, a speech of Arcite in which he substantially reproduces the thought of the entire *prose*. Cf. also 6-8 and *Troi.* 3. 1691-2; 54-6, on the doctrine of Epicurus, and A336-8, E2021-3; 63-6 and *Troi.* 5. 762; 77-9 and *Truth* 2, 10, 15, A490, B4029.

m2. Comparisons from nature showing that all men by instinct seek the highest good. Cf. 27-9, 15-22 and F608-17, H160-74.

p3. In the analysis of false felicity, riches are first taken up, as they were first taken up in describing the gifts of Fortune. Again the conclusion is reached that riches may not bring happiness. Cf. 24-6 and *Parliament of Fowls* 90-1, *Complaint to Pity* 99-105, *Complaint to his Lady* 47-8, *Anelida and Arcite* 203, G958, we want what we do not have and we have what we do not want; 71-2 and *Truth* 2, 10, 15, A490, B4029, contentment in little things as in 2. p5, the previous discussion of riches.

m3. All the riches in the world do not bring happiness.

p4. "Dignitees" do not bring happiness. As in the previous discussion of this theme, the conclusion is reached that "unto vertu longeth dignitee." Cf. *Gentilesse* 5; 44-48 and D1139-49.

m4. Nero, as in the first discussion of dignity, is an example of the uselessness of dignity in the ordinary sense of the word. Cf. 1-3 and B3658-60.

p5. Power does not bring happiness. The short *prose* is summed up in B3429-36. Cf. also 23-5 and D1187-8; 34-41 and B3685ff; 51 and E1784.

m5. Power is nothing, unless one have power over his own dark passions.

p6. Glory, especially glory coming from family name, is nothing; true gentility consists in virtue. Here comes Dame Philosophy's celebrated discussion of true nobility in which she shows that it may not be inherited by son from father; that it consists in goodness; that it is inherited from God alone, the father of all, as He is the source of all goodness. Her discussion is very practical in that she shows through it how man may realize in life the supreme good which she is presently to describe. Cf. 24-38, m6 and the poem *Gentilesse, Legend of Good Women* 1819-24, D1109-1176, E155-61, 424-5, F684-94, 1460-70. For the general discussion of gentilesse see pp. 94-103.

m6. Gentilesse comes from God alone.

p7. Pleasures of the body bring not happiness, but sorrow.

m7. Such pleasures, like bees, give honey, but sting.

p8. A summary of all that has been said of false felicity.

Cf. 22 and B295-9; 10-12, 35-9 and C294-6. The *Parson's Tale* contains just such a summary in lines 471-74.

m8. Alas, why do people look in the wrong places for happiness?

p9. The explanation of true felicity begins. All supposed forms of felicity added together make the true felicity, and this felicity may not be divided into parts; indeed, the trouble is that men do try to divide it, or to part what may not be parted. Cf. D2214.

m9. Before the next step, Philosophy invokes God in prayer. She gives a fervent account of God, the creator, mover, governor, the cause of all, and alludes to the Platonic conception that God created the world from the ideal form of the world in his thought. Cf. 8-10 and *Legend of Good Women* 2228-30, G327. Cf. also 1-2 and F865-7; 5-7 and A2987-93, *HF.* 81-2; 12-16 and *Parliament of Fowls* 380-1 and *HF.* 738-46. Chaucer thus gathers many of the attributes by which he describes the deity from this *meter.*

p10. Philosophy proves that true felicity, described in the previous *prose,* is in God, and that God is in sovereign good. Cf. 18-22 and A3004-9, the nature of things did not proceed from that which is imperfect, but from that which is whole and absolute and which descends down into things, of themselves empty and without fruit; cf. 85-6 and E1638, there may not be two perfect goods.

m10. God is the refuge and light of wretches. The shining of the gems of all the rivers of Asia will not lighten the darkness of the soul. Cf. 9-14 and *Former Age* 30.

p11. Good, as has been shown, is the composite substance of all the imagined forms of good, is, therefore, the One. Experience shows that, if one or a whole is divided into parts, the one perishes. The next step is this: All animate things, both plant and animal, all inanimate things, by a powerful natural force, desire to live, to have a "perdurable dwelling," to escape destruction. Therefore all things desire to dwell with the good, for, if they become separated from the good, the One, thus scattered into parts, perishes. Good is essential to existence, is the end of life. Men must be merged with it. This conception, colored as it is by Platonism, is the "middel sothfastnesse," the "prikke" of Dame Philosophy's argument. Cf. 37-40 and D1968-9, a thing is stronger when it is one than when it is scattered; 46-51 and *Troi*. 1. 960-1, he that is parted is not whole; 56-137 and *HF*. 737-56, all things, animate and inanimate, seek a permanent dwelling; 166-7 and *Legend of Good Women* 2586-8. For the discussion of the poem *Truth* in relation to this passage see pp. 112-15. The passages which Chaucer drew from this prose indicate that he understood it thoroughly.

m11. Who-so seeks truth, he will find it implanted naturally within himself. As Dame Philosophy says, this is the Platonic conception that truth exists by nature in the soul and needs only to be discovered to shine forth. 5. m4 takes up the opposite view of the Stoics that impressions come through the senses from without and are recorded in the soul as reflections in a mirror; Chaucer was greatly interested in this *meter*. For the discussion of Chaucer's poem *Truth*, see pp. 104-19. Cf. also 7 and *Troi*. 4. 200, the black cloud of error prevents us from seeing what is best.

p12. Boethius professes himself satisfied. Dame Philosophy, however, suggests again the very question which Boethius asked in 1. m5, how may God, who is goodness, who by His bounty governs the world, who, in the language of Parmenides, turns the world and the movable circle of things, permit evil, the direct contrary of good. Boethius thinks that he is being played with, that he is wound up in an argument as intricate as was the Labyrinth. Cf. 117-8 and *HF* 1920-1, the house of Daedalus; 145-7 and B145-7, the moving firmament; 152-3 and *Lack of Steadfastness*, A741-2, H207-10, the word must be cousin to the deed.

m12. Happy is he, who, unbound from the burdens of the world, may see the clear well of good. Unhappy is he who looks back on the low things of the world, as Orpheus and Eurydice looked back upon the mouth of hell from which they were escaping. Cf. 28-30 and *Troi*. 1. 786-8, 3. 592, 4. 791, allusions to Tityus, Tantalus, and Orpheus and Eurydice; 37-9 and A1164-6.

Book IV

In the discussion of evil in this book, the fatalistic conception of the *Consolation* is developed.

p1. Boethius asks again why the evil flourish and the good suffer. Philosophy consents to explain, and, thus, to do one more thing to bring him back to his "country." Cf. 30-33 and D100.

m1. The flight of Boethius, in thought, through the moving heavens to his "country." Cf. *Truth* 19; 1-5 and *HF.* 972-8; 6 and B295-9.

p2. The wicked really are impotent, because they do not obtain the good which they, as explained in 3. p11, instinctively desire. No one is mighty if he may not obtain what he wishes. Cf. 9-10 and *Troi.* 1. 637-46; 22-4 and D1187-8.

m2. The mightiest tyrant may himself be tyrannized over by vices.

p3. The punishment of the wicked is that they do not attain to that unity in the good for which all things strive. Instead of being like gods, they are like beasts.

m3. Vices turn men into beasts more than Circe, the enchantress, turned the companions of Ulysses into beasts.

p4. Philosophy proves several paradoxical statements: that wicked men are more unhappy when they succeed in doing evil deeds than when they fail; that they are more happy if they receive punishment than if they do not receive it; that they are more unhappy than those upon whom they inflict wrong. Evil-doers, in not being able to attain the good which they desire, are diseased, and really deserve more pity than the good people upon whom they inflict wrong, because they miss the great reward, the good, which is the end of life. Cf. 132-3 and *Parliament of Fowls* 599-600. Chaucer borrows less from the *proses* just mentioned than from any part of the *Consolation* yet considered. It will be recalled that his characters, although they consider the question of evil, do not attempt to explain why it exists.

m4. Why does hatred run rampant in the world? We should love good folk and pity wicked folk; thus none will be left to be hated.

p5. Although Boethius accepts all that has been said of the wicked, he can yet see no reason why the good should suffer. Philosophy explains that his failure to understand this is because he does not understand the divine causes.

m5. The causes, hid in heaven, trouble the thoughts of men.

p6. This *prose,* in which Philosophy explains the hidden

causes of things, sets forth the fatalistic conception advanced in the *Consolation*. Philosophy shows that Providence works in the world through destiny and other agencies, that the destinal order constrains the deeds and fortunes of men by a bond of causes which may not be escaped, that nothing is done for evil, but that, as there are countless examples to prove, all is done for the best. As I have tried to show elsewhere (p. 117-18), this is the *prose* which explains Chaucer's line "And trouthe shal delivere, hit is no drede." Chaucer borrows far more from it than from all the rest of Book IV together. Cf. 35-54 and *Fortune* 65-70, *Troi.* 3. 617-22, 5. 1-3, A1663-65, the relation of Providence and destiny; 49-51 and *Troi.* 2. 526-8, God leads all things to their end by "purveyaunce"; 57-60 and *Troi.* 1. 1065-71, a man who builds a house plans beforehand; 62-71 and D1483, E1671-3, 1967-9, the instruments of Providence; 101-6 and A2994-9, 3011-15, God establishes life and death by progressions; 106-17 and *Troi.* 4. 1654, E1975, God knows the causes; 114-19, 149-54 and A1251-4, B481-3, F886-7, God does all for the best, although men do not understand the causes; 180-6 and E 1155-62, God scourges men with adversity.

m6. God rules the constellations and the elements by love, and turns all back to good. Cf. 13-9 and A2987-93, bond of love; 15-20 and *Parliament of Fowls* 380-81 and *HF* 738-46, hot cold, heavy light, etc.; 31-40 and A3035-40, God turns all things to good. The long speech of Theseus (A2987-93, 3035-40) is in the spirit of this *meter* and the preceding *prose*.

p7. The use of Fortune, as an instrument of Providence, is that it gives men training in character. Cf. 55-6 and *Troi.* 4. 1587-9, he is lord of Fortune who rises above her.

m7. Examples of men who have triumphed over Fortune. Cf. 20-43 and B3285-3300, the exploits of Hercules.

Book V

Book V explains how it is possible for man to have free will notwithstanding the destinal ordinances.

p1. As a related question, Philosophy defines chance, "hap or elles aventure of fortune." It may be from the last expression that Chaucer derives "cas or aventure," as explained before (pp. 62-4). Cf. 65-69 and E1972, F1031-4. Cf. also 1. m6.

m1. Fortune and chance are ruled over by the divine ordinance. Cf. *Fortune* 65-9 and *Troi.* 5. 1541-4.

p2. Boethius raises the question of free will and necessity. Philosophy explains that necessity is of different kinds, although she does not yet explain in full. Cf. *Troi.* 4. 958-9, 961-6.

m2. God sees all things, past, present, and future.

p3. Argument of Boethius against free will, a large part of which is translated in *Troilus.* Cf. 7-71 and *Troi.* 4. 974-1078; 70-71 and B4528; 96-9 and *Troi.* 4. 989-92. For a discussion see pp. 71-79.

m3. Alas, that the soul of man, beclouded by its contact with the body, is not able to see the whole truth. This *meter* is also a part of the speech of Boethius.

p4. Philosophy in the following *proses* and *meters* shows that there is a difference in degree between the knowledge of man and the knowledge of God and that, if one understands this difference, he will be able to reconcile divine prescience and man's free will.

m4. Man, although he sees imperfectly, has within his soul the principles of truth, always questioning, desiring to know, and to receive confirmation from without; he should follow these inward promptings. The Stoics were wrong in thinking that the soul was passive; that it received impressions only from without and did not have quickening impulses within itself any more than a mirror receiving reflections of things outside itself. Cf. 1-13, 29-32 and *Troi.* 1. 295-8, 365-7, 2. 981, E1579-82, 2178, F829-34.

p5. The "wit" of animals, like oysters, that cannot move, and the "imagination" of higher kinds of dumb animals cannot comprehend the reason of man. Likewise man's reason cannot understand the "intelligence" of God.

m5. Look up to God, not down, as do beasts. Cf. *Truth* 18-19.

p6. God sees past, present, and future in an eternal present. His grasp of eternity is comparable to man's grasp of the moment. His prescience, therefore, may no more imply a constraining force on the acts of men than the gaze of a spectator implies a constraining force on the movements of a chariot-driver whom the former is observing. The necessity which obtains in such a case is only a "conditional necessity," occasioned merely by the fact that an act beheld must be true. There are, however, certain immutable laws like the law of death . In such a case the necessity is "simple necessity." Cf. 12-17 and *Troi.* 5. 764-9, man's limited powers of embracing time; 126-152 and B4435, 4439-40, simple and conditional necessity.

The list just concluded shows several facts concerning the nature of Chaucer's indebtedness to Boethius. In the first place, except for some of the steps of the argument in Books IV and V, Chaucer has left hardly any of the *proses* and *meters* of the *Consolation* untouched. Secondly, the borrowings indicate that he had so entirely mastered and assimilated its thought at all points that he had complete command of it, and, except for the longer borrowings, would not need to resort to the text of the *Consolation* for using it in his poetry; for illustration, I have frequently found after the analysis of a particular *prose* or *meter* in the list above, that Chaucer's borrowing from it neatly summed up its content. Lastly, the list shows that Chaucer emphasized most the important steps in the argument of Dame Philosophy. The parts which he thus emphasized are the following: 1. m5, raising the question why evil exists and starting the discussion; 2. p2, the defense of Fortune by herself, and 2. p4, on fortitude and self-mastery, the first "point" of happiness; 3. p2 on the different kinds of felicity; 3. p6, on true gentility, a practical discussion on how to obtain true felicity in life; 3. p11 and m11 on true felicity and truth; 4. p6, on fate; 5. p3, on whether or not free will is possible (as explained elsewhere Chaucer emphasizes the question of Boethius rather than the answer of Dame Philosophy).

CONCLUSION

The thesis shows that Chaucer worked over the *Consolation of Philosophy,* in his translation of that work, earnestly, making use of the Latin original and a French translation, not to mention the commentary of Trivet and his possible recourse to various texts of the original; that he attempted, although not always quite succeeding, to reproduce the thought of the *Consolation* faithfully and to reproduce its spirit by a stateliness of tone and by embellishments of style; that he subsequently incorporated in extended passages here and there throughout his poetry and in individual poems almost all of the *Consolation*—what it has to say of fortune, of false felicity, power, fame, and riches, of true gentility, of the two "points" of blissfulness, fortitude of spirit and truth, of fate, and of the connected subjects, the relation of evil and free will to a benevolent and all-powerful deity, although he seems to have emphasized fate at the expense of the latter two; that his grasp of the *Consolation* was so firm that he was able beautifully to express its central teachings in the short poem *Truth* as counsel to Sir Philip la Vache and to put it to uses so original that its influence, although possibly profound, is transmuted almost beyond recognition as in the *House of Fame;* that the *Consolation,* as it concerns the most important question of life, the end or "fyn" of existence, went far to determine his mental attitude, his conception and disposition of the characters in the *Knight's Tale* and especially in *Troilus,* two poems presumably written when he was fresh from the translation; that the *Consolation* was a lasting, if a diminishing influence, throughout the *Canterbury Tales,* especially in the discussions of gentilesse.

How much the *Consolation* determined Chaucer's own attitude toward life, it is difficult to determine with precision. At the least, it may be said that Boethius and Chaucer were compatible in point of view and that Chaucer found in Boethius, in many ways, a congenial spirit. At the most, it may be said that Boethius was an influence so profound that he completely determined Chaucer's view of the meaning of life and of the way in which life should be conducted. The truth no doubt lies somewhere between the two extremes, and Boethius probably accentuated and extended views which Chaucer already had temperamentally. Furthermore, the *Consolation of Philosophy,* as it thus gives expression to a philosophy of life which so much interested Chaucer, presents an opportunity to determine what Chaucer's conception of the ideal philosopher would be. Chaucer's ideal philosopher would be a man who understood and brought into practice the two "points" of the *Consolation.* First, as the aged Egeus, father of Theseus, he must understand the transmutation of the world from woe to weal and back to woe again, and, unheeding worldly joys and woes alike, must stand steadfast, at peace with himself, though the world fall in ruin about him. But he must do more than stand stoically and grimly at bay. He must realize, somewhat like Plato, that there is an ideal good and that this good is unalterable; that, through a study of astronomy, so as to understand the harmony of divine law and to obtain a just perspective of petty worldly concerns, and through gentilesse and through the truth within him, he must try to associate himself with the universal good. When one remembers Chaucer's *Astrolabe, Melibeus,* and *Parson's Tale,* his retirement from life poring over old books, his broad and sympathetic view of his fellow men of all degrees and conditions, it is almost possible to believe that Chaucer himself was this kind of philosopher, although, as he himself says, "no man is al trewe, I gessé." The above pages help to show that Chaucer was sometimes a very serious poet and that he, not always earth-bound, had visions of eternal truths such as the greatest poets have had.

BIBLIOGRAPHY

In the preparation of this thesis I have consulted chiefly the following books and publications.

ALANUS DE INSULIS. Planctus Naturae and Anticlaudianus. In Vol. II of Anglo-Latin Satirical Poets (Record Ser.). Ed. T. Wright.

BARBOUR, JOHN. Bruce. Ed. W. W. Skeat. 1874-7. E. E. T. S. Ex. ser. 21, 29.

BOETHIUS, ANICIUS MANLIUS SEVERINUS. De Philosophiae Consolatione. Ed. R. Peiper. Leipzig. 1871.

BRADWARDINE, THOMAS. De Causa Dei. London. 1618.

CHAUCER, GEOFFREY. The Complete Works. Six Volumes. Ed. W. W. Skeat. 2nd ed. Oxford. 1894-1900.

COLVILLE, GEORGE. Boethius' Consolation of Philosophy tr. from the Latin in 1556. Bax edition. London. 1897.

DANTE, ALIGHIERI. Il Convito. Ed. G. Barbèra. Firenze. 1900. La Divina Commedia. Ed C. H. Grandgent. Boston. 1909-13.

ELIZABETH, QUEEN OF ENGLAND. Englishings. Ed. Caroline Pemberton. 1899. E. E. T. S. Orig. ser. 113.

FANSLER, D. S. Chaucer and the Roman de la Rose. Columbia University Studies in English and Comparative Literature. 1914.

FURNIVALL, F. J. Trial Forewords to my Parallel-text edition of Chaucer's Minor Poems, Part I. Chaucer Soc. Pub. 1871. 2nd ser. 6.

GALPIN, S. L. Fortune's Wheel in the Roman de la Rose. Pub. of the Mod. Lang. Ass. Vol. XXIV.

GODEFROY, F. Dictionnaire de l'ancienne langue française. 8 vols. Paris. 1881-94.

GOWER, JOHN. The Complete Works. Ed. G. C. Macaulay. Oxford. 1899-1902.

GUIDO DELLE COLONNE. Historia Trojana. Strasburg. 1489.

HAMMOND, E. P. Chaucer: A Bibliographical Manual. New York. 1908.

JEAN DE MEUN. Roman de la Rose. Elzévirienne edition. Paris. 1878.

KITTREDGE, G. L. Chaucer and his Poetry. Cambridge. 1915.

LANGLOIS, ERNEST. La Traduction de Boèce par Jean de Meun. Romania. Vol. 42. Origines et Sources du Roman de la Rose. Paris. 1890.

LIDDELL, M. H. Announcement of Chaucer's use of the French translation in his own translation of Boethius. Academy. 1895. Announcement of Chaucer's use of the Pseudo-Aquinas. Nation. 1897. Edition of Boece in the Globe Chaucer.

LINDNER, FELIX. The Alliteration in Chaucer's Canterbury Tales, in Essays on Chaucer. Chaucer Soc. Pub. 2nd ser. 2.

LOUNSBURY, T. R. Studies in Chaucer. 3 vols. New York. 1892.

LOWES, J. L. Chaucer and Dante's "Convivio." Modern Philology.

Vol. XIII. The Prologue to the Legend of Good Women. Pub. Mod. Lang. Ass. Vols. XIX, XX.

LYDGATE, JOHN. Troy Book. Ed. H. Bergen. E. E. T. S. Ex. ser. 97, 103, 106. Parts I, II, III.

MACROBIUS, AUR. Theodosius. Opera. London. 1694.

MACHAULT, GUILLAUME. Remède de Fortune. Oeuvres. Ed. Hoepffner. Société des Anciens Textes Français. Vol. II.

MORRIS, R. Chaucer's Translation of Boethius's "De Consolatione Philosophiae." 1868. E. E. T. S. Ex. ser. 5.

PETERSEN, K. O. Chaucer and Trivet. Pub. Mod. Lang. Ass. Vol. XVIII.

PIERS THE PLOWMAN. Ed. W. W. Skeat. 2 vols. Oxford. 1886.

PLATO. Republic, tr. into English by J. L. Davies and D. J. Vaughn. London. 1886. Golden Treasury Ser.

RICKERT, EDITH. Thou Vache. Modern Philology. Vol. XI.

ROOT, R. K. The Poetry of Chaucer. Boston and New York. 1906.

ROSSETTI, W. M. Chaucer's Troylus and Cryseyde comp. with Boccaccio's Filostrato. Chaucer Soc. Pub. Ser. 1, 44.

ST. AUGUSTINE. De Dei Civitate. Teubner text.

STEWART, H. F. Boethius, an Essay. Edinburgh and London. 1891.

SYPHERD, W. O. Studies in Chaucer's Hous of Fame. Chaucer Soc. Pub. 2nd ser. 39.

TATLOCK, J. S. P. The Development and Chronology of Chaucer's Works. Chaucer Soc. Pub., 2nd Ser., 37. 1907.

Chaucer and Dante. Modern Philology. Vol. III.

TOYNBEE, PAGET. Dante in English Literature. London. 1909.

UEBERWEG, FRIEDRICH. History of Philosophy from Thales to the present, tr. by G. S. Morris. New York. 1873.